vabnf   VAL
347.732634 ROBIN

Robin, Corey, 1967- author
The enigma of Clarence Thomas
33410016862817   11-20-2020

W9-ANW-941

DISCARD

Valparaiso Public Library
103 Jefferson Street
Valparaiso, IN 46383

ALSO BY COREY ROBIN

The Reactionary Mind:
Conservatism from Edmund Burke to Donald Trump

Fear: The History of a Political Idea

THE ENIGMA OF
CLARENCE THOMAS

THE ENIGMA OF

CLARENCE THOMAS

COREY ROBIN

METROPOLITAN BOOKS

HENRY HOLT AND COMPANY   NEW YORK

m

Metropolitan Books
Henry Holt and Company
Publishers since 1866
120 Broadway
New York, New York 10271
www.henryholt.com

Metropolitan Books® and m® are registered trademarks of
Macmillan Publishing Group, LLC.

Copyright © 2019 by Corey Robin
All rights reserved.
Distributed in Canada by Raincoast Book Distribution Limited

Library of Congress Cataloging-in-Publication Data

Names: Robin, Corey, 1967– author.
Title: The enigma of Clarence Thomas / Corey Robin.
Description: New York : Metropolitan Books, Henry Holt and Company,
    2019. | Includes bibliographical references and index.
Identifiers: LCCN 2019012026 | ISBN 9781627793834 (hardcover)
Subjects: LCSH: Thomas, Clarence, 1948– | Judges—United States—
    Biography. | Political questions and judicial power—United States. |
    Conservatism—United States.
Classification: LCC KF8745.T48 R63 2019 | DDC 347.73/2634—dc23
LC record available at https://lccn.loc.gov/2019012026

Our books may be purchased in bulk for promotional, educational, or business use. Please
contact your local bookseller or the Macmillan Corporate and Premium Sales Department at
(800) 221-7945, extension 5442, or by e-mail at MacmillanSpecialMarkets@macmillan.com.

First Edition 2019

Designed by Kelly S. Too

Printed in the United States of America

1 3 5 7 9 10 8 6 4 2

For Carol,
though she be but little she is fierce

I am invisible, understand, simply because people refuse to see me. . . . When they approach me they see only my surroundings, themselves, or figments of their imagination—indeed, everything and anything except me.

—Ralph Ellison, *Invisible Man*

CONTENTS

THE ENIGMA OF
CLARENCE THOMAS

Introduction

Clarence Thomas is the longest-serving justice on the current Supreme Court. When he joined the Court on October 18, 1991, the Soviet Union was a country, Hillary Clinton was Arkansas's First Lady, and Donald Trump was declaring the first of his businesses' six bankruptcies.[1] Since then, Thomas has authored more than seven hundred opinions, staking out controversial positions on gun rights, campaign finance, and other issues that have come to command Supreme Court majorities.[2] "Thomas's views," Yale legal scholar Akhil Reed Amar has said, "are now being followed by a majority of the Court in case after case." That was in 2011. In subsequent years, Thomas has been joined on the Court by Neil Gorsuch, who frequently signs on to Thomas's opinions, and Brett Kavanaugh, who will push the Court even further in Thomas's direction.[3]

Ever since he became a candidate for the Court, Thomas has spoken to and for the most revanchist elements of the American right. During his Senate confirmation hearings, his nomination was championed by Republican operative Floyd Brown, who made the notorious Willie Horton ad that helped sink the presidential campaign of Michael Dukakis. After George H. W. Bush's election in 1988, Brown formed a new organization to advocate for Bush's Supreme Court nominees. He called it Citizens United. Throughout the Obama years, Thomas was known as the "Tea Party justice." His blistering dissents were welcomed by many in the movement, and his wife, Virginia, worked closely with Tea Party leaders.[4]

With the election of Trump, Thomas's influence has grown. Not only has he authored several important opinions in recent years—about abortion and the First Amendment, the police and probable cause—but his former law clerks also play a leading role in and around the Trump regime.[5] Ten former clerks hold high-level positions in the administration—defending Trump's travel ban and other immigration policies in court; signing amicus briefs in *Masterpiece Cakeshop*, the Colorado gay wedding cake case; eliminating or rewriting Obama-era regulations—or have been appointed to the Offices of the United States Attorneys.[6] Eleven former clerks have been nominated to the federal bench, seven of them to the Court of Appeals, just one step away from the Supreme Court.[7] No other justice under Trump has had as many clerks appointed to the judiciary.[8]

Thomas is also a black nationalist.

When he was nearly forty years old, just four years shy of his appointment to the Court, Thomas set out the foundations of his political vision in the *Atlantic Monthly*: "There is nothing you can do to get past black skin. I don't care how educated you are, how good you are—you'll never have the same contacts or opportunities, you'll never be seen as equal to whites." No moment's indiscretion, this was the distillation of a lifetime of learning, which began in the segregated precincts of Savannah during the 1950s and continued through his college years in the 1960s. As a militant undergraduate at the College of the Holy Cross, Thomas came into contact with the tenets and practices of black nationalism and Black Power. He devoured the speeches of Malcolm X, which he listened to on records and was still reciting from memory two decades later.[9] In the 1970s, Thomas began moving to the right. In 1981, he joined the Reagan administration, first as an assistant secretary of education and then as chair of the Equal Employment Opportunity Commission (EEOC). Despite his political turn, Thomas has never lost touch with the racial separatism of his early encounters. "I've been very partial to Malcolm X," he told a conservative magazine in 1987, six years into his tenure in the Reagan administration. "There's a lot of good in what he says."[10] On the Court, Thomas has continued to believe—and to argue, in opinion after opinion—that race matters; that racism is a constant, perhaps ineradicable feature of American life; and that the best hope for black people lies within themselves, not as individuals but as a separate community with separate institutions, apart from white people. This is the man Donald Trump has called his favorite justice.[11]

With the conclusion of the 2018–19 term, Thomas has finished his twenty-eighth year on the Court. At the age of seventy-one, he is far younger than Justices Ruth Bader Ginsburg and Stephen Breyer, who are eighty-six and eighty, respectively, and Anthony Kennedy, who retired in 2018 at the age of eighty-two. Should Thomas remain on the Court another nine years, he will be the longest-serving justice in the history of the United States. His imprint will be broad and deep. Despite that, the only things most Americans know about him are that he once was accused of sexual harassment and that he almost never speaks from the bench.

IN THE 3,300-PAGE transcript of Thomas's Senate confirmation hearings, the word "enigma" appears thirty times.[12] "Clarence Thomas may be more of an enigma than any Supreme Court nominee in recent history," one liberal organization stated in opposition to his nomination. Initially, people were puzzled by the disparity between Thomas's liberal-sounding testimony and his record as a right-wing ideologue and government official. On the witness stand, Thomas warmly declared, "So many others gave their lives, their blood, their talents. But for them I would not be here. Justice [Thurgood] Marshall, whose seat I have been nominated to fill, is one of those who had the courage and the intellect. He is one of the great architects of the legal battles to open doors that seemed so hopelessly and permanently sealed." Just three years earlier, however, Thomas had dismissed Marshall's liberal views as "exasperating and incomprehensible," his rendition of the Constitution a race-baiting vision that "alienates all Americans" and "pits blacks . . . against the Founders." On the stand, Thomas paid homage to Fannie Lou Hamer, Rosa Parks, and other women of the black freedom struggle, proudly affirming their creed of solidarity and mutuality as the keystone of his success. A decade earlier, however, he had publicly sneered at his impoverished sister, struggling to make ends meet in Georgia with the help of the government: "She gets mad when the mailman is late with her welfare check. That is how dependent she is."[13]

But once Anita Hill stepped forward with credible allegations that Thomas had sexually harassed her, and Thomas denied them, and other women stepped forward with additional credible allegations of sexual harassment, it was obvious to everyone but his most hard-bitten defenders that Thomas would say anything to get his seat on the Court.[14] The disparity between the witness and the ideologue, the man on the stand and the man in the square, no longer seemed puzzling or surprising. Given the record of Senate confirmation hearings since then, where witnesses increasingly duck questions about their views on constitutional issues or offer bland assurances of impartiality that no one believes, our presumption of a nominee's credibility or veracity has diminished considerably.[15] Artful dissembling, if not outright lies, is what we have come to expect from our Supreme Court nominees.

Yet the enigma of Clarence Thomas remains.

Thomas is not a conservative man who happens to be black. Thomas is a black man whose conservatism is overwhelmingly defined by and oriented toward the interests of black people, as he understands them. In popular and academic discussion, African American concerns are associated with liberalism and the left. The same is true in discussions of the Court: liberals stand for civil rights and voting rights; conservatives oppose them. Yet Thomas has long been committed to a conservatism that speaks to and for African Americans. In a 1987 speech to the Heritage Foundation that was widely shared at the time of his nomination, Thomas claimed that a "principled" conservatism should "make it clear to blacks that conservatives are not hostile to their interests but aggressively supportive" of their interests. Such a conservatism would appeal to African Americans not by ignoring race but by breaking the left's stranglehold on African American allegiances and issues. "If you could get the whole racial issue out of the context of liberal and conservative," he said in an interview, most black people would see that they "are really conservative."[16]

This race-conscious conservatism is not just a theory for Thomas. It is a politics, a set of values and beliefs, policies and prescriptions, that he has long hoped to cultivate in the black community. "He talked about changing the way our people thought," says a close friend of his during the 1970s. "That was a clear dream. He talked about a time when we would not be so foolish to be enslaved by just one particular view, or leaders who were clearly captured by one political party." According to Thomas, "I saw the prospects of proselytizing many young blacks who, like myself, had been disenchanted with the left; disenchanted with so-called black leaders; and discouraged by the inability to effect change or in any way influence the thinking of black leaders in the Democratic party."[17] That project has accompanied Thomas onto the Court, where he continues to speak to and for a constituency of potential black conservatives.[18]

Thomas is the first to recognize that forging a black conservatism, breaking the links between African Americans, liberalism, and Democrats, is a tall order. He knows how unwelcome his views and jurisprudence are in the black community: "It pains me deeply, more deeply than any of you can imagine, to be perceived by so many members of my race as doing them harm."[19] His goal, however, is to speak to African Americans not as they are but as they might be, to persuade African Americans that there is nothing to be gained—and everything to be lost—from their allegiance to liberalism and the Democratic Party.[20] To turn his imagined community into a real constituency, he has sought to show not only that conservatism will "help black America," but that race matters in ways blacks don't often realize, producing a liberal jurisprudence that is more beneficial to whites than it is to blacks.[21]

In pursuit of this project, Thomas has benefited enormously from his immersion in black nationalism. Such a claim may seem improbable to readers for whom black nationalism is associated with Third World internationalism and the romance of revolution, notions that Thomas roundly rejects.[22] Nor does Thomas embrace other principles that are often considered the keystones of black nationalism, such as black territorial self-determination or a unified black culture. But strict adherence to those propositions is not the only way to be a black nationalist. As the Harvard philosopher Tommie Shelby has noted, many black nationalists throughout American history have opted for a looser, more pragmatic "program of black solidarity and group self-organization" rather than an insistent demand for a black state. That approach, what another scholar calls "community nationalism," captures a good deal of Thomas's thinking over the years.[23] Like most ideological commitments, Thomas's black nationalism is selective. Still, many elements of the program he embraced in the 1960s and 1970s—the celebration of black self-sufficiency, the scathing attack on integration, the support for racial separatism and black institutions, the emphasis on black manhood as the pathway to black freedom, the reverence for black self-defense—remain vital parts of his jurisprudence today.

Thomas's black nationalist conservatism is not a pose or a posture. It's rooted in the deepest traditions of African American political thought. In both black conservatism and black nationalism, there is a suspicion of white liberalism and its African American allies, skepticism of the state, pessimism about integration, a focus on the family, an emphasis on traditional morality, an appreciation of black business, and a belief in the saving power of black men. While the two traditions are by no means identical, they overlap in multiple respects.[24] That is why Thomas has been able to forgo the left for the right without having to give up the black nationalism that can be found on either side of the spectrum.

Among the few to have noticed this at the time of his nomination was the right-wing intellectual Murray Rothbard. Before he died in 1995, Rothbard came to a late-life vision of a coalition of libertarians and white nationalists. Forging alliances with Pat Buchanan and Ron Paul, Rothbard anticipated the merger of America's two great manias—

racism and capitalism—that are the hallmark of the Trump regime. "Black separatism, or black nationalism," Rothbard said of Thomas's philosophy, "has long struck me as far more compatible with human nature, as well as far more libertarian, than the compulsory integration beloved of left-liberalism." A "modern, updated version of the Black Nation idea," Rothbard added, "would set the American blacks free at last, free from what they see as white racism and what many whites see as parasitism over the white populace (through crime or welfare payments). Independent at long last, liberated from what they see as the institutionalized legacy of slavery, the blacks would finally be free to find their own level."[25] Three decades later, Rothbard's statement still offers a useful road map to Thomas's jurisprudence.

From the perspective of American—and, indeed, European—history, however, Thomas's politics are not that surprising. A long if unstoried tradition of black conservatism in this country extends from Booker T. Washington to the black novelist and social critic George Schuyler and the black economist Thomas Sowell. The travels of Schuyler and Sowell from left to right in the early and middle decades of the twentieth century anticipate Thomas's journey at the end of the century.[26] Conservatism, moreover, has consistently needed, and sometimes heeded, the voice from the margins. Since its beginnings in the reaction against the French Revolution, the right in Europe and in the United States has sought to appeal to those on the bottom, to forge a mass politics of privilege by making alliances between the lower and higher orders.[27]

What is surprising, and truly enigmatic, about Clarence Thomas is that he is a Supreme Court justice. Not only has he fused these elements of black nationalism and black conservatism, but he's also managed to infuse them into his opinions on the Court—all the while remaining a hero to some of the most racist elements of the American polity.[28] This country has seen black conservatives. It has seen black nationalists. It has seen conservative black nationalists. It has never seen a conservative black nationalist on the Supreme Court. Thomas, moreover, has injected his beliefs into the Court not through any philosophy of a "living Constitution"—that is, a Constitution that evolves over time, adapting to new values and the inclusion of new citizens and voices—but through the original Constitution, the Constitution as it was adopted in 1789, the very Constitution that Thomas acknowledges was written by and for racists and slaveholders.[29] That Thomas has managed to take his peculiar blend of black nationalism and black conservatism and find a place for it in the most unaccommodating and anachronistic vision of the Constitution, that he has managed to fit this alien and intransigent politics into that most traditional and stylized genre of the American canon, the Supreme Court opinion—that truly is surprising, and enigmatic.

And most surprising of all: outside of a few observers, hardly anyone has noticed.

THOMAS'S BELIEFS AND jurisprudence are not tucked away in an inaccessible archive. In writing this book, I did not have to travel the country, trekking to far-off hamlets in search of Thomas's long-lost friends and relatives, hoping to nudge them toward explosive revelations. The central claim of this book—Thomas is a black nationalist whose conservative jurisprudence rotates around an axis of black interests and concerns—is a secret hiding in plain sight. All the evidence I've relied upon is from public interviews and speeches he has given over the years, the congressional record, academic articles and journalistic biographies, and most important of all, Thomas's Supreme Court opinions.

Before Thomas joined the Supreme Court, he was a prolific writer and speaker on the right and a prominent figure in the Reagan administration. In those writings and speeches, as well as in two widely noticed articles—one, an interview with the libertarian magazine *Reason*; the other, a profile by Juan Williams in the *Atlantic*—Thomas discussed frankly and openly his radical past, setting out the reading and experiences that led to and undergirded his conservatism. Typically, it was black journalists like Williams and black scholars like Harold Cruse, Manning Marable, and Niara Sudarkasa who picked up on these nationalist elements in his thinking.[30] Thomas's black nationalism did become a brief flashpoint during his confirmation battle when it came to light that he had given two speeches in 1983 praising Louis Farrakhan, the head of the Nation of Islam. But Farrakhan's anti-Semitism wound up obscuring the question of Thomas's black nationalism.[31] Seven years after Jesse Jackson's first run for the presidency, in which Jackson's reference to New York City as "Hymietown" sparked a months-long controversy, Thomas's dalliance with Farrakhan got absorbed into the more general unsettlement about black anti-Semitism, a discourse of concern among white intellectuals and the media that was still alive in the 1990s.[32] And then all of it got overshadowed by and forgotten in the wake of Anita Hill.

The journalists who wrote books on the Thomas-Hill story after Thomas's confirmation—including Jane Mayer and Jill Abramson, who would go on to prominent careers at the *New Yorker* and the *New York Times*—briefly reported on Thomas's black nationalist past, but merely as prelude to the larger story of sexual harassment and Anita Hill.[33] The three biographies of Thomas that have since been written—as well as one group biography of Thomas and his circle of friends who integrated Holy Cross—discuss his black nationalist past, as did an insightful profile in the *New Yorker* in 1996.[34] One of those biographies, Kevin Merida and Michael Fletcher's *Supreme Discomfort*, delves deeply into the intensity of Thomas's hostility to whites and his strong racial identifications. But like Thomas's other biographers, Merida and Fletcher are more interested in Thomas the man, his biography off the Court, than the jurist and his jurisprudence. The connections between Thomas's black nationalist past and jurisprudential present are occasionally made but seldom explored.

There have been two full-length academic studies of Thomas the jurist, both by conservative scholars. Aside from a couple stray sentences in one of the volumes, neither book discusses these elements in his biography or jurisprudence.[35] Among legal scholars, there is a handful of articles, most of them by scholars of color, addressing the influence of black nationalism on Clarence Thomas or the persistent race-consciousness of his thought. One of them, by a former Thomas clerk, is even called "Clarence X."[36] Yet of the 6,612 academic articles in law reviews and journals that discuss Thomas, only 99—that's

1.5 percent—mention black nationalism, usually as a reference to a title in a footnote or in the most cursory fashion.[37]

Thomas and his beliefs, in other words, are right there for all to see. Despite the frequent complaint that Thomas doesn't speak, he does speak. A lot. He gives speeches and interviews, which are televised, transcribed, and reported in the press. He writes articles. He writes opinions: in the last decade, an average of thirty-four a year—often the most of any justice.[38] Yet he and they remain unseen. There's a character in American literature whose experience looks remarkably like this. "I am an invisible man," reads the first line of his story. "I am invisible, understand, simply because people refuse to see me." Ralph Ellison's *Invisible Man*, as it happens, is one of Thomas's two favorite novels. Richard Wright's *Native Son* is the other.[39]

From the moment of his ascension to the Supreme Court, Thomas has been dismissed as an intellectual nonentity, a dim bulb in a brightly lit room. The claims are by now familiar: Thomas doesn't ask questions during oral argument because he's sleeping or lazy or doesn't know what to ask. (Most studies show that oral argument plays little to no role in the outcome of a case, and most justices use oral argument merely to shoot down the positions of their opponents on the bench.)[40] Thomas has his clerks write his opinions for him. Before Justice Antonin Scalia's death in 2016, Thomas was often called "Scalia's puppet."[41] Thomas himself joked bitterly about those rumors. "I have here a book called *My Grandfather's Son*," an interviewer once said, holding up a copy of Thomas's memoir. Before he could finish his sentence, Thomas cut him off: "written by Justice Scalia." Despite the fact that Supreme Court reporter Jan Crawford Greenburg showed long ago what an active presence Thomas is in the Court's deliberations, despite her rebuttal of the myth that Thomas followed Scalia—the evidence indicates just the opposite—the myth persists.[42]

There's only one other Supreme Court justice in recent memory who has been subject to all of these kinds of insinuations. Thurgood Marshall, whom Thomas was appointed to replace, was also deemed the puppet of a white ideological ally (Justice William Brennan). Law clerks on the Court called him "Justice Brennan-Marshall" behind his back. Archibald Cox—legendary liberal law professor at Harvard, solicitor general under John F. Kennedy and Lyndon Johnson, and Watergate special prosecutor whom Richard Nixon ordered to be fired in the Saturday Night Massacre—said that "Marshall may not be very bright or hard-working but he deserves credit for picking the best law clerks in town." Marshall's dozing visage graced a 1989 cover of *National Review* with the caption "While Justice Sleeps." The article wondered: "Of the 15 or so opinions the court assigned to [Marshall] during the term, how many does he, not his clerks, actually write?" In their best-selling book *The Brethren*, Bob Woodward and Scott Armstrong claimed that Marshall watched TV during the day and that his fellow justices appreciated him for his dirty jokes rather than for his arguments or opinions.[43] Marshall, it hardly need be said, is the only other black Supreme Court justice in American history.

THE AIM OF this book is to make the invisible justice visible, drawing on the facts of Thomas's biography to see how that biography, and the beliefs and ideologies that developed with it, have found their way into his opinions, structuring and informing his jurisprudence. At issue are not just Thomas's opinions on affirmative action, which are what have gotten the most attention from the small group of scholars attuned to Thomas's past, but Thomas's views on a variety of constitutional questions: voting rights, property rights, federalism, the Commerce Clause, freedom of speech, the Privileges or Immunities Clause, gender equality, the right to bear arms, the rights of individuals in relation to the powers of judges, juries, police, and prisons.

For many Court watchers and scholars, particularly in law schools, this is perilous ground. Supreme Court justices are supposed to be disembodied voices of the law, their opinions far removed from politics or personality, their decisions the dictates of text, doctrine, and precedent. Thomas periodically indulges this conceit: "I show no personality in my opinions," he declared in 1999. Yet Thomas is also the first to admit that "judges do not cease to be human beings when they go on the bench." Indeed, few judges have made their biographies so central to their understanding of what it is that they do as judges. While Thomas insists that judging involves the impartial application of relevant principles, he's quick to add that "reaching the correct decision itself is only half the battle. Having the courage of your convictions can be the harder part."[44]

Character matters, in other words, and Thomas attributes his to his life experiences. And where the discipline of judging places great emphasis on the restraint of personality, the submersion of self in the impersonality of law, Thomas is insistent about the need to reveal oneself through one's words rather than hiding behind the forms of law or mannered codes of disagreement. There is "an overemphasis on civility," Thomas said in 2001. "Civility cannot be the governing principle of citizenship or leadership." When pressed by friends and allies after the Anita Hill controversy to go on the road and present himself to the public, to reveal the real Clarence Thomas to a suspicious nation, Thomas replied, "Let them read my opinions. I say what I have to say in my opinions."[45] It is in Thomas's opinions, in other words, that we'll find not only the mind but also the man.

Before he became a Supreme Court justice, Thomas was, like many justices in the nineteenth and twentieth centuries, a political actor. Unlike his colleagues on the Court, he was not an esteemed legal scholar, an accomplished litigator, or an experienced jurist. Aside from brief stints in the Office of the Attorney General of the State of Missouri, as a corporate attorney for Monsanto, and an appellate judge in the D.C. Circuit, Thomas had little legal experience. After law school, he spent much of the following two decades angling for position and principle in the world of right-wing politics. That makes his profile more like that of Justice Hugo Black, who also had little legal experience before his appointment to the Court, whose background was exclusively political (he had been a senator), and who spent years writing solo opinions only to see them gradually accepted as the consensus of the Court.[46] Like Black, Thomas turned to judging not to abandon politics but to do it in a different way. If we're to understand Thomas's politics, we must read his opinions not only as legal arguments or doctrinal rulings but as revelations of a comprehensive worldview.

Thomas's jurisprudence features little of the consistency of legal high principle that his conservative admirers wish to claim for him, but neither is it the opportunistic hash that his liberal critics try to make of it. Thomas's mind is less juristic than it is political—that is where its consistency lies—but it is not narrowly partisan. In some instances, and on certain occasions, his opinions can be read as doing little more than fulfilling the imperatives of the Republican Party or the needs of the conservative movement. Thomas, after all, is a conservative justice appointed by a Republican president. When it comes to issues like unions, war powers, and gay marriage, his opinions reflect that fact. But precisely because these opinions are mostly right-wing boilerplate, they warrant little discussion here. I will focus instead on those emblematic opinions in which Thomas develops a distinctive constitutional and political vision.

Neither a straightforward biography nor a strictly legal analysis of cases and doctrines, this book is an interpretation of a profoundly political man who has chosen to express himself and his politics through a medium that puts severe constraints on how that politics and self may be expressed. Constitutional law is a stylized language. It has its norms and forms, forcing Thomas to render his largest political beliefs as the smallest of legal claims. To read Thomas, then, we must perform an act of translation. We have to hear the political arguments and beliefs that reside in his opinions—not behind or underneath them, for the most part, but in the words—and return them to their original language. That will require us to wrench each opinion out of its narrow legal context, to see in it a larger world.

As an intellectual and political biography, this book is structured in an unorthodox manner. Rather than organize Thomas's life story around a chronology of biographical facts—born in Georgia in 1948; heads north to Holy Cross in 1968, graduates in 1971; enrolls in Yale Law School in 1971, graduates in 1974; heads out west to Missouri in 1974 to work for Republican John Danforth, the state's attorney general, with an accompanying shift to the right; joins the Reagan administration in 1981; appointed by George H. W. Bush to the U.S. Court of Appeals in 1990; appointed to the Supreme Court in 1991; and then more than a quarter-century tenure on the Court—I've chosen to tell Thomas's life story in relation to the three central elements of his jurisprudence.

Race is the foundational principle of Thomas's philosophy and jurisprudence. It is his first political idea, which he comes to as a young boy growing up in the segregated South and as a politicized student in the desegregating North. It is the ground of his thinking about morals and politics, society and the law. Biographically, the first chapter of Part I ("Race") takes us from Thomas's youth in Georgia through his training at Yale Law School. During those years he develops his philosophy of race, which he will take with him, essentially untouched, onto the Court. The remaining chapters of Part I examine Thomas's opinions, from his first year on the Court through the most recent term, that deal directly with the question of race. The topics of these cases range from affirmative action to desegregation to cross burning to jury trials to prisoners' rights to campaign finance. Rather than focus on discrete areas of constitutional doctrine—a section on equal protection, another on cruel and unusual punishment—these and subsequent chapters on Thomas's jurisprudence look to extract the coherence of his political ideas from statements and claims scattered across the tidy doctrinal lines of case law.

In the mid-1970s, Thomas began thinking hard about capitalism, about the relationship between states and markets, particularly as those issues pertain to African Americans. He slowly came to a political economy, informed by many of his ideas about race as well as the history of slavery and Jim Crow. The opening chapter of Part II ("Capitalism") takes up Thomas's biography from his 1974 move to Missouri through the end of his tenure at the EEOC, where the workplace economy was a central concern, and the obligation of law and government to address that economy the animating mission. In the rest of Part II, I examine those Supreme Court opinions in which Thomas sets out his political economy of states and markets. These chapters also cover crosscutting terrain, with constitutional questions as varied as voting rights, the First Amendment, the Commerce Clause, the Takings Clause, and the Fourteenth Amendment.

Thomas's views about the Constitution did not emerge until the mid-1980s, when the possibility of a judicial appointment opened in the second term of the Reagan administration. The first chapter of Part III ("Constitution") takes us from that period in his life all the way through his Senate confirmation hearings, including the allegations made by Anita Hill. Thomas's ideas about the Constitution, as we'll see, are suffused with assumptions about gender and race, about the role of black men and women, which find their way into his jurisprudence. The confrontation with Anita Hill thus takes on a new and surprising importance. More than a story of sexual harassment or perjury, it is the Rosetta Stone of Thomas's two competing visions of the Constitution—what I call "The Black Constitution" and "The White Constitution"—that are found in his opinions about federalism, the Privileges or Immunities Clause, and the crime and punishment amendments of the Bill of Rights.

I reject virtually all of Thomas's views. In presenting his vision, however, I've opted for interpretation and analysis rather than objection and critique. I've included dissenting voices—either my own or those of other justices or analysts in the media and academe—only when they amplify lines of argument or assumption in Thomas's jurisprudence that might otherwise be inaudible. As a longtime reader of the right from the left, I know how tempting it is for people on one side of the spectrum to dismiss those on the other as unthinking defenders of partisan advantage. Because the temptation to dismiss is even greater in Thomas's case—perversely mimicking the dismissal of Marshall—and because it's sufficiently difficult to get people to believe that Thomas *has* a jurisprudence, much less to hear it, the imperative to let him speak without the interruption of easy criticisms is that much more acute.

Thomas's is a voice that unsettles. His beliefs are disturbing, even ugly; his style is brutal. I want to make us sit with that discomfort rather than swat it away. This is not so that we adopt Thomas's views, but so we see the world through his eyes—and realize, perhaps to our surprise, that his vision is in some ways similar to our own. Which should unsettle us even more.

THE STORY OF Clarence Thomas is the story of the last half century of American politics and the long shadow of defeat that hangs over it: the defeat not only of the civil rights movement and the promise of black freedom, but also of a larger vision of democratic transformation, where men and women act deliberatively and collectively to alter their estate. The citizens of the freedom struggle believed that society was made and could be remade through politics. Their successors, of whom Thomas is one, no longer believe that kind of change is possible, particularly when it comes to race. A deep and abiding racial pessimism now pervades our politics, transcending the divisions of left and right. Thomas's black nationalism is mirrored not only by the white nationalism of Trump (reprising an ancient fraternity of opposites— from Marcus Garvey and the Ku Klux Klan to the Nation of Islam and the American Nazi Party—that believed in the permanence of racial enmity), but also by the racial despair of the left.[47] From that bipartisan pessimism about race flow a great many other pessimisms about politics: that the state is not a sphere we should look to for social transformation; that a democratic concert of activists on the ground and actors in the government is neither possible nor desirable; that coalitions of solidarity cannot be forged from situations of divergent interest.

It's no accident that race, capitalism, and the Constitution are the primary categories of Clarence Thomas's jurisprudence. These are the totems of our culture, the fetishes of our fixity. They denote a world that is as immovable as it is inviolate. If we're going to come out of the shadow of defeat, we're going to have to get past these totems. But to get past them, we have to go through him.

PART I

RACE

1

Race Man

Clarence Thomas began elementary school in 1954, three months after the Supreme Court declared segregation unconstitutional. But it wasn't until 1964, when he switched to an elite Catholic boarding school outside Savannah, that he would share a classroom with whites—initially as one of two black students, in less than a year as the only black student.[1] By his own report, Thomas spent his first sixteen years in an "entirely black environment." The only white people at the schools he attended were the nuns who taught him. From the age of sixteen onward, however, he moved in a white world. When the FBI asked him in his background interview for the Supreme Court if he ever had been a member of an all-white club, he was tempted to reply, "Yes, I was, when I was in high school." (Years later, he fantasized about being asked the same question and responding that the only all-white club of which he was a member was the Court itself.) Looking back on his childhood, Thomas minced no words about Jim Crow: "I grew up under state-enforced segregation, which is as close to totalitarianism as I would like to get." Why, then, with each step across the color line, did he experience a loss, one he would forever associate with the end of Jim Crow? "I don't fit in with whites, and I don't fit in with blacks," Thomas says. "We're a mixed-up generation—those of us who were sent out to integrate society."[2]

The classic American autobiography narrates a pilgrim's progress, originating in chaos and ending in clarity. Even when the conclusion is tragic, there is an ascension to the light of the sort Bigger Thomas experiences in the final pages of *Native Son*. Awaiting trial and execution, Bigger realizes how constrained and fated his life has been, how his every action has been a preordained attempt to escape Jim Crow. But now he can see beyond the brambles to a clearing of the mind. Clarence Thomas refuses that narrative. His autobiography reads like an unironic Henry Adams, never reaching illumination and mastery, never attaining that sense of sovereignty that characterizes stories of the self in America. Imagine "a young black man, who hasn't spent much time with whites" and "suddenly finds himself among almost all whites," he said in 1995. "You can feel lost. . . . You may find you're never fully accepted up ahead, that you've landed between two worlds. That's the way I feel sometimes, even now, and it can make you angry."[3] He had been on the Supreme Court for four years.

THE STORY BEGINS in Pin Point, Georgia, an impoverished black community founded by freed slaves after the Civil War, where Thomas was born in 1948. The precision of its name is echoed in the specificity of his prose: "Myers [Thomas's younger brother] and I skipped oyster shells on the water with our cousins and caught minnows in the creeks. We rolled old automobile tires and bicycle rims along the sandy roads. . . . We were supposed to stick close to home, but no sooner did the adults leave for work each day than we ran for the sandy marshes, in which we hunted for fiddler crabs."[4] The family's move to Savannah at age six brought this pastoral to an end. A world of natural immediacy, a bountiful harmony of found objects and child's play, gave way to a city of muck and mire. In the movies Savannah conjures images of cobblestone and moss, canopied paths and oak-lined streets. Thomas's memories are different.

When I was a boy, Savannah was hell. Overnight I moved from the comparative safety and cleanliness of rural poverty to the foulest kind of urban squalor. . . . I'll never forget the sickening stench of the raw sewage that seeped and sometimes poured from the broken sewer line. Pigeon [Thomas's mother] preferred to use a chamber pot, and one of my Saturday-morning chores was to take it outside and empty it into the toilet. One day I tripped and tumbled all the way down the stairs, landing in a heap at the bottom. The brimming pot followed, drenching me in stale urine.[5]

In Pin Point, Thomas fed himself directly from the land and the water, feasting on "a lavish and steady supply of fresh food: shrimp, crab, conch, oysters, turtles, chitterlings, pig's feet, ham hocks, and plenty of fresh vegetables." In Savannah, he spooned up "cornflakes moistened with a mixture of water and sweetened condensed milk."[6]

Thomas was quite young when he moved to the city, so his memories of life in Pin Point are likely to be more invented than recalled. They are a useful chapter in a political tale of rural innocence ruined. Thomas's loathing of the city thus breaks with classic American autobiographies in a second way: Ben Franklin discovered opportunity in Philadelphia; Frederick Douglass found interracial cooperation in Baltimore; Malcolm X saw worldliness and achieved power in Harlem. In African American autobiographies, in particular, the countryside is often a place of horror, the site of the slave plantation that Douglass escaped; the big city is an answer to the rural. The great exception to that is Booker T. Washington, who also viewed the city with suspicion. Though Thomas frequently invokes Douglass, whose photograph hangs behind his desk in his chambers in the Supreme Court, his urban gothic fits more closely with the anti-urban pastoral of Washington.[7]

Thomas's first experience of racism in Savannah was not at the hands of whites, with whom he had little contact. "We knew it was there all along," he says of the color line, but it was an abstraction. "We never had to come face to face with it 24 hours a day. You didn't have to meet it in the shower. You didn't have to meet it in the bathroom.

You didn't have to meet it in the classroom. You didn't have to meet it walking down the street. You didn't have to meet it on the ballfield." The hostility Thomas did suffer came from blacks. His nickname in the schoolyard and the streets was "ABC," short for America's Blackest Child. "If he were any blacker," his friends and classmates jeered, "he'd be blue." "Before it was popular for all of us to be black and proud, as James Brown used to cheer us on, having Negroid features was not exactly popular," Thomas later observed. "It provided a rich source of insults."[8] Color was code for class. Though Thomas and his brother eventually moved into their grandparents' home in Savannah, where they enjoyed greater material comfort than other black children, the darkness of his skin—along with the Gullah/Geechee dialect and accent he retained from Pin Point—remained a sign of his lowly status and origin. "Clarence had big lips, nappy hair, and he was almost literally black," a classmate recalled. "Those folks were at the bottom of the pole. You just didn't want to hang with those kids."[9]

The wounds Thomas has suffered from white people remain acute, but the cruelties of the black community are a lifelong hurt. "People love to talk about conflicts interracially," he says. "They never talk about the conflicts and tensions intraracially. The ones we had to deal with most often and most frequently were the intraracial ones." From an early age, the primary racial inequity Thomas had to confront was the privilege of black wealth and light skin. "You had the black elite, the schoolteachers, the light-skinned people, the dentists, the doctors. My grandfather was down at the bottom," Thomas says. "They would look down on him. Everybody tries to gloss over that now, but it was the reality."[10]

The intertwined divisions of class and color are an old topic in African American politics and culture; Marcus Garvey voiced a similar animus toward light-skinned black elites.[11] What distinguishes Thomas's antipathy is that it gets channeled into a dislike of black liberals such as Patricia Harris, who was Jimmy Carter's Secretary of Health, Education, and Welfare, and Drew Days, who served as Bill Clinton's solicitor general.[12] In Thomas's view, black liberalism is the language of light-skin privilege. The black elites "know which fork to use," Thomas claims Margaret Bush Wilson—chair of the NAACP National Board of Directors, pillar of the black community in Saint Louis, an attorney who helped get the Supreme Court to strike down restrictive covenants—once told him. Because light-skinned black elites have the skills and cultural capital to represent the race, to put African Americans in the best possible light to white people, they see themselves as the public face and natural leaders of the black community.[13] They are not just the voices of black liberalism; to Thomas's mind, they are the front men and women, the emissaries, of white supremacy, a notion that recalls some of the more caustic commentary of W.E.B. Du Bois in the early 1930s.

> This leaves a mass of untrained and uncultured color folk and even of trained but ill-mannered people and groups of impoverished workers of whom this upper class of colored Americans are ashamed. They are ashamed both directly and indirectly, just as any richer or better sustained group in a nation is ashamed of those less fortunate and withdraws its skirts from touching them. But more than that, because the upper colored group is desperately afraid of being represented before American whites by this lower group, or being mistaken for them, or being treated as though they were part of it, they are pushed to the extreme of effort to avoid contact with the poorest classes of Negroes.[14]

If the move from rural Pin Point to urban Savannah introduced Thomas to one aspect of the color line, his journey north introduced him to another. Thomas arrived at all-male Holy Cross in August 1968, one of nineteen young black men recruited by the legendary Father John Brooks, a Jesuit priest who would serve as the college's president for nearly a quarter century. Having completed one year of college at a Catholic seminary in Missouri, Thomas enrolled as a sophomore. His tight-knit circle of black friends included Edward P. Jones, who would go on to become a Pulitzer Prize–winning novelist; Ted Wells, now a white-collar defense attorney who's represented everyone from Scooter Libby to Eliot Spitzer and Michael Milken; and Stan Grayson, whose peregrinations between Wall Street and City Hall would come to define membership in New York's power elite.[15] As a poor southerner, Thomas was atypical of his black cohort, yet he was part of a vast movement of southern black students who began integrating northern institutions of higher education in the late 1960s.[16]

Located in Worcester, a small city forty miles west of Boston with a black population of 2 percent, Holy Cross was even whiter than its environs. The summer before the arrival of Thomas's class, the college contacted incoming white students to see if they would object to having a black roommate; black students were never asked if they objected to having white roommates. In a survey, a quarter to a half of Thomas's fellow students agreed that blacks "have less ambition" and "looser morals" than whites and that they "smell different."[17]

Alienated by the whiteness of the campus, evident in everything from the music played at parties to the books assigned in class, black students were subject to a combination of scrutiny and condescension from their white professors and white peers. In a 1987 letter to the editor in the *Wall Street Journal*, responding to an article titled "Black College Students Are Viewed as Victims of a Subtle Racism," Thomas wrote: "A new media fad is to constantly harp on the plight of black college students on predominantly white campuses. Believe it or not, the problems are the same as they were 20 years ago when I attended college. The major difference is that the media paid little attention to them then."[18] The slow, halting, and sometimes hostile integration of black students at Holy Cross offered Thomas a mild preview of more vicious and violent battles to come. As he would write of the busing crisis that divided Boston several years later:

> I wasn't surprised by the explosion of white rage that threatened to rip the city in two. It was in Boston, not Georgia, that a white man had called me nigger for the first time. I'd already found New England to be far less honest about race than the South, and I bristled at the self-righteous sanctimony with which so many of the northerners

at Yale glibly discussed the South's racial problems. Now that their own troubles were on national display, I was unsympathetic.[19]

There's reason to be skeptical of Thomas's claim that Boston was the first place he heard someone call him "nigger." Thomas has spoken on multiple occasions of the racism he did suffer from whites in the South—"Not a day passed that I was not pricked by that ever-present trident of prejudice"—a fact confirmed by journalists who've written about his upbringing in Savannah. Even if a white man had never called him "nigger" in the South, he'd heard the word plenty. There was the time, for instance, when one of his white high school classmates had cried out, upon seeing football player Jim Brown play on television, "Look at that nigger go!" There's another reason to be skeptical of the claim: on some occasions, Thomas has gone to the extreme of claiming that the South was an idyll in which race was scarcely discussed. "To my knowledge," he declared in 2014, "I was the first black kid in Savannah, Georgia, to go to a white school. Rarely did the issue of race come up." Not only do we know that race came up at that white school—virtually every night, after lights out, when Thomas's classmates would taunt him that they couldn't see him in the dark—but the oxymoron of the statement, in which he is the first black student at a segregated school where race goes unremarked, belies the calm and composure of the memory.[20]

Yet Thomas is not alone in claiming that the racism he encountered in the North was somehow more shocking than what he had experienced before. Some of this had to do with expectations. Many southern black students of Thomas's generation, sent north to integrate colleges and universities, thought they were heading to the promised land. Says one woman who traveled from Saint Louis to Wellesley in 1965: "This was Massachusetts, the home of abolitionists. I thought I was escaping segregation." "I chose a Northern school," reports another black woman who went from Birmingham to Northwestern, "so there would be no racism."[21] What they found was the opposite. Whether Thomas's story about being called "nigger" for the first time in Boston is fictitious or not, it reveals a truth: that the North was not without its racism, and that it was in the North, in the New England of dashed expectations, that he first began thinking seriously about racism and race.

BEFORE HEADING NORTH, Thomas had a situation, not a story.[22] He knew Jim Crow and, like many African Americans, endured or witnessed the viciousness of its defenders and shape-shifting violence of its demise. He had read and loved Richard Wright: "He's an angry black novelist, and I was an angry black man." But he hadn't yet come to a worldview about race and its role in his development. In the North, Thomas found that worldview—in the black nationalism that inspired many African Americans and frustrated radicals of the era. Thomas was one of "Malcolm's children," the generation of black students who took inspiration from Malcolm X, Stokely Carmichael, the Black Panthers, and Black Power.[23]

Within months of their arrival at Holy Cross, Thomas and his friends organized themselves into the Black Student Union, toggling back and forth between aspirations toward inclusion and demands for separation. Their very name was a political choice: "Black Student Union" was a term that signaled an understanding and affirmation of "blackness" as "a deliberate political and cultural stance," in the words of Malcolm X, rather than as "an inherited set of physical characteristics."[24] The BSU founding statement called for the admission of more black students, the hiring of black faculty, courses in black literature and history, and campus events to showcase black artists and culture. They prefaced their demands with a rousing affirmation of black identity: "We, the Black students of the College of the Holy Cross, in recognizing the necessity for strengthening a sense of racial identity and group solidarity, being aware of a common cause with other oppressed peoples, and desiring to expose and eradicate social inequities and injustices, do hereby establish the Black Students Union of Holy Cross." Thomas typed up the document and was elected secretary-treasurer of the organization.[25] The BSU also published an eleven-point manifesto, which included these rules:

1. The Black man must respect the Black woman. The Black man's woman is the most beautiful of all women.

. . .

3. The Black man must work with his Black brother.

. . .

7. The Black man wants . . . the right to perpetuate his race.

. . .

9. The Black man does not want or need the white woman. The Black man's history shows that the white woman is the cause of his failure to be the true Black man.[26]

That last rule caused some playful friction within the group when some members got involved with white women from the areas around the campus. After the BSU learned that a member was dating a white woman, they convened a mock trial, found him guilty, and broke his Afro comb as a punishment. Thomas took the rule more seriously, particularly after meeting Kathy Ambush, a black woman whom he would marry in 1971 and divorce in 1984. In a poem, "Is you is, or is you ain't, a brother?," he set out the obligations of black men to black women. Even in the BSU milieu, friends recall, Thomas's "edgy race consciousness" stood out. When he saw an interracial couple strolling on campus he loudly demanded, "Do I see a black woman with a white man? How could that be?" Up until 1986, when Thomas met Virginia Lamp, who is white and would become his second wife, he opposed interracial sex and marriage.[27]

That Thomas and his classmates would affirm their solidarity in such heavily gendered terms is no surprise. "Masculinism," as historian Steve Estes has argued, is central to the struggle for black freedom. Masculinism "uses the traditional power wielded by men to woo supporters and attack opponents. It rallies supporters to a cause by urging them to be manly or to support traditional ideas of manhood." It argues that men "should have control over their own lives and authority over others." Black nationalists were hardly the only masculinists in the black freedom struggle (or other movements of the left, for that matter), and there were sharp debates about gender equality within groups like the Panthers. Still, the second half of the 1960s brought with it a heightened masculinist rhetoric, often expressed through intensified homophobia, ambient sexism, and outright misogyny. It was common to find militants like Thomas and his campus comrades framing their demands for black freedom in the idiom of black male honor, which could only be met by recognition from white men and deference from black women. While that honor code might sometimes impose an obligation on black men to show respect to black women, such behavior was mostly meant to enhance the standing of black men in a white world. "The black man never will get anybody's respect until he learns to respect his own women," Malcolm X argued in his *Autobiography*, outlining a belief system from his early years in the Nation of Islam in which respect for black women was only a means to a more important end.[28]

Thomas read the *Autobiography* in his first year at Holy Cross. He put up a poster of Malcolm X in his dorm room. He collected records of his speeches. Two decades later, he could still recite passages from memory. "I'd been very partial to Malcolm X, particularly his self-help teachings," Thomas explained in 1987. "There is a lot of good in what he says, and I go through it for the good." (Thurgood Marshall, by contrast, dismissed Malcolm X as "a bum . . . about as lowlife as you can get.") Well into the second term of the Reagan administration, Thomas was summoning Malcolm as a witness for the prosecution against the liberal establishment: "I don't see how the civil-rights people today can claim Malcolm X as one of their own. Where does he say black people should go begging the Labor Department for jobs? He was hell on integrationists. Where does he say you should sacrifice your institutions to be next to white people?" Even after he became a Supreme Court justice, Thomas felt Malcolm's pull, writing in defense of racial separatism and against integration, and enthusing over Spike Lee's 1992 film *Malcolm X*.[29]

In college, Thomas wore a Panthers-style leather jacket and beret. He sported Black Power buttons, including one that said, "No Vietnamese ever called me Nigger" (attributed, wrongly, to Muhammad Ali). He signed his letters "Power to the People." He championed the cause of Black Panther leaders and of Communist Party member Angela Davis, in flight from the government after being charged in connection with a politically fraught kidnapping and murder.[30] In a 1996 public conversation with Kay Cole James, now president of the Heritage Foundation, Thomas described his politics thus:

THOMAS: I was truly on the left.

JAMES: How far left were you?

THOMAS: Well, there was nobody on the other side of me. Let's just put it this way. I thought George McGovern was a conservative.

. . .

JAMES: How did you go from a McGovern liberal to . . .

THOMAS: I was never a liberal.

JAMES: What were you?

THOMAS: I was a radical.[31]

Like other politicized black students at the time, organizing on almost two hundred college campuses, Thomas was an activist. Asked at his Senate confirmation hearings what he majored in, Thomas said English literature; asked what he minored in, he said, "I think protest."[32] His first trip to Washington, D.C., was to march on the Pentagon in protest of the Vietnam War. The last rally he attended, in Cambridge—one of the most violent in the city's history, in which two thousand cops assaulted three thousand protesters—was to free Black Panther leaders Bobby Seale and Ericka Huggins. At the rally, he chanted "Ho, Ho, Ho Chi Minh" in support of the Vietnamese communist leader and the cause of a united and independent Vietnam. He also remembers a policeman yelling at him and his friends, "This must be the nigger contingent from Roxbury."[33] The Panthers, Thomas believed, offered "another way." With their guidance, he and other members of the BSU organized a free breakfast program modeled on one the Panthers had pioneered in Oakland and elsewhere, serving daily meals out of a church in Worcester to about fifty poor children—most of them, as it turned out, white (not surprising, given the city's demographics).

While his Holy Cross friends were less than diligent in their duties, Thomas rose at five in the morning to do his part for the movement.[34]

Thomas also played a leading role in what by all accounts was the defining racial crisis of those turbulent years at Holy Cross. It was the fall of 1969, Thomas was a junior, and fifty-four students had staged a sit-in to protest General Electric recruiters on campus, blocking access to other students seeking an interview with a company that was a major military contractor and had been accused of discriminating against black workers. After the protesters refused to cede the space, the administration brought sixteen of them up on disciplinary charges. Only five of the fifty-four protesters were black, but four of them were among the sixteen now facing disciplinary action—a stark preview of the racial disproportionality in the criminal justice system Thomas would confront on the Court.

The BSU debated what to do. Members wanted to take over a building or take up arms. Thomas proposed that all black students walk out, quitting the campus in solidarity with the black students facing expulsion. Make visible the removal of black faces from a campus that had worked so hard to make itself look less white. "I don't know about you guys," Thomas said, "but the way I was raised was that if someone is treating me unfairly, they are demonstrating to me that I am simply not welcome." After a last-ditch attempt at negotiations with the administration failed, virtually every one of the campus's sixty black students did walk out, fists clenched in the air, ready to never return. White students on campus began organizing a sympathy strike, the story generated national headlines, and within two days the administration reversed itself.[35] In a triumphant editorial, Thomas called the walkout "an action for liberation." It showed black students "that nothing is more important than being the black men that they are. . . . For the black students this Exodus is one more step in the direction of complete liberation from the slavery that whites—whether knowingly or otherwise—persist in foisting upon the black man. . . . The blacks acted as men, and that was all that counted. They did not plan to compromise manhood for a 'good' education, and didn't."[36]

To say that Thomas was steeped in the black nationalism of the late 1960s may be to say both too much and too little. Like many students of any era, Thomas was in an extended period of experiment, oscillating between dramatically opposing styles of thought and action without reaching center or settlement. He often took dissenting positions in arguments with his friends, pressing a contrary viewpoint in the hope that a dogma might be averted or a depth achieved. One night, he'd push a hard line of black and white; the next, he'd soften it with shades of gray. Sometimes he urged more integration and less confrontation. Then he'd reverse himself. Despite his separatist positions, he seemed personally more at ease with white people than his black friends were—not unlike LeRoi Jones (en route to becoming Amiri Baraka), whose racially charged visions did not preclude close relationships with whites or marriage to a white woman, and whose most welcoming audiences in the early 1960s were often white.[37]

Like all ideologies, black nationalism is a contested tradition, whose exponents and analysts seldom agree on its basic tenets.[38] While a stringent definition might entail a belief in the separate cultural identity of African Americans and a commitment to their gaining a sovereign state, black nationalists frequently have taken up one position without the other, larding both with a thick layer of pragmatism. The hope of many black nationalist leaders has been that if African Americans act in solidarity with each other, they or their allies might use these nationalist claims—particularly the demand for a separate black state—to leverage more limited advances, as well as some level of self-determination and community control, within the American polity.[39] It wouldn't have been difficult for Thomas to claim the mantle of black nationalism as a student without conforming to a strict set of beliefs.

When Thomas was in college, black nationalism was fast becoming the universal grammar of even the most conventional black politics. "We are first and foremost black nationalists," declared Julian Bond, an early leader of the Student Nonviolent Coordinating Committee and a representative in the Georgia House of Representatives, in 1970. "Nation Time" was the chant at the 1972 National Black Political Assembly in Gary, Indiana, where legions of mainstream black politicians and activists gathered to chart an electoral course for the future in the wake of waning black protest and rebellion in the streets.

As Kenneth Gibson, Newark's black mayor, had explained two years earlier to the thousands assembled at the Conference of African Peoples in Atlanta: "You have to understand that nobody is going to deal with our problems but us. . . . Nationalism is simply the expression of our recognition of the fact that in the final analysis it is Black people who must solve the problems of Black people."[40] That fusion of solidarity and separatism, of collective self-reliance and self-help, which so often has been the calling card of black nationalism, was rife throughout the black freedom struggle of the time.

But precisely because black nationalism was the sea in which so many swam, it would be a mistake to underestimate the effects of Thomas's immersion in it. "I was a kid who found it hard to go to a white college in Worcester, Massachusetts," he says. Moving to a white institution in the North repeated the trauma of moving to a white seminary in the South, which Thomas described in an interview with the *Crisis*, the magazine of the NAACP, thus: "So you leave that [all-black environment] and go into an environment where you are the only black and you are in a setting where you live day in and out and attend classes and the only blacks you see are the two women who work in the kitchen and the rest are white people. You . . . go through some changes." Going through those changes in the charged context of an integrating northern college campus, surrounded by the tenets and texts of black nationalism, transformed him. "It was a special time in my life," he says. In later years, Thomas would downplay the presence of black nationalism in his mature thinking, hotly declaring, "I'm not a nationalist." Yet he never disavowed its role in his development, going so far as to invoke Malcolm X as an analog or precedent for his biography: "I have been angry enough in my life, and there are some points where I'm sure my attitudes approached black nationalism. I'm certain you could say the same thing about Malcolm X."[41]

In college, Thomas's black friends loved to tease him about the fervor of his commitment and the seriousness of his study: "What woman would want this man anyway? He's . . . into books and Black Power." But even as a Supreme Court justice looking back on his youthful development, Thomas refused to mock the moment: "I was an angry black man," he wrote in his memoir. "The more I read about the black power movement, the more I wanted to be a part of it."[42]

THOMAS GRADUATED FROM Holy Cross in 1971; Michael Harrington, the democratic socialist, delivered the commencement address. Thomas considered wearing a dashiki but opted not to. He ranked ninth in a class of 521. Along with nineteen other students, he was elevated by the faculty to a prestigious national honor society of Jesuit scholars.[43] That fall, he entered Yale Law School, which he had chosen over Harvard because Yale was more liberal. There he was flattened by a blast wave of white paternalism. One of twelve black students, Thomas was the beneficiary of an affirmative action program—precisely the sort of race-conscious initiative he would come to revile. Yale had decreed that 10 percent of the incoming class was to be students of color.[44] The program was more stringent and selective than one Yale had adopted two years before; still, Thomas felt himself the object of the most intense snobbery and suspicion. "You had to prove yourself every day because the presumption was that you were dumb and didn't deserve to be there on merit," he later recalled. "Every time you walked into a law class at Yale it was like having a monkey jump down on your back from the Gothic arches." Thomas had long experience of proving himself before a hostile audience, of being the "black spot on the white horse."[45] But now the competition was stiffer and the stakes higher. The scrutiny was coming not just from fellow students but also from liberal whites acting as his patrons and protectors. In the South—and even at Holy Cross, where he had been recruited—Thomas saw himself forcing his way into and through the meritocracy by the power of his intelligence and will; all Father Brooks had had to do was notice him. At Yale, where he was just one of many talented students, and by no means the most talented, his accomplishments felt divested of their authorship. No matter how hard he worked, he could not claim the authority of his arrival. "I was among the elite," he recalls, yet "no amount of striving would make me one of them."[46] Never an equal, he would forever remain the object of white largesse.

Throughout his life, Thomas has repeatedly been told that he owes his success, whether admission to Yale or elevation to the Court, to affirmative action. President Bush may have declared that he chose Thomas for the Court because he was the most qualified candidate, but virtually no one believed him. "Candidly," the esteemed black jurist A. Leon Higginbotham wrote in a humiliating public letter to Thomas after his confirmation, "I do not believe that you were indeed the most competent person to be on the Supreme Court." Higginbotham quoted Charles Bowser, a distinguished African American Philadelphia lawyer, who said, "I'd be willing to bet . . . that not one of the senators who voted to confirm Clarence Thomas would hire him as their lawyer." Such jibes make Thomas smart: "I don't think black people are indebted to anybody for anything. Nobody has done us any favors in this country, buddy. This thing about how they let me into Yale— that kind of stuff offends me. All they did was stop stopping us."[47] Yet Thomas also acknowledges he has been the repeated beneficiary of affirmative action—"I have been both deterred and preferred by racially conscious policies." It is a fact he is constantly reminded of, by friends and enemies, on the left and on the right.[48] No reservoir of inner resolve and self-confidence has ever been enough to overcome the fact that his race, once a social liability, is now counted an unearned asset. A sympathetic Yale professor once compared affirmative action to the admissions preferences schools give to the children and grandchildren of alumni. The analogy was meant to lighten the load, but Thomas only felt burdened by it. "As much as it had stung to be told I'd done well in [high school] despite my race," he wrote, "it was far worse to feel that I was now at Yale because of it."[49]

At Yale, Thomas developed an understanding of racism he would never shake. Whites—southern and northern, liberal and conservative, rural and urban—are racists. The causes of that racism are unclear. Racism "has complex and, to a certain degree, undiscoverable roots."[50] Not knowing the beginnings of racism, we can't know its end. Without an analysis of its origins, we can have no vision of its abolition. Race is pervasive—and perdurable. Even as a conservative, Thomas would insist that racism and all its manifestations were here to stay. (Since the 1970s, by contrast, most conservatives and Republicans have claimed to believe that America is a color-blind society, where the problem of racism and discrimination has been essentially solved.)[51] "Will discrimination ever disappear?" Thomas was asked by the *Washington Post* in 1983. "I'm not one who believes that it will," he replied. In 1985, Thomas told the graduating class of Savannah State College: "I have no delusions about discrimination, racism, or bigotry. I am not among those who believed that this unholy triumvirate went some place—disappeared. . . . I am here to say that discrimination, racism, and bigotry have gone no place and probably never will." That same year, he declared in an influential conservative magazine, "I don't think the society has ever been color-blind. I grew up in Savannah, Georgia, under segregation. It wasn't color-blind and America is not color-blind today. . . . Racism has existed from time immemorial. Discrimination still exists." Four years before his nomination to the Supreme Court, Thomas's views remained unchanged: "I'd have to say there is still racism and there are still attitudes based on race." "There is nothing you can do to get past black skin," he told Juan Williams in 1987. "I don't care how educated you are, how good you are—you'll never have the same contacts or opportunities, you'll never be seen as equal to whites."[52] According to Williams, who Thomas claims is his closest friend in the media:

> Ultimately, he said to me one day, turning away as if to avoid revealing some private hurt, it doesn't matter that black and white Americans are unlikely ever to see each other as anything but blacks and whites. It doesn't matter that a black in America is only rarely judged on the basis of his character rather than that of his color. It does not really matter that the dream of racial integration—of uplift through education, of gradual absorption into the social and economic mainstream—has not worked for most black Americans, even for those who, like him, have leaped the boundaries of the ghetto and, it would seem, "made it" in a white world. For when you get right

down to it, Thomas said, successful blacks don't particularly like the kind of integration that whites have crafted for them in the past thirty years. Increasing numbers of middle-class blacks see integration simply as window dressing; blacks may be present and visible, but only a few have any real power.[53]

Because white racism is not going to disappear, the most that can be hoped for is that whites will be honest about their racism. Honesty is demonstrated through crude statements of personal animus or intellectual professions of racial inequality. Dishonesty takes the form of denial of one's racism coupled with sympathetic offers and extensions of help. Dishonesty is worse than honesty. It lulls blacks into a false sense of security, assuring them that they are safe when they are not. Racial sincerity is what distinguishes the South from the North, conservatives from liberals, good country folk from city-dwellers. It is praiseworthy even in the extreme case of the Southern Confederacy. According to one of his co-workers at his first job after law school, Thomas liked to say that "you knew exactly where you stood with the Confederacy. Today people discriminate but they are sneaky. But I just as soon that people be honest."[54]

During his time in the Reagan administration, Thomas often criticized the right's hostility to African Americans: "The Republican Party and conservatives have shown very little interest in black Americans and have actually done things to leave the impression among blacks that they are antagonistic to their interests," he said. "Conservatives don't exactly break their necks to tell blacks that they're welcome." In 1987, Thomas declared in a speech before the Heritage Foundation, "Unfortunately, I would have to characterize the general attitude of conservatives toward black conservatives as indifference—with minor exceptions. It was made clear more than once that, since blacks did not vote right, they were owed nothing. . . . And our treatment certainly offered no encouragement to prospective converts. It often seemed that to be accepted within the conservative ranks and to be treated with some degree of acceptance, a black was required to become a caricature of sorts."[55] Thomas knew whereof he spoke. Referring to Thomas's time at the Equal Employment Opportunity Commission, South Carolina senator Strom Thurmond once remarked, "I've known Clarence since he was head of the Unemployment Commission"—just one of the many slights and oversights Thomas received at the hands of conservatives and Republicans.[56]

Yet despite these blistering assessments of the Reagan administration and the conservative movement, Thomas continued to deploy the calculus of race sincerity to exonerate the right. "Yes, there are a lot of racists in the Administration," he told Williams. "So what? There may be more here now, they may be more out front. I don't care. I prefer dealing with an out-and-out racist anyway to one who is racist behind your back."[57] One of Thomas's favorite songs is the 1971 hit "Smiling Faces Sometimes" by the Undisputed Truth, which he first listened to at Yale Law School. Its classic lyric—"Smiling faces, smiling faces tell lies"—resonates with his experience of northern white liberals, from Yale to his Senate confirmation hearings.[58] Among the virtues of the Reagan administration, he once said, was its "honesty," the fact that no one working for it was "smiling in your face."[59]

In making sincerity the litmus test of American racism, Thomas took a strand of the black nationalism that influenced his early development and wove it into a near entire philosophy of race. In the 1920s, at the nadir of another moment of racist reaction in the United States, Marcus Garvey also found succor in the promise of racial candor—the uglier, the better. "They are better friends to my race for telling us what they are, and what they mean, than all the hypocrites put together with their false gods and religions, notwithstanding," Garvey said of the Ku Klux Klan. "I like honesty and fair play."[60]

Not only did Thomas borrow from the substance of black nationalism; he also mimicked its style. He wrote: "At least southerners were up front about their bigotry: you knew exactly where they were coming from, just like the Georgia rattlesnakes that always let you know when they were ready to strike. Not so the paternalistic big-city whites who offered you a helping hand. . . . Like the water moccasin, they struck without warning."[61] The imagery of his language, with its use of animal prototypes for conservative and liberal racism, mirrors that of Malcolm X.

> The white conservatives aren't friends of the Negro either, but they at least don't try to hide it. They are like wolves; they show their teeth in a snarl that keeps the Negro always aware of where he stands with them. But the white liberals are foxes, who also show their teeth to the Negro but pretend that they are smiling. The white liberals are more dangerous than the conservatives; they lure the Negro, and as the Negro runs from the growling wolf, he flees into the open jaws of the "smiling" fox.[62]

For Thomas, liberal dishonesty was not only about race; it was connected to class. However well-intentioned white liberals were about remedying racial inequality, their elitism was steadfast. No matter what, they wished to maintain the hierarchies of American society, in which they and their children were guaranteed a place at the table, secured through networks of friendship and family and coveted spots at schools and universities. White liberals were as protective of the privileges of their education and the social capital they acquired in college as the most hidebound conservative was of his. At Yale, some of Thomas's classmates would query the absence of class rankings and grades. "You are the cream of the crop of law schools in the world," a professor responded. "You do not separate cream from cream. It is your fate as a Yale Law School student to become one of the leaders in the legal profession. It will happen, not because of you personally, but because you are here. That is what happens to Yale Law School students." Blacks at Yale and other white institutions, however, were consistently separated from the cream. Indeed, the absence of grades and rankings at Yale was used to effect that separation. After graduation, when Thomas tried to secure a position at an elite law firm in Atlanta that had no black associates, one of the marks against him was that he had no grades: Even if he came from Yale, how could his employers know how good he was?[63]

Something about the class position of liberal whites drove them to lend a helping hand to blacks and to remind blacks of the help they had received. Offering help to the help—aid that only elite whites were able to provide—was a way to express the combined privileges of race and class. That is a running theme of *Native Son*: a poor black man from the slums of Chicago, Bigger Thomas is given an opportunity to overcome his situation when a wealthy white family, impassioned by a sense of social mission and liberal purpose, hires him to work as their chauffeur. The notion that blacks can advance only with the help of whites is anathema to Clarence Thomas, who has identified with Bigger throughout his life.[64] It reinforces the status of whites as patrons and the sense of blacks as being patronized. "The most devastating form of racism is the feeling that blacks are inferior," writes Thomas, "so let's help them." It was a lesson Thomas learned at Yale and would take with him to the Supreme Court.[65]

Even if whites never followed up their proffers of help with acts of harm, their help was a harm because the helping hand was white. White benevolence denies African Americans the pride of achievement, the knowledge that their success is theirs—not as individuals (Thomas has repeatedly acknowledged that he could not have succeeded without the help of others) but as African Americans.[66] If one is black and overcomes the barriers of Jim Crow, one can be assured that one's achievements are real, as real as the color line itself. That clarity is a necessary constituent of race pride, of the robust sense of equality that Thomas claims he saw in his grandparents. Despite Jim Crow's drastic abridgments of freedom, his grandparents managed to acquire property and to support themselves and their extended family, their friends and neighbors. They understood that "the rewards of our efforts were not commensurate with those of whites." But the knowledge that blacks "had to work twice as hard to get half as far" ensured, however far they got, that the distance would be theirs: again, not as individuals but as members of the black community. Armed with that knowledge, "they knew we were inherently equal under God's law."[67]

When blacks succeed in the shadow of their white benefactors, that clarity and certainty are lost. After Jim Crow was dismantled and integration was pursued as policy, blacks were deprived of "the chance to savor the triumph over adversity." That "ability to endure adversity and to use it for gain," Thomas once wrote, is "the core of human dignity." It is what "gives us our measure as individuals."[68] The struggle against adversity is also where we find our freedom. The "dirty little secret of freedom," according to Thomas, is that it "is often very, very difficult"—and it must remain difficult. If the goods of life come too easily, we cease to exercise our power to get them. The elimination of adversity deprives blacks of the opportunity to exercise their power, thereby undermining that sense of dignity and freedom.[69] Now blacks "owe all their achievements to the 'anointed' in society who supposedly changed the circumstances—not to their own efforts."[70]

In Thomas's view, this benevolent tendency of white liberalism, with its ease and excuse-making, has only grown stronger since the end of Jim Crow. "You all have a much tougher road to travel," he told the students of Savannah State College in 1985. "Not only do you have to contend with the ever-present bigotry, you must do so with a recent tradition that almost requires you to wallow in excuses. . . . Unlike me you must not only overcome the repressiveness of racism, you must also overcome the lure of excuses. You have twice the job I had." Or, as he said to a group of black conservatives in 1985, "What we had in Georgia under Jim Crow was not as bad as this."[71]

That is the loss that Clarence Thomas has suffered since his youth: not of the color line but of its clarity. "It was more difficult for me to live in Massachusetts than it was for me to live in Savannah," he told an interviewer. "In Savannah, the rules were indeed clear." The advantages of clarity are not that they make social life easier to navigate, assuring one of a place in the social order; Thomas's is not a traditionalist vision of a social cohesion destroyed. It's that they make black achievements more exigent and easier to identify, easier to measure and avow. That loss of clarity is something Thomas associates with liberalism, the North, cities, and, above all, integration. "I never worshipped at the altar" of integration, he declared five years after his ascension to the Supreme Court. "The whole push to assimilate simply does not make sense to me."[72] It is a loss that he has set out—from his early years as a radical black nationalist at Holy Cross through his current tenure as a conservative black nationalist on the Court—to reverse.

2

Stigmas

On the Supreme Court, Thomas has argued that racism is a fact of American society. It is not going away. It is everywhere, even in cases that don't appear to involve race. This last point is especially important to Thomas. As a conservative black nationalist, Thomas seeks to show that race matters but not in the ways liberals or conservatives think it matters. Where liberals and conservatives have identified a set of provisions in the Constitution that they believe define and delimit the domain of race—the Equal Protection Clause, say, or the Fifteenth Amendment, which protects the right to vote—Thomas raises the banner of race in precincts that neither liberals nor conservatives believe involve race at all.

Take campaign finance. In the controversial 2010 case *Citizens United v. Federal Election Commission*, the Court's conservative majority, including Thomas, held that the First Amendment stops the government from restricting corporate spending on election-related activities, such as corporations airing their own political ads in support of a candidate or campaign.[1] In his dissent, the liberal Justice John Paul Stevens denounced the Court for overturning a century-long tradition of regulating corporate spending. The fountainhead of that tradition, wrote Stevens, is the Tillman Act of 1907, which bans any direct contributions from corporations to federal candidates. Stevens returned repeatedly to that legislation, citing it as a touchstone of good governance, a testament to Congress's recognition of the "recurrent need to regulate corporate participation in candidate elections."[2]

For Thomas, the Tillman Act, named after longtime South Carolina senator Benjamin Tillman, evoked something else entirely. Five months after the Court decided *Citizens United*, Thomas wrote a blistering opinion in an unrelated gun rights case that hinged, in part, on a Reconstruction-era interpretation of the Second Amendment. Rehearsing at length the murderous consequences for African Americans who were denied guns under Jim Crow, Thomas made a point of calling out a particular figure in this reign of racial terror.

> Take, for example, the Hamburg Massacre of 1876. There, a white citizen militia sought out and murdered a troop of black militiamen for no other reason than that they had dared to conduct a celebratory Fourth of July parade through their mostly black town. The white militia commander, "Pitchfork" Ben Tillman, later described this massacre with pride: "[T]he leading white men of Edgefield" had decided "to seize the first opportunity that the negroes might offer them to provoke a riot and teach the negroes a lesson by having the whites demonstrate their superiority by killing as many of them as was justifiable." . . . None of the perpetrators of the Hamburg murders was ever brought to justice.
>
> Organized terrorism like that perpetuated by Tillman and his cohorts proliferated in the absence of federal enforcement of constitutional rights.[3]

With a nod to Stevens's dissent in *Citizens United*, Thomas drily noted, "Tillman's contributions to campaign finance law have been discussed in our recent cases on that subject."[4] In a speech at a law school in Florida that same term, Thomas was less circumspect. Defending the majority opinion in *Citizens United*, he drew a direct link between Stevens's favorite campaign finance reformer and white supremacy.

"Go back and read why Tillman introduced that legislation," he told the audience. "Tillman was from South Carolina, and as I hear the story he was concerned that the corporations, Republican corporations, were favorable to blacks and he felt that there was a need to regulate them."[5] For Thomas, even the seemingly non-racial subject of campaign finance is, like so many constitutional questions, deeply enmeshed in race.[6]

Sometimes there is an instrumental purpose to Thomas's declarations that race matters. In certain cases, where Thomas is trying to reason his way to a conservative outcome, race affords him easy access to that destination, or at least a quick way to undermine liberal positions. Such invocations of race can lead to the suspicion that they are merely opportunistic, a cheap playing of the race card. An instance of this occurs in Thomas's criticism of the Court's refusal in 2018 to hear *Silvester v. Becerra*, also a Second Amendment case. Like many states, California imposes a waiting period on the purchase of handguns, but California's ten-day wait is longer than that of most other states, and it applies not only to first-time gun buyers but also to people who already own guns. Jeff Silvester sued California, claiming that the state's unusually restrictive waiting period violates the Second Amendment.[7] The Court refused to take the case, prompting a furious dissent from Thomas. Even though the Court had previously ruled that gun ownership is a constitutional right protected from state and federal infringements, Thomas accused liberals of treating it as "a disfavored right." Liberals are much less worried about abridgments of the right to bear arms, he claimed, than they are about the right to an abortion or freedom of speech—even racist speech: "I . . . suspect that four Members of this Court would vote to review a 10-day waiting period on the publication of racist speech, notwithstanding a State's purported interest in giving the speaker time to calm down," he wrote.[8] The implication was as crude as it was clear: liberals care more about controlling guns than fighting racism.

But if Thomas is being opportunistic, the question is: Opportunistic for what? Invocations of race, particularly in situations that are not obviously connected to race, are not necessary to achieve conservative outcomes. Indeed, other conservative justices often reach the same conclusions as Thomas in gun rights and campaign finance cases without the race-conscious detour. Something else is going on here. Thomas is weaving blackness into a new constitutional cloth, one that is race-conscious, even race-centric, but with race located in different places and generating different claims from those we have come to expect from contemporary constitutional discourse.

Though Thomas understands racism as primarily a form of individual prejudice—not as the product of impersonal institutions whose policies and practices reproduce the inequality of black people, intentionally or unintentionally—he does believe that this prejudice has a social life and social consequences. Racism does not reside only in people's conscious beliefs and opinions. It lies beneath and below those opinions, in the unconscious prejudices white people bring to their interactions with black people. Racism expresses the yawning gulf between whites and blacks, how differently they see and experience the world, how differently they receive its benefits and bear its burdens. For Thomas, the most important form that racism takes is the stigma or mark it puts on black people, designating them as less worthy or capable than white people. None of these arguments will be unfamiliar to liberal anti-racists: indeed, the notions of racial stigmas and unconscious bias are among the leading elements of the contemporary social science of race. What distinguishes Thomas's jurisprudence is that he accepts these liberal claims about the secret and not-so-secret life of race, while refusing the conclusions that liberals believe must follow from them.

IN ONE OF his first opinions on the Court, in 1992, Thomas wrote: "Conscious and unconscious prejudice persists in our society. Common sense and common experience confirm this understanding."[9] Ten years into his tenure on the Court, he was still reaffirming that common sense: "If society cannot end racial discrimination, at least it can arm minorities with the education to defend themselves from some of discrimination's effects."[10] That "if" flies by so quickly the reader may not notice what Thomas is doing: rather than setting up a conditional about American society, he sets out the inability to end racial discrimination as *the* condition of American society.

Thomas made a similar move in the 2007 school desegregation case *Parents Involved in Community Schools v. Seattle*. The Court's liberal dissenters argued that one of the reasons it was important for Seattle to take more interventionist measures to integrate its schools was that integration would teach "social cooperation" between students of different races. The problem with that argument, wrote Thomas, is that teaching cooperation between the races would require Seattle to impose desegregation measures with "no durational limit." As he put it, "It will always be important for students to learn cooperation among the races. If this interest justifies race-conscious measures today, then logically it will justify race-conscious measures forever."[11] Once again, the "if" says more than we might realize. Why, after all, should the need to teach racial cooperation today mean that it must be taught forever? There may once have been a need to teach cooperation between Protestants and Catholics, but it doesn't follow that one needs to teach that cooperation in perpetuity. At some point, social conflicts go away. Not when it comes to race, says Thomas.

By way of contrast, notice how the liberal justice David Souter justified a federal affirmative action program that benefited construction firms owned or controlled by racial and ethnic minorities. After conceding that whites may be "hurt" by this system of preferences and incentives, Souter argued that one of the reasons this "price is considered reasonable" is that it is "to be paid only temporarily." In Souter's account, racism will be eradicated by anti-racist measures, ultimately making those measures unnecessary: "If the justification for the preference is eliminating the effects of a past practice, the assumption is that the effects will themselves recede into the past, becoming attenuated and finally disappearing."[12] That is not Thomas's vision of the future.

In its crudest form, racism is found in the negative attitudes and prejudices of whites, upon which they are willing to act, sometimes to devastating effect. In *Georgia v. McCollum* (1992), the Court ruled that criminal defendants—in this case, three whites accused of assaulting two African Americans—should not be allowed to strike down potential jurors based on their race. Allowing defendants to make racially based "peremptory challenges" would violate the Equal Protection Clause, denying black citizens the right to serve on juries merely because they are black.[13] The Court already had held that prosecutors, as agents of the state, could not use peremptory challenges to reject potential jurors on the basis of their race. *Georgia v. McCollum* now applied that same rule to the defense. Even though criminal defendants are not state actors, the Court reasoned that defendants are relying on a privilege or power of the state (the peremptory challenge) in a state institution (the jury trial). Because their case and tools are authorized by the state, defendants are required to obey the Constitution's guarantee of equal protection, which binds the state and state actors. "We hold that the Constitution prohibits a criminal defendant from engaging in purposeful discrimination on the ground of race in the exercise of peremptory challenges," wrote the liberal Justice Harry Blackmun for the Court.[14]

All four of the Court's conservatives—Thomas, Scalia, William Rehnquist, and Sandra Day O'Connor—dissented or wrote concurrences that demurred from part of the majority's opinion. The main, if not sole, objection of the three white conservatives was to the majority's claim that criminal defendants should be thought of as state actors. Scalia called that position "sheer inanity."[15] Being tried for a crime, defendants are acted upon by the state; they do not act for the state. Thomas scarcely touched that issue. His concern, shared by no other justice, liberal or conservative (save for one brief mention by O'Connor at the very end of her opinion), lay not with the actual defendants in this case but with a hypothetical black defendant. Facing the prospect of a majority-white or all-white jury, such a defendant might find himself wishing to use a peremptory challenge to strike down potential white jurors and thereby secure a more racially balanced jury. "I am certain," Thomas warns, "that black criminal defendants will rue the day that this Court ventured down the road that inexorably will lead to the elimination of peremptory strikes."[16]

Flipping the racial script of the Court's judgment, Thomas used race to undo the liberal jurisprudence of race. Instead of staying with the fact that the defendants were white, Thomas made them black. Instead of seeing the subject of rights as a prospective black juror, he focused on the right of black defendants. Having constructed the racial hypothetical in this way, Thomas evoked the 1880 case *Strauder v. West Virginia*, which struck down state prohibitions on blacks serving on juries. In *Strauder*, wrote Thomas, "we reasonably surmised, without direct evidence in any particular case, that all-white juries might judge black defendants unfairly."[17] The liberal majority in *McCollum* held that to strike a potential juror, there had to be direct evidence that he "harbors racial prejudice" and is "incapable of confronting and suppressing [his] racism." In Blackmun's words, "This Court firmly has rejected the view that assumptions of partiality based on race provide a legitimate basis for disqualifying a person as an impartial juror."[18] Thomas countered that even when there is no evidence of such racism, it is fair to assume that "the racial composition of a jury may affect the outcome of a criminal case." The fact that whites are racist, and will act on that racism when in a group, must be acknowledged. Despite a century's agitation for racial equality, concluded Thomas, "I do not think that the basic premise of *Strauder* has become obsolete."[19] So persistent is the significance of race.[20]

FOR THOMAS, RACE has a social existence; it lives in the world. Race signals the lack of commonality between whites and blacks, how differently they see the world, how conflicting are their interests and combustible their hatreds. Sometimes, the settings for these differences are familiar and near—in schools, for example. In Ohio, the state government had created a voucher program, giving students in any local school district that had been placed under a federal court order the opportunity to use public money to attend private schools, including religious schools. Cleveland was the only such district in the state. The state's program was targeted at poor students: about 60 percent of the Cleveland students receiving the vouchers were at or below the poverty line.[21] The constitutional question raised by the school voucher program, which came before the Court in *Zelman v. Simmons-Harris* (2002), concerned the Establishment Clause: Does the First Amendment ban on the establishment of religion prohibit the state from allowing students to use public money to attend religious schools? That was the question all the Court's justices—whether in the five-member majority, which ruled in favor of the voucher program, or in dissent—focused on. All except Thomas.

In his concurring opinion, Thomas transformed the constitutional question at stake in *Zelman* from religious freedom to racial equality. The majority of Cleveland's population was black. Almost two-thirds of those living under the poverty line were black, in one of the poorest large cities in the United States.[22] Do "failing urban public schools," which do not provide a decent education to black students, violate the Equal Protection Clause, the state's obligation to treat blacks and whites equally?[23] Opening and closing with passages from Frederick Douglass—Thomas is just about the only justice to cite both Douglass and W.E.B. Du Bois in his opinions—and references to Reconstruction, Thomas made the centerpiece of his decision the claim that education is an instrument of black emancipation.[24] By not providing an equal education to black children, he wrote, "many of our inner-city public schools deny emancipation to urban minority students." The failings of Cleveland's public schools "disproportionately affect minority children most in need of educational opportunity." While other justices mentioned in passing the failings of Cleveland's public schools, only Thomas saw those failings as a denial of equal protection. Where the Court's white justices saw religion, Thomas saw race. Opponents of the voucher program "raise formalistic concerns about the Establishment Clause," he wrote, "but ignore the core purposes of the Fourteenth Amendment": namely, that whites and blacks be treated equally, that the state ensure an equal education to white and black students.[25]

In *Virginia v. Black* (2003), Thomas performed a similar maneuver, using race to leverage a shift in perspective in what was constitutionally at stake in a case. The case grew out of two incidents of cross burning in Virginia. The first was at a Klan rally held by Barry Black on private property with the consent of the owner. Though several hundred yards from the road, the cross was visible to neighbors; a visitor to an adjacent property reported feeling "very . . . scared." The second incident involved three people setting fire to a cross on the property of a black man. A provision in a Virginia statute dating back to the days of segregation stipulated, in effect, that any cross burning was by definition an act of intimidation designed to terrorize individuals.[26] Striking down the provision, the Court held that while many acts of cross burning were in fact acts of intimidation, an intention to intimidate could not be inferred simply from the act of cross burning. There remained some elements of cross burning that could be purely expressive, designed to communicate an idea rather than terrorize an individual or group of individuals. As Justice O'Connor wrote for the majority: "A burning cross is not always intended to intimidate. Rather, sometimes the cross burning is a statement of ideology, a symbol of group solidarity."[27] To the extent that cross burning was expressive, it was protected by the First Amendment.

In his dissent, which was joined by no one, Thomas mobilized the archive of African American history to argue that no act of cross burning contained a purely expressive element. At least in the United States, cross burning was always an act of racial terrorism. (Indeed, Thomas approvingly cited a statement identifying the Ku Klux Klan as "the world's oldest, most persistent terrorist organization"—less than two years after 9/11, when discussions of terrorism in the United States were particularly fraught.)[28] In his view, cross burning raised no First Amendment questions at all.

In her majority opinion, O'Connor also recited at length the historical links between cross burning and racial terror. Unlike Thomas, however, she opened her history of cross burning with an almost lyrical invocation of its medieval origins and Gothic romance. "Cross burning originated in the 14th century as a means for Scottish tribes to signal each other," she wrote. "Sir Walter Scott used cross burnings for dramatic effect in The Lady of the Lake, where the burning cross signified both a summons and a call to arms." Though she was quick to acknowledge that cross burning "long ago became unmoored from its Scottish ancestry" and was now "inextricably intertwined with the history of the Ku Klux Klan," O'Connor insisted on keeping open a space for cross burning as something other than an act of racial terrorism, even when it involved the Klan. For members of the Klan, cross burning "was a sign of celebration and ceremony." Such events were "potent symbols of shared group identity and ideology."[29]

Thomas, by contrast, opened his dissent by noting that "in every culture, certain things acquire meaning well beyond what outsiders can comprehend." At first, it looks as if the outsiders in question would be non-Americans, or perhaps white Northerners who can't understand the Southern code. Over the course of his dissent, though, it becomes clear that the outsiders Thomas has in mind are whites on the Court "imputing an expressive component" to cross burning—that is, every other Supreme Court justice. Anyone who would even think that Virginia's ban on cross burning intrudes "into the zone of expression," he wrote, "overlooks not only the words of the statute but also reality." Though Thomas averred that this insight about cross burning "is not limited to blacks," his dissent critically depends on African American history—and not only on the facts of that history but also on how that history looks to African Americans. By holding Virginia's ban unconstitutional, by refusing to accede to the fact that all cross burning is an act of intimidation, he declaimed, "the Court ignores Justice Holmes' familiar aphorism that 'a page of history is worth a volume of logic.'"[30] While the history may be American, it requires a race-conscious interpretation to see it plain. The prism of race transforms the case from a question of the First Amendment to one that involves no constitutional question at all.[31]

The bleakness and brutality of Thomas's racial vision are most evident, however, when he shifts his gaze to more extreme settings in society. When male inmates enter a state prison in California, they are racially segregated for up to sixty days: black men are housed with black men, white men with white men, and so on. California claims that such segregation is necessary to prevent racial conflict and violence between prison gangs. Garrison Johnson, a prisoner in the state system, argued that prison segregation violated the Equal Protection Clause. By the time the case reached the Court in *Johnson v. Califor-*

nia (2005), the question had become whether practices of this sort should be treated deferentially by the courts—on the assumption that prison officials have more intimate knowledge of what is necessary for order and stability in prisons than do judges and justices—or should be subject to strict scrutiny, the most demanding standard an institution must meet in order to avoid the Court's inquiries. The Court held that California's prison practice was subject to strict scrutiny, sending the case back to the lower courts to be examined under that exacting standard of review.[32]

In a sharp dissent, Thomas offered an analysis similar to that deployed by the Court in *Plessy v. Ferguson*, the infamous 1896 case that formally legitimized legal segregation and was later overturned in *Brown v. Board of Education of Topeka*. It is as if the jail were a microcosm of Jim Crow and the organization of the jail an elaboration of a persistent social norm. "In pairing cellmates," Thomas acknowledged, California makes "race . . . indisputably the predominant factor." That posed no problem for Thomas: it matched his view of the world. Far from choosing to make race matter, California's policy reflected a social reality to which the state was adapting. That reality was that gangs "are organized along racial lines."[33] In separating cellmates by race, the government was not creating or reinforcing a social reality, but merely accommodating that reality. And it was doing so not for the purpose of creating racial hierarchy—like the *Plessy* Court writing about Jim Crow, Thomas held that California's segregation policy "is neutral" between the races, favoring neither white nor black—but for the sake of safety and security, the comity and well-being of the mini-society that is the prison. (Thomas's argument for the legitimacy of segregation so long as it is for the sake of stability and social peace is also reminiscent of *Plessy*, which held the goal of segregation laws to be "the preservation of the public peace and good order.")[34] As Thomas explained it, "The risk of racial violence in public areas of prisons is high, and the tightly confined, private conditions of cells hazard even more violence. Prison staff cannot see into the cells without going up to them, and inmates can cover the windows to prevent the staff from seeing inside the cells. . . . The risk of violence caused by this privacy is grave, for inmates are confined to their cells for much of the day." While California's practices may seem extreme, Thomas reminded the Court that jailers racially segregate their prisoners across the United States—not temporarily, as California does, but permanently.[35]

If William Blake saw the world in a grain of sand, Thomas sees it in the cell of a jail. The prison makes Thomas's racial vision plain, but he brings the same philosophy to other domains as well. Two years after *Johnson v. California*, Thomas invoked a version of the same argument—indeed, cited that very case—in the far more benign setting of a Seattle school. In *Parents Involved in Community Schools v. Seattle* (2007), the school desegregation case mentioned above, the Court's liberals had claimed that integrating the city's schools would lead to increased contact between students of different races, and this contact would lead to an improvement in racial attitudes. Thomas took issue with each step of that argument. The mere fact that white and black students attend the same school, he wrote, does not mean that they will come into contact with each other. Schools track students by academic performance, which can produce classrooms "with high concentrations of one race or another." Even if schools do not track students, white and black students often self-segregate in social settings, and even if they do interact, "it is unclear whether increased interracial contact improves racial attitudes and relations. . . . Some studies have even found that a deterioration in racial attitudes seems to result from racial mixing in schools." Here, Thomas evoked the California prison case, suggesting that relations between black and white schoolchildren in Seattle mirror the racial animus of racially organized gangs in prison. Because of the Court's decision in *Johnson v. California* to strike down segregation, Thomas noted pointedly, there was "race rioting" in California's prisons in which "inmates were killed."[36]

Even when Thomas is not invoking the specter of racial hostility and violence, he still finds a yawning divide between the races. Terry Campbell, a white man, had been indicted for second-degree murder of another white man by a grand jury in Evangeline Parish, Louisiana. He filed a motion alleging a history of racial discrimination in the parish: over a sixteen-and-a-half-year period, not a single African American had held the position of jury foreperson even though the parish was 20 percent black. (In Louisiana, the foreperson is directly placed on the grand jury by the judge, bypassing the regular juror selection process; the choice of foreperson thus partly determines the composition of the grand jury.) The motion was thrown out on the grounds that a white person had no standing to challenge the parish's history of excluding black people from grand jury positions. Campbell was tried, convicted, and sentenced to life in prison without parole. But in *Campbell v. Louisiana* (1998), the Court ruled in favor of Campbell: a white criminal defendant could challenge the constitutionality of his indictment if the process of selecting the jury that issued that indictment had been biased against African Americans. Though Thomas concurred with part of the Court's decision, he sharply dissented from the claim that a white man had standing to challenge the exclusion of black people from a jury pool.[37]

Writing for the majority, Justice Kennedy didn't ignore Campbell's race. Yet he seemed to find it blandly immaterial, almost an abstraction: "Regardless of his or her skin color, the accused suffers a significant injury in fact when the composition of the grand jury is tainted by racial discrimination."[38] Thomas, by contrast, refused to let go of the fact that it was a white man claiming constitutional harm because black citizens had been excluded from the jury passing judgment on him. He began his opinion on a harsh note with a sharp racial edge: "I fail to understand how the rights of blacks excluded from jury service can be vindicated by letting a white murderer go free." He then hammered that note, forcing the Court to hear the racial dissonance beneath its monotonic assertions of color-blind formality: "There was simply no basis for the Court's finding of a 'close relation[ship]' or 'common interest' between black veniremen [potential jurors] and white defendants. Regardless of whether black veniremen wish to serve on a particular jury, they do not share the white defendant's interest in obtaining a reversal of his convictions. Surely a black venireman would be dismayed to learn that a white defendant used the venireman's constitutional rights as a means to overturn the defendant's conviction."

Thomas could easily have made the same argument for the absence of common interests between any juror and any defendant without referencing race. He could have noted, for instance, the divide between the impartial face of the law and the disfigured face of the criminal. But though Thomas made a gesture in that direction ("of course, the same sense of dismay would arise if the defendant and the excluded venireman were of the same race"), he tucked that point inside a footnote. The rest of his opinion depends for its sense of dismay upon a repetition of the irrepressible conflict between white and black—and on a dig at his white colleagues, who, Thomas suggests, unjustifiably assume that black jurors will find "an ambient fraternity" with a white murderer in danger of losing his rights.[39]

THOMAS'S INVOCATION OF race may be used to highlight hostility between the races, as in the California prison case or *Georgia v. McCollum*. It may point to the absence of common interests between the races, as in *Campbell v. Louisiana*. Race may generate unequal opportunities, as in Cleveland and other urban school systems, or produce different ways of knowing and looking at the world, as in cases involving the Klan and the cross. But the most pervasive and toxic expression of race, the most grievous and direct form of racism, in Thomas's worldview, is the marking of individuals by the color of their skin in ways that diminish or deny their personal talents, capacities, skills, and strengths.

From his earliest days in the Reagan administration, Thomas has voiced concern about how black people are stereotyped and harmed by that stereotyping. They are harmed, he believes, not just by people acting upon stereotypes but also by the mere existence of the stereotypes, which turn black people into lesser beings in the symbolic space of popular culture and public opinion. "I'm tired of blacks being thought of only as poor people, people on welfare, people who are unemployed," Thomas declared in 1980.[40] That lament—the negative ways in which black people are depicted and thought of—is at the center of much of Thomas's jurisprudence of race.[41]

There's a personal dimension to Thomas's concern with racial stigmas. In addition to causing suspicions about his abilities at Yale Law School, racial stigmas played a large role in his Senate confirmation hearings. After Anita Hill's accusations of sexual harassment, Thomas cried out to the Senate Judiciary Committee, "I have been harmed. I have been harmed." The harm was not only that he might now not be confirmed to the Court; it was the fact of Hill's accusations themselves. By playing to stereotypes of black men as overly sexual beings, the charges depicted him in a lurid light, eclipsing everything he had done in his life. Once made, the accusations could not be unmade; they would forever attach themselves to Thomas, leaving "an indelible mark on me." "These are the kind of charges that are impossible to wash off," he lamented. That was the "high-tech lynching" Thomas spoke of at the hearings: not the attempt to deny him a seat on the Court but the imposition of an irremovable stigma. Even if it did not carry with it any material consequences or differential treatment, the stigma was a form—the form—of harm. "I have been harmed worse than I have ever been harmed in my life," Thomas proclaimed. "I wasn't harmed by the Klan, I wasn't harmed by the Knights of Camelia, I wasn't harmed by the Aryan race, I wasn't harmed by a racist group. I was harmed by this process which accommodated these attacks."[42]

On the Court, Thomas has offered a more comprehensive account of how stigmas work and why they are harmful. At its most basic level, the stigma of race associates blackness with inferiority or second-rateness. "It never ceases to amaze me," he declared in one opinion, "that the courts are so willing to assume that any thing that is predominantly black must be inferior."[43] The stigma of inferiority may register a moral deficit—the sexual depravity Thomas spoke of during his confirmation hearings, for example—but usually it references a deficit of skill, intellect, or talent, a limitation of mental capacity rather than moral character or physical ability.

Thomas does not believe that all mentions of skin color—or even some differential treatments based on race, as he made clear in *Johnson v. California*—qualify as racial stigmas. The problem arises when the notation signals some deficit in the person who is its object. It does not matter if the notary's intention is to overcome that deficit, as happens with affirmative action. The mere fact of pointing to a supposed deficit will overwhelm or override the underlying intention: all that society will see and conclude is that this person, and the group to which he belongs, are defective.[44] Being singled out for help brands African Americans with—here Thomas borrows directly from the language of *Plessy v. Ferguson*—"a badge of inferiority."[45] In a competitive society that measures the worth of its citizens by their success—education, economic, or political—marking someone as deficient, in need of assistance, is the cruelest cut of all.

When the state and public institutions identify a subordinate group as beings in need of help, each and every member of that group becomes someone who once needed and will always need help. Thomas mentions "women and minorities," but his writing suggests that he believes the point applies with special force to African Americans. Having once been identified as a group in need, they have come to be known as a group that is "permanently disabled and in need of handouts."[46] It doesn't matter if some African Americans succeed without help. The stigma of deficiency taints them and their achievements too. In the same way that the enslavement of people of African descent marked all people of color, whether free or slave, as inferior, so does the stigma of a need for help mark all African Americans—at whatever rung of society they stand, and however they reached it—with the badge of inferiority.

Without saying so, Thomas is reprising a move memorably described by the Columbia historian Barbara Fields.[47] Blacks, Fields argued, are the only race in America. A white man can identify, and be identified, in multiple ways: as a Catholic, as an Italian American, as a New Yorker, as an individual. When it comes to identity, whites have the luxury of choice. They are agents and subjects. Blacks, on the other hand, are the persistent and pervasive objects of identification. They have no choice; the choice is made for them. A black man may wish to affiliate and identify himself with his social class, his religion, his hometown, his profession, his inner soul; but whatever his wish may be, he will be publicly identified as black. Blacks will be identified as black and nothing else, and any negative characteristic exhibited by one black person will be viewed as the inherited trait of all. Fields was attempting to deconstruct and undermine that phenomenon. Thomas enacts it.[48] Not because he wishes it to be that way, but because, to his mind, that is the way it is.

The specificity of Thomas's conception of racial stigma—that the deficiency it marks is not one of physical capacity or moral character but of intellect and mental capacity—is suggestive of the class politics of his jurisprudence. When it comes to stigmas, black people, in Thomas's conception, do not need to prove that they are physically capable or even morally upstanding. Perhaps it is because he thinks the stereotype of the strong black man or righteous churchwoman—the stolid icon of the southern civil rights movement, prepared to bear disciplined witness against a world seething with racism—is sufficiently present in American culture, or at least the culture of Hollywood and the liberal media, as to not require much counteracting pressure. Thomas's concerns arise from and speak to a more rarefied world of rank and status. His account of racial stigma—where the black person's dignity is called into question in educational and workplace settings rather than in police departments or prisons, where his standing is sullied by associations of blackness with welfare, poverty, and unemployment— is a jurisprudence of the black professional class. The victim of racial stigmas Thomas has most in mind is not a poor black person racially profiled by the police but the ambitious black striver condescended to by liberal whites. The victim he has in mind is someone like him.

Racial stigmas need not be expressed explicitly. Like many contemporary social psychologists of race, who focus on implicit bias rather than overt belief, on racial attitudes embedded in quicksilver reactions rather than in deliberative action, Thomas has found racist notions less in formal propositions and statements than in deeper layers of unconscious sentiment. In order to spot that sentiment, one must look to the gaps in arguments about race and understand that those arguments only make sense if one assumes a connective tissue of racial assumptions. Thomas did just that with a lower court's argument that the fact of "racial isolation" in schools—that is, continuing segregation of black and white schools, without formal state compulsion and with no unequal distribution of resources—is a constitutional injury to black schoolchildren. "If separation itself is a harm," Thomas wrote, "and if integration therefore is the only way that blacks can receive a proper education, then there must be something inferior about blacks." Having identified that deeper association between blackness and inferiority, Thomas then interpreted the court's surface concern for the harm of segregation as reflecting a covert belief in black inferiority. Seemingly egalitarian policies like integration thus become deeper claims of the racial inferiority of blacks, which then provide Thomas with the grounds he needs to reject the seemingly egalitarian policy of desegregation: "We must forever put aside the notion that simply because a school district today is black, it must be educationally inferior."[49]

Thomas's argument here evokes that of Stokely Carmichael and Charles Hamilton's *Black Power* and other statements of black nationalism. Integration, Carmichael and Hamilton wrote, "reinforces, among both black and white, the idea that 'white' is automatically superior and 'black' is by definition inferior. For this reason, 'integration' is a subterfuge for the maintenance of white supremacy." At the 1972 Gary Convention, delegates from South Carolina proposed a resolution declaring busing "a bankrupt, suicidal method of desegregating schools, based on the false notion that Black children are unable to learn unless they are in the same setting as white children."[50]

THOMAS OFTEN CLAIMS that identifying an individual as needing assistance is an assault on that person's "dignity" and standing as a citizen.[51] But exactly why—and when—such marks on citizens threaten their dignity is an unsettled question in his jurisprudence. It can wind up tying him in knots, with Thomas left to claim that some policies, such as affirmative action, undermine dignity while other policies, like the ban on gay marriage, do not. While that is intelligible as Republican Party dogma, Thomas provides no accounting for it as argument. Instead, he offers two contradictory claims about dignity with no obvious way to reconcile them.

On the one hand, in the context of the ban on gay marriage, Thomas

has argued that dignity is "innate"—so innate that no act of humili-
ation, degradation, or oppression by the state could deprive a person
of it. "Slaves did not lose their dignity (any more than they lost their
humanity) because the government allowed them to be enslaved,"
Thomas wrote in one opinion. "Those held in internment camps did
not lose their dignity because the government confined them. And
those denied governmental benefits certainly do not lose their dignity
because the government denies them those benefits. The government
cannot bestow dignity, and it cannot take it away."[52]

Here Thomas seems to suggest the presence of an almost imperturbable self, surrounded by a perimeter that cannot be breached. This
is the self of Stoic lore: no matter how exigent the world, the self rises
above it, surveying its injuries and indignities from an august and aus-
tere remove. As Thomas put it in a 1996 law review article, "I am
reminded of what Saint Thomas à Kempis wrote more than five hundred years ago about the human spirit. His standard is a useful one for
thinking about the instruction that our law should be offering: '[T]ake
care to ensure that in every place, action, and outward occupation you
remain inwardly free and your own master. Control circumstances, and
do not allow them to control you. Only so can you be a master and
ruler of your actions, not their servant or slave; a free man.'"[53] (It is
no accident that Stoicism often is associated with slavery.)[54]

On the other hand, Thomas also argued, in an opinion on affirmative action, that "every time the government places citizens on racial
registers and makes race relevant to the provision of burdens or benefits, it demeans us all."[55] How such an imperturbable self could be
demeaned, have its dignity diminished or called into question by the
actions of an unforgiving world, when the dignity of the slave remains
untouched, is left unexplained.

3

Separate but Equal

Since the 1990s, much of the liberal program for racial justice has focused on the call for inclusion and diversity, most visibly in higher education, the culture industry, and corporate offices. Thomas takes sharp exception to that move. A leading critic of affirmative action, he has authored opinion after opinion attacking virtually every effort to bring African Americans into mainstream white institutions. These opinions have led Thomas's critics to accuse him of hypocrisy: having benefited from affirmative action at the most elite institutions, he is now closing the door to younger African Americans seeking to follow him there. As Rosa Parks said in 1996, "He had all the advantages of affirmative action and went against it."[1] Other critics on the left as well as Thomas's defenders on the right believe that Thomas is simply hewing to the conservative line on affirmative action: that it is a form of reverse discrimination, which fails to treat blacks and whites as individuals; that, like all race-conscious measures, it imposes illegitimate harms on a racially defined set of victims; that it is similar if not identical to the race-conscious regime of Jim Crow, the only difference being the identity of the victims. "Jim Crow laws are bad," Justice

Scalia said in an interview. "I just don't think it is any better when it is directed at the majority."[2] That, it's said, is Thomas's position as well.[3]

In fact, Thomas's claims against affirmative action are considerably more radical and unorthodox than that. Based on his vision of racial stigmas, Thomas advances the position that the entire enterprise of diversity is the most recent attempt by white people to brand and belittle black people as inferior and deficient. Far from seeking more anodyne or color-blind forms of inclusion, as many white conservatives claim they are doing, Thomas posits the separation of blacks and whites to be a necessary condition of black flourishing and advancement.[4]

THROUGHOUT HIS CAREER, Thomas has tended to avoid the conservative claim that the race-conscious measures of Jim Crow and of affirmative action are equivalent, that the victims of affirmative action are analogous to the victims of Jim Crow.[5] At the height of the Reagan years, Thomas pleaded with his conservative allies to "remember that affirmative action has been put in place because minorities and women have been discriminated against in the past." Though he vacillated over the legitimacy of affirmative action, he was leery of the argument that "consideration of race or ethnicity for any purpose is illegal 'racism.'"[6] To critics of affirmative action who said it was racism in reverse, swapping out one violation of the Constitution for another, Thomas thundered in a speech in 1983: "I say to you what is more immoral than the enslavement of an entire race? What is more immoral than the vicious cancer of racial discrimination? What is more immoral than the fabrication of a legal and political system which excludes, demands and degrades an entire race? Those who seek to invoke morality today, must first address the pervasive and persistent immorality of yesterday."[7] He criticized the "hypocrisy and irony of repeated calls for color-blind legal remedies in a country which has tolerated color-conscious violations of the law for so much of its history."[8] Five years after he joined the Court, Thomas was still voicing his discomfort with the conservative critique of affirmative action:

"Most significantly, there is the backlash against affirmative action by 'angry, white males.' . . . For some white men, preoccupation with oppression has become the defining feature of their existence. . . . They must remember that if we are to play the victim game, the very people they decry have the better claim to victim status."[9]

In one of the few instances on the Court when Thomas spoke of whites as victims of affirmative action, he immediately went on to stress that affirmative action causes greater harm to African Americans who are supposed to benefit from it: "There can be no doubt that the University's discrimination injures white and Asian applicants who are denied admission because of their race. But I believe the injury to those admitted under the University's discriminatory admissions program is even more harmful."[10] Thomas's other references on the Court to whites suffering constitutional harm are glancing and undeveloped, quick asides to which he pays little attention, and which play little role in his opinions.[11] Speaking up for the proverbial white ethnic, by contrast, Justice Scalia stated simply that the main victim of affirmative action is "the Polish factory worker's kid."[12]

Thomas's most radical claim against affirmative action is not that its tools formally mirror white supremacy but that it is a continuation of white supremacy. In the one case when Thomas did seem to equate affirmative action and Jim Crow—"I believe that there is a 'moral [and] constitutional equivalence' . . . between laws designed to subjugate a race and those that distribute benefits on the basis of race in order to foster some current notion of equality"—it is clear that the equivalence he has in mind is that African Americans are the victims in both cases. For Thomas, what unites Jim Crow and affirmative action is that both regimes are premised on "racial paternalism" toward African Americans.[13]

Throughout much of American history, racism has been the ideology by which white Americans reconciled their declared commitment to freedom with the realities of legal domination. By defining blacks as distinctive beings, implicitly or explicitly lesser—in court cases and official statements, in laws and policies—whites could proclaim their belief in the egalitarian principles of the Declaration of Independence while denying those principles to people of African descent, with no exigent sense of contradiction.[14] Thomas believes that affirmative action performs a similar function today: without disrupting the deep facts of white privilege and black subordination, diversity talk allows white elites to reconcile their rhetoric of racial equality with the realities of racial inequality.

According to liberals, the race-conscious jurisprudence of affirmative action departs from the race-conscious jurisprudence of Jim Crow because the aim of affirmative action is to help, not harm, African Americans. Even if the architects of Jim Crow and the architects of the liberal state employ the same tools of racial classification, they are designing different edifices: one of racial hierarchy versus one of racial equality. In Justice Stevens's words, "There is no moral or constitutional equivalence between a policy that is designed to perpetuate a caste system and one that seeks to eradicate racial subordination. Invidious discrimination is an engine of oppression, subjugating a disfavored group to enhance or maintain the power of the majority. Remedial race-based preferences reflect the opposite impulse: a desire to foster equality in society."[15]

But there is nothing special about liberal claims for the beneficence of their race-conscious program, says Thomas. From slavery through Jim Crow, all defenders of racial domination in the United States have justified their systems of race classification by claiming a benefit to black people. As Thomas noted in an affirmative action case, "Slaveholders argued that slavery was a 'positive good' that civilized blacks and elevated them in every dimension of life." For evidence, he cited everything from an 1837 speech by John C. Calhoun ("never before has the black race of Central Africa, from the dawn of history to the present day, attained a condition so civilized and so improved, not only physically, but morally and intellectually") to an 1835 article in a Southern periodical (slavery "has done more to elevate a degraded race in the scale of humanity; to tame the savage; to civilize the barbarous; to soften the ferocious; to enlighten the ignorant, and to spread the blessings of [C]hristianity among the heathen, than all the missionaries that philanthropy and religion have ever sent forth") to an 1858 address by Senator James Henry Hammond ("they are elevated from the condition in which God first created them, by being made our slaves"). "A century later," Thomas wrote, "segregationists similarly asserted that segregation was not only benign, but good for black students. They argued, for example, that separate schools protected black children from racist white students and teachers."[16]

Given the history of white supremacy in America, it is neither surprising nor dispositive that liberal defenders of a race classification scheme claim that their system benefits—indeed, is designed for the benefit of—African Americans. Racial paternalism is intrinsic to the practice of rule by race.[17] Here again, Thomas repeats lines of argument from the most radical moments of the 1960s: An "overriding sense of superiority," Carmichael and Hamilton declared in *Black Power*, "pervades white America. 'Liberals,' no less than others, are subjected and subject to it. . . . No matter how 'liberal' a white person might be, he cannot ultimately escape the overpowering influence—on himself and on black people—of his whiteness in a racist society."[18]

AFFIRMATIVE ACTION REPRODUCES white supremacy in two ways, claims Thomas. First, it reinforces the stigma of inferiority that already marks African Americans. Thomas is well aware that other groups also receive preferential treatment in the United States—that the children of alumni are favored in college admissions, for example.[19] Those preferences, however, are not implemented against a background stigma. The preferment given to some legacy students does not taint all children of alumni. Because of the preexisting stigma, however, all blacks are tainted by the preferences some blacks receive. When some African Americans are accepted to institutions of higher education through affirmative action programs, asks Thomas, "Who can differentiate between those who belong and those who do not?" There is an interconnection between black and black that is not at work among other groups. Even those African Americans who do not benefit from affirmative action "are tarred as undeserving," Thomas says:

This problem of stigma does not depend on determinacy as to whether those stigmatized are actually the "beneficiaries" of racial discrimination. When blacks take positions in the highest places of government, industry, or academia, it is an open question today whether their skin color played a part in their advancement. The question itself is the stigma—because either racial discrimination did play a role, in which case the person may be deemed "otherwise unqualified," or it did not, in which case asking the question itself unfairly marks those blacks who would succeed without discrimination.[20]

Liberals counter that race-conscious measures will help erode that stigma of race.[21] But Thomas, deeply pessimistic about the possibilities of transcending race, and deeply skeptical of the motivations of the people who would administer these measures of transcendence, disagrees: "I have never understood the notion that we could continue to focus on race in order to get over race. I've never understood that— that we have to continue to identify us, to be race conscious, in order not to be race conscious." This claim is less moral or logical than it is sociological. Given the persistence of racism (asked by an interviewer, "How should we best combat racism in our society?," Thomas threw up his hands and replied, "I'd love to say I know"), affirmative action only reinforces the notion that black people cannot succeed without the "patronizing indulgence" of white people.[22]

Thomas is not the only member of the Court to deploy this account of racial stigmas in opposition to affirmative action. At an earlier moment in his tenure, Justice Stevens made a similar claim against affirmative action.[23] By the time Thomas joined the Court, however, Stevens had come to radically qualify that position. Whether affirmative action programs caused "psychological damage" to their beneficiaries, Stevens wrote, was a "judgment the political branches can be trusted to make." The issue of stigmas was too contested to provide the Court with a firm basis to strike down affirmative action. As for Thomas's claim that there was continuity between the race-consciousness of Jim Crow and that of affirmative action, Stevens now said that it was simply not the case.[24] Likewise, while in earlier affirmative action cases

Justice O'Connor had signaled her sympathy with the racial stigma argument, by the time she stepped down from the Court the claim had all but disappeared from her opinions on affirmative action.[25]

The second way that affirmative action continues white supremacy, in Thomas's view, is by elevating whites to the status of benefactors who dole out scarce privileges to the few African Americans they decide to reward. Instead of empowering black people, he believes, affirmative action deepens the power of white people. The most remarkable element of Thomas's affirmative action jurisprudence, what makes it unlike that of any other justice on the Court, is how much attention it devotes to whites not as victims but as perpetrators, as the lead actors in a racial drama of their imagination. Put simply, Thomas believes that affirmative action is a white program for white people.

In the early 1990s, the University of Michigan Law School adopted a race-conscious admission policy in order to create a more diverse student body. Barbara Grutter, a white applicant who was denied a place at the law school, alleged that she was a victim of racial discrimination, and that the affirmative action policy violated the Fourteenth Amendment. In *Grutter v. Bollinger*, a 5–4 majority ruled that because the program involved "a narrowly tailored use of race," with a candidate's race weighted only as one factor among many, the program was not unconstitutional. (Had race been the sole or overriding consideration, applicants would not have been treated as individuals but as members of a given race, violating the Fourteenth Amendment's Equal Protection Clause. But even with its affirmative action program, the majority ruled, the law school still assessed each candidate as an individual, making its approach permissible.)[26] Chief Justice Rehnquist dissented, arguing that there was nothing narrow or tailored about the program. It was more like a crude quota, he wrote, "designed to ensure proportionate representation . . . from selected minority groups."[27] In treating applicants as members of racial groups rather than as individuals, Rehnquist said, the law school failed to give each applicant equal consideration.

Thomas also dissented in *Grutter*. But his dissent focused, uniquely, not on Grutter herself or other putative white victims of the law school's affirmative action program but on what the law school's program revealed about its creators and caretakers. The most salient characteristic and commitment of the leaders of the law school, said Thomas, was their elitism. An institution of the American ruling class, the law school was primarily concerned about "its exclusivity and elite status," which it maintained through an "elitist admissions policy."[28] The elitism was what made the law school a truly national institution, "a way station for the rest of the country's lawyers, rather than a training ground for those who will remain in Michigan."[29]

Affirmative action reflected that elitism. According to Thomas, the simplest, most effective way to diversify the law school would have been for it to stop relying on standardized testing, since black students tended not to do well on the LSAT.[30] (Thomas did not explain why the LSAT is racially skewed, but given his oft-declared belief that students of color are as intelligent as white students, one can assume he believed students of color did not get adequate preparation for standardized tests.) Instead of using the LSAT, the law school could have chosen to accept any applicant who had graduated from a certified educational institution or passed an exam testing his knowledge. Standardized testing, Thomas noted, was an "imperfect" diagnostic tool, its ability to "'predict' academic performance . . . a poor substitute for a system that gives every applicant a chance to prove he can succeed in the study of the law."[31] Yet despite being aware of the LSAT's flaws, the law school continued to rely on it as a key component of a highly selective admissions policy that, were it not for affirmative action, would yield a nearly all-white student body.

The reason the Michigan Law School and other elite academic institutions refused to adopt more inclusive and accessible measures was not, Thomas made clear, because they were committed to meritocracy.

The rallying cry that in the absence of racial discrimination in admissions there would be a true meritocracy ignores the fact that the entire process is poisoned by numerous exceptions to "merit." For example, in the national debate on racial discrimination in higher education admissions, much has been made of the fact that elite institutions utilize a so-called legacy preference to give the children of alumni an advantage in admissions. This, and other, exceptions to a "true" meritocracy give the lie to protestations that merit admissions are in fact the order of the day at the Nation's universities.[32]

Rather, they were committed to exclusivity, determined to be an enclave of elites.[33]

That is why elite institutions turn to affirmative action. Affirmative action enabled them to alter, ever so slightly, their racial skew without jeopardizing their exclusivity. Affirmative action allowed for an exception to the iron law of whiteness without disrupting the overall exclusions of white privilege. It was a "solution to the self-inflicted wounds of [an] elitist admissions policy."[34] Because the law school wished to maintain "an exclusionary admissions system that it knows produces racially disproportionate results," the only way for it to diversify itself was to rely on discretionary measures that explicitly consider race.[35] Given the insistence on exclusivity, there was no way to achieve diversity other than to make race-laden judgments of individuals. It was "the interest in remaining elite and exclusive," in other words, and not a simple, unalloyed commitment to racial justice, that led to the use of standardized tests, which produced racially skewed results, which then had to be remedied by race-conscious measures like affirmative action.[36] The result, ironically, was to increase the racial prerogatives of white elites, enhancing their ability to bestow the blessings of society upon a few lucky African Americans whose fortunes those white elites chose to advance.

While an elite institution's desire to diversify itself without sacrificing its exclusivity is a socially intelligible praxis, that desire was not a constitutional value that the Court need recognize.[37] As Thomas put it, "there is nothing ancient, honorable, or constitutionally protected about 'selective' admissions."[38] Liberals on the Court, however, did wish to validate that desire, said Thomas, which explained their refusal to find other ways for these institutions to diversify themselves. "The Court will not even deign to make the Law School try other methods . . . The same Court that had the courage to order the desegregation of all public schools in the South now fears, on the basis of platitudes rather than principle, to force the Law School to abandon a decidedly imperfect admissions regime that provides the basis for racial discrimination."[39] In the same way that white southerners under slavery once used race consciousness to reconcile their commitments to freedom and to domination, so did liberal whites now use race consciousness to reconcile their commitments to diversity and to elitism.

ONE OF THE key arguments of affirmative action proponents is that diversity in an educational setting has an educational benefit: surrounded by men and women from other backgrounds and experiences, students will be exposed to different and challenging views and voices. That was the ground of the Court's *University of California v. Bakke* decision, the landmark 1978 ruling permitting affirmative action in higher education: not that affirmative action was a legitimate means to redress past injustices or current inequality but that it was an educational good, offering diversity in the classroom and on campus from which all students would benefit.[40] Thomas rejects that argument. If it were the case that diversity is the keystone of academic excellence, he wrote in *Grutter*, if diversity were as educationally important as its proponents claim, elite institutions would do everything necessary, including overhauling their admissions process and forgoing exclusivity, to produce the greatest diversity. The fact that they don't "suggests that the educational benefits" of diversity "are not significant or do not exist at all."[41]

What these institutions do believe, Thomas has argued, is that diversity in the institution "prepares . . . students to become leaders in a diverse society."[42] Diversity, in other words, does not benefit students academically: it does not improve their grades, polish their writing, or enhance their learning. Instead, it lends a future ruling class "a facade" of color. It burnishes the credentials, image, and style of those students—mostly white—who will go on to run American society. The unstated premise or implication of Thomas's argument is that diversity does not teach students skills they will need to lead or negotiate a multicultural and multiracial world. It does not improve their ability to understand alternative views, or empathize with experiences and backgrounds other than their own. It does not "produce better leaders" in that sense. What diversity does do is make "the class look right." According to Thomas, "classroom aesthetics"—the look of the student body at elite institutions—are critical to the self-image of the ruling class.[43] ("Aesthetic," "aesthetics," "racial aesthetics," and "aestheticists" are words and phrases that recur throughout Thomas's opinions on affirmative action and desegregation.)[44] That aesthetic is important not because a diverse elite is necessary in a diverse society; Thomas doesn't believe the ruling class is so outward-looking. The aesthetic of the classroom is important for the self-image of the ruling class, for its sense of itself as a class. It is how white elites signal to other white elites their sophistication, taste, and cosmopolitanism. "All the Law School cares about is its own image among know-it-all elites."[45]

Affirmative action doesn't just reflect white elitism; it reinforces that elitism. As Thomas wrote in another affirmative action case, affirmative action "teaches" white people that "minorities cannot compete with them without their patronizing indulgence." It "engender[s]"— "inevitably," said Thomas—"attitudes of superiority" among white people, whereby it is the duty of whites, like the masters of old, to look out and care for their racial inferiors.[46] During the Gilded Age, a conservative Supreme Court also invoked the specter of paternalism, striking down progressive wage and health and safety laws on the ground that those laws reflected a view of workers as unable to fend for themselves without the help of the state. Thomas has given that conservative position a racial twist, sharpening the accusation of white paternalism against a background in which the presence and presumption of white supremacy, even in liberal institutions, is all too apparent.[47]

The racial variety of paternalism is particularly "poisonous and pernicious," in Thomas's view, because it presumes and reinforces the fundamental disparity in power between whites and blacks.[48] It leaves whites in the position to act, blacks in the position to be acted upon. In the same way that any slaveholder's assumption of responsibility for the fate of his slave—even if that assumption promoted the health and well-being of the slave—reinforced the inequality of power between them, so does the liberal elite's assumption of responsibility for the fate of black people, even if meant to help them, reinforce the inequality between them: "The paternalism that appears to lie at the heart of this program is at war with the principle of inherent equality."[49] Affirmative action, for Thomas, is not only the product of liberals being unwilling to confront their own elitism; it is also a symptom of their desire to display that elitism through acts of beneficence to the less fortunate—acts that will not jeopardize their privilege, and the stigma of which will be borne by African Americans.

What lends Thomas's position its toxic and unsettling force is that he and his readers, white and black, know that a large portion of the institutions that are preaching and practicing affirmative action, including the Supreme Court, are white. They are led by white people, funded by white people, and managed by white people. If such an institution decides to implement affirmative action, the deciders will be white. It is this backdrop—the existence of white supremacy as a social practice and institution, the fact that the circles of power in which debates over affirmative action occur still tend to be white—that allows Thomas to do what he does: transform the demand for affirmative action into a program and practice of white agency.

There's little doubt that Thomas is having his cake here and eating it too. Thomas is a member of a generational cohort of upwardly mobile African Americans who managed to ascend to these white institutions and become a part of the American leadership class. The very fact that Thomas is in a position to advance the opinions he does on the Supreme Court is testament to that fact. Yet Thomas also believes that the increased presence of black people like himself at the middle and upper rungs of power only proves his point that affirmative action is a project of the American ruling class. The vast majority of blacks are simply "too poor or uneducated" to be eligible for inclusion in the nation's colleges and universities; affirmative action doesn't touch them or their lives.[50] The African Americans who are interested in affirmative action, says Thomas, the ones who have helped design and implement it, are upwardly mobile professionals. These are the same light-skinned, wealthier African Americans who have long tormented him, the black people who "go to Yale or Harvard or Princeton" and want "a BMW or Mercedes"—the Margaret Bush Wilsons who see themselves as ambassadors to the white world, who believe that it should be they, not the black working class or black poor, who integrate elite white institutions. Black defenders of affirmative action are entirely separate from "my people," says Thomas; his people are the black "masses."[51]

The truth of Thomas's account is debatable. (Thomas may not own a fancy foreign car, but he does drive a limited-edition Corvette and own a luxury mobile home, and there's little evidence that the black masses are flocking to him or his program.)[52] But it remains the case that when he opened his opinion in *Grutter* with a statement from Frederick Douglass—"The American people have always been anxious to know what they shall do with us. . . . I have had but one answer from the beginning. Do nothing with us!"—he was not issuing a simple libertarian cry for noninterference from the state, as his conservative admirers claim.[53] He was asking—demanding—that white liberals cede their place at center stage of the African American drama, that they cease their imaginings that black fate is in white hands.

THROUGHOUT HIS FIRST decade on the Court, Thomas would meet regularly with high-achieving students of color from Washington's poorer neighborhoods. (At least into the aughts, Thomas also met with student groups at high schools in poor neighborhoods and neighborhoods of color. When Justice Sonia Sotomayor joined the Court, she did the same.)[54] One meeting during his fourth year on the Court—with Cedric Jennings, a high school student just a few months shy of graduation—was immortalized by the journalist Ron Suskind in the July 1998 issue of *Esquire*. After several hours of warm and friendly conversation, Thomas asked Jennings what his plans were for college. "I'm off to Brown," Jennings replied. Thomas frowned. "Well, that's fine, but I'm not sure I would have selected an Ivy League school.

You're going to be up there with lots of very smart white kids, and if you're not sure about who you are, you could get eaten alive. It's not just at the Ivies, you understand. It can happen at any of the good colleges where a young black man who hasn't spent much time with whites suddenly finds himself among all whites. You can feel lost."[55] It is no exaggeration to say that much of Thomas's jurisprudence is dedicated to avoiding this situation: that of the young black man, thrown into a white world, where he flounders and fails.[56]

Thomas is no advocate of legally mandated segregation, except in prisons. But neither is he an advocate of desegregation or integration.[57] "Some people think that the solution to all the problems of black people is integration," Thomas declared in 1997. By his own admission, he is not one of them.[58] Looking back on his education in an all-black environment, Thomas has admitted to wanting to "turn the clock back" to a time "when we had our own schools." In a lengthy 1982 research article (published with an acknowledgment of "the invaluable assistance of Anita F. Hill"), Thomas noted pointedly that "it must be decided what the standard of integration will be and whether integration *per se* should be a primary goal." Thomas believes that *Brown* rightly ended legal segregation, if for the wrong reasons.[59] But he also thinks the push for desegregation after *Brown* produced bad policy. More than a decade after *Brown*, he wrote, "we discovered that *Brown* not only ended segregation but required school integration. And then began a disastrous series of cases requiring busing and other policies that were irrelevant to parents' concern for a decent education."[60]

At Thomas's Senate confirmation hearings, Republican senator Arlen Specter of Pennsylvania pressed Thomas on that statement: "If you end segregation, doesn't it necessarily mean that you are requiring school integration?"[61] Thomas dodged the question at the hearings but has since given his answer on the Court. Though he accepts the *Brown* principle that separate but equal is inherently unequal, he understands that principle in a narrow legal sense. It is only the state's requirement of the separation of the races that is inherently unequal; the mere social fact of separation or "racial isolation" is not.[62] Many white conservatives agree with the claim that the Constitution only strikes down the laws and policies, not the social fact, of segregation. They claim, however, to be making that distinction in the service of a specific moral ideal: that of a color-blind society. Color-blind policies, they say, promote a color-blind world, or reflect such a world to the extent that it already exists. Thomas rejects that vision. As he put it in the *Wall Street Journal*, "Much of the current thinking on civil rights has been crippled by the confusion between a 'colorblind society' and a 'colorblind Constitution.' The Constitution, by protecting the rights of individuals, is colorblind. But a society cannot be colorblind, any more than men and women can escape their bodies."[63]

Once the legal requirement of race-blind policies has been met, Thomas's social vision can come awfully close to separate but equal, where the only question at stake is not the mixing of races but the distribution of resources. From his earliest days in the Reagan administration in the Department of Education's Office of Civil Rights, Thomas has aggressively pursued that vision. "Within a month of taking that job," he says, "I was terrified by the possible effects of the desegregation effort on black colleges." During the 1960s, radical students in the Black Power movement, particularly in the South, fought hard to preserve historically black colleges and universities from the opposition of both white racists and black integrationists. More than a decade later, Thomas waged a version of that campaign in the Department of Education. Arguing against those—many of them holdovers from the Carter administration—who sought to dismantle historically black colleges and universities, Thomas "approached enforcement with great care. I insisted that the state plans have as a major objective the enhancement of black institutions. This means better libraries, better programs, upgraded faculty and more funds. In that way, equality of educational opportunity was best realized."[64] In that same 1982 article where Thomas raised the question of whether integration should be the goal of education policy, he also noted that desegregation had failed to make African Americans the equal of white Americans, or even to give them schooling equal to that of white Americans. This failure, he said, demanded "that we rethink notions of desegregation and refocus on the original goal of education quality. Perhaps we will find directing our energies toward providing quality education for minorities better promotes the goal of educational equality."[65]

On the Court, Thomas has continued his campaign on behalf of separate black institutions and against the idea of race mixing. In the 1995 case *Missouri v. Jenkins*, the Court's conservative majority ruled that the federal courts could not force Missouri to adopt school policies designed to entice suburban white students to enroll in predominantly black urban schools. Thomas joined the majority. In the Court's private deliberations about the case, he argued, in the paraphrase of *New Yorker* writer Jeffrey Rosen:

> I am the only one at this table who attended a segregated school. And the problem with segregation was not that we didn't have white people in our class. The problem was that we didn't have equal facilities. We didn't have heating, we didn't have books, and we had rickety chairs. . . . All my classmates and I wanted was the *choice* to attend a mostly black or a mostly white school, and to have the same resources in whatever school we chose.[66]

That private sentiment made its way into Thomas's public statement. Thomas's concurrence in *Missouri v. Jenkins* is "the only opinion" in the case, argues legal scholar Mark Graber, "that questioned whether desegregation was a constitutional value."[67] If anything, Thomas believes that the state should—where it can, within the law—support the separation of the races. Thomas's jurisprudence, in other words, is dedicated to undoing not simply affirmative action but also the "grand experiment" of mixing the races that he believes himself to be the victim of: "I have been the guinea pig for many social experiments on social minorities. To all who would continue these experiments, I say please 'no more.'"[68]

In keeping with his conservative black nationalism, Thomas sees in the integration of the races real harm to black people and in the separation of the races the condition of black flourishing. In educational settings, where he has addressed this issue most directly, the harms come in a variety of forms. There is, first of all, risk of a "mismatch" between underprepared black students and elite white institutions, leading black students to do less well than their classmates, lose confidence, switch to "less competitive" majors and programs, or perhaps drop out.[69] If they do succeed at these institutions, their success may come through an insidious form of social promotion: they may receive decent grades and "a communal, rubber-stamp credentialing process," but they will not get the "knowledge and skills" they need. Sooner or later, in the workplace if not before, their lack of preparedness will be exposed, and they will "no longer" be "tolerated." This is not only a problem at elite white institutions, Thomas asserts: black students encounter it at white schools and colleges at all levels.[70]

The problem is not simply a lack of preparedness for the rigors of top schools. Thomas believes that the very fact of race mixing can be a harm to black people. When white liberals trumpet the benefits of diversity—thinking mostly of the white students who will go on to lead a diverse society, or of abject black students in desperate need of exposure to the mind and manners of whites—they overlook the fact that "racial (and other sorts of) heterogeneity actually impairs learning among black students." Whatever gains in social contacts and prestige are to be had, those gains will be counterbalanced by the significant failures in learning—as evidenced by lower grades, higher dropout rates, and the choice of easier majors—that result from that contact.[71]

When African Americans attend predominantly and historically black institutions, Thomas writes, they "experience superior cognitive development" and enjoy "higher academic achievement."[72] According to a Carnegie Commission report that Thomas cites approvingly in *United States v. Fordice*, a 1992 desegregation case from Mississippi, such institutions provide "educational opportunities for young blacks at all levels of instruction" and enhance "the general quality of the lives of black Americans."[73] Why that is, Thomas doesn't explain. Occasionally he will invoke studies purporting to demonstrate the benefits of separation and the harms of race mixing, but it would be a mistake to take seriously his fidelity to or interest in social science. When it comes to research, Thomas is all over the map, claiming, within the space of the same opinion, that the research is "hotly disputed among social scientists," that the research shows that the positive effects of diversity have been overstated, that the evidence demonstrates the negative effects of diversity, that the methodology is flawed, that the research is inconclusive. He will claim that the Court should not defer to "the evanescent views of a handful of social scientists" but then will cite directly from a handful of social scientists, or at least offer anecdotal examples from that handful that supposedly demonstrate "the fact of black achievement in 'racially isolated' environments."[74]

One clue as to why Thomas believes what he believes about the educational value of segregation can be gleaned from his oblique reference, in *Fordice*, to the "distinctive histories and traditions" of historically black colleges and universities. What those distinctive histories and traditions are, he also doesn't say—except to invoke the possibility that they "might disproportionately appeal to one race or another." It is an institution's racial identity, the fact that it is predominantly and historically black, that lends it its specific history and tradition, which Thomas sees as not only the source of its appeal to black people but also an "undisputable" reason for its success in fostering black achievement. The fact that these institutions, again quoting that Carnegie Commission report, are "a source of pride to blacks who have attended them and a source of hope to black families who want the benefits of higher learning for their children" becomes the "sound educational justification" for keeping them. While no state is required to maintain such institutions, Thomas says, no state should be required to eliminate them either, particularly not just for the sake of race mixing and diversity. States, in fact, might want to encourage them, for those institutions "sustained blacks during segregation." They "survived and flourished" under Jim Crow.[75] Recalling his understanding of freedom and dignity as forms of persistence and survival in the face of adversity, Thomas sees these black institutions—which he fully acknowledges were created by Jim Crow—as the keystone of future black success.

Ever since his youth, when he repeatedly found himself the only black person in a white world, Thomas has wondered at and about the price of integration. The blessings of diversity fall mostly to whites; the burdens, as he sees them, are borne by blacks. To that extent, liberal programs of bringing together the races repeat some of the longstanding patterns and problems of American history, where white people profit from the sacrifice of black people. It's not merely that whites flourish in diverse elite institutions, flaunting their openness and urbanity, their culture and sophistication. It's that their flourishing comes at black expense. It is the black body, or psyche, that pays. Perhaps African Americans should find a better way.

PART II

CAPITALISM

4

White State, Black Market

If conversion narratives are to be believed, Clarence Thomas had his on the road to Saint Louis. In 1974, Thomas graduated from Yale Law School. Having failed to secure a position at an elite firm on the East Coast, he set out for Jefferson City, the capital of Missouri, to work for John Danforth, the state's Republican attorney general. At the time, Thomas was not a Republican. He was disaffected. By his lights, the most conservative thing he had done was to vote for George McGovern in 1972: "Still a bit too conservative for my taste," Thomas said of the Democratic candidate, but "he would have to do."[1] Thomas was in transit, however, retreating from a black left that disquieted him and white liberals who looked down on him. He also needed money. He had student loans, which he still would be paying off at the time of his appointment to the Supreme Court. The day after his graduation from Holy Cross, he had married Kathy Ambush; two years later, they had a son. They named him Jamal Adeen Thomas; decades later, the Arabic name would prompt Thomas to remark, "You know where my head was when I named that child."[2] Desperate for a job that would support his family and provide interesting work, unhappy with the ideological options on offer, Thomas headed west.

Within two years of his arrival in Missouri, a friend called Thomas about an exciting new book that had just been reviewed in the *Wall Street Journal*. The book was *Race and Economics*; the author was the conservative black economist Thomas Sowell. Sowell himself had once been on the left. With a doctorate from the libertarian-leaning University of Chicago, he now was a critic of the left, particularly its commitment to government intervention in matters of race and the economy. "Clarence," the friend said, "there's another black guy out here who is as crazy as you are. He has the same ideas that you have. There are two of you!" In law school, a classmate had given Thomas a different book by Sowell. Thomas had hurled it into the trash. This time, he was ready. "It was like pouring half a glass of water on the desert," he recalled later. "I just soaked it up."[3] Thomas ordered six copies of *Race and Economics*, one for him, the rest to share with friends and colleagues. He read and underlined his copy and made the two-hour pilgrimage to Saint Louis to get an autograph from Sowell, who was in town to debate an up-and-coming law professor by the name of Ruth Bader Ginsburg. Sowell "didn't turn me into a conservative, much less a Republican," Thomas recalls, but *Race and Economics* did set him on that path.[4]

In 1976, Thomas registered as an independent and voted for Gerald Ford. He became the most conservative attorney in an office that included John Ashcroft, darling of the radical right in the Senate in the 1990s and in George W. Bush's White House in the 2000s.[5] In 1980, Sowell invited Thomas to a gathering of mostly conservative African American intellectuals, politicians, and officials at the Fairmont Hotel in San Francisco. In a widely read *Washington Post* dispatch from the conference titled "Black Conservatives, Center Stage," Thomas was featured as the face and future of black conservatism. Four months later, he went to work for Reagan.[6]

It's not difficult to see how *Race and Economics* would have appealed to a twentysomething Clarence Thomas. A mix of Malcolm and Milton (Friedman), Sowell's arguments for black self-help and his skepticism about white liberalism reminded Thomas "of the mantra of the Black Muslims I had met in college: *Do for self, brother.* Now I began to see more clearly why they had impressed me."[7] But deeper in Sowell's text is a more contentious claim, which would push Thomas to pivot further, and harder, to the right—without forsaking the race consciousness he had forged on the left. In the black experience, argues Sowell, economics has always been more important than politics. Politics is the sphere of white domination and rule; economics, the medium of black transformation and progress.[8] At the moment of African Americans' greatest degradation and despair, at the moment of their most acute powerlessness, it was the laws of capitalism— specifically, the imperative of production for profit that came from the slaveholder's dependence on the market—that did the most to mitigate and constrain the despotism of white America. "Although a slave-owner's power to punish a slave was virtually unlimited by either law or custom, there were economic limits on the profits to be derived in this way. . . . While sufficiently severe and thoroughgoing repression could theoretically stop all of this [slave protest, rebellion, and sabotage], the cost of an army of guards or extraordinarily formidable fences and obstacles around a plantation would have eaten up the profits that might have been achieved by more severe slave control."[9] With all his supremacist hauteur, the white man was not the master of his house. His posture of superiority, his sense of power, was pushed and pulled by forces beyond his control: by the laws of nature, as refracted through the imperatives of the capitalist market.

> Whatever the *inclination* of slave owners, their actual behavior was limited by the crop they were growing and this in turn was limited by the climate and soil where they were. The land most suitable for cotton production became the land where plantation slavery was most concentrated. In turn, the attitudes and ideologies of this region of slave-driving were those providing the strongest justification for slavery in terms of the most degraded picture of the Negro race. Those parts of the South least adaptable, by climate and soil, to plantation slave crops were those in which racism did not achieve the same degree of fervor in word and deed.[10]

This notion—that capitalism was the one power that could bring the white slaveholder to heel, that the economy was the one force that the white man could not control, that the market was the one institution to which the white man would have to yield—is a through line of *Race and Economics*. For Thomas, it was a lifeline. From the wonky, often turgid sentences of a Chicago-trained black economist emanated a vision of white constraint so potent, so satisfying, it could seem like, well, half a glass of water in a desert.[11]

CONVERSION NARRATIVES ARE like that: a pilgrim is heading one way, has a life-altering experience, then changes course. Political journeys are more circuitous. Despite Thomas's claim that his right turn was "a 'Road to Damascus' experience," the roads to Damascus are many; Saul is always and already becoming Paul.[12] Long before Thomas met Sowell, while he was still working in the precincts of the left, there were signs that he was looking for the exits. There was a moment in college—the morning after that violent demonstration in Cambridge, which had descended into looting, rioting, and tear gas—when Thomas woke up in his dorm room, awash in feelings of repulsion at the mob around him, shame at the mob within him. He went to chapel, prayed for release from the anger that was consuming him, and resolved to focus on his studies. Law school beckoned.[13]

There was the summer after college, when Thomas read Ayn Rand's *The Fountainhead* and *Atlas Shrugged*. The novels inspired in him a resolution to be black on his own terms, without hewing to a specific politics or aesthetic. If he preferred, he could listen to Carole King over Hugh Masekela. (On the Court, Thomas opens every term with a screening of *The Fountainhead*, which his clerks are required to attend.)[14] There was the moment at Yale in 1972 when he met John Bolton, who would one day serve as Donald Trump's national security advisor. Thomas had lost his wallet; Bolton found and returned it. Touched by the kindness of a white man, who turned out to be his classmate and neighbor, Thomas struck up a friendship with this outspoken conservative from working-class Maryland. They got into a heated discussion over helmet laws and seatbelt requirements. Thomas favored them; Bolton opposed them. "Clarence," Bolton said, "as a member of a group that has been treated shabbily by the majority in this country, why would you want to give the government more power over your personal life?" The question "stopped me cold," Thomas reports; years later, he still felt its effects.[15]

Conversely, even after he had begun his migration to the right, Thomas held on to the symbols and substance of the left. He may have hung the Confederate flag in his Law School apartment, thumbing his nose at the liberals he loathed, but he was careful to place the Pan-African flag next to it. After he had joined the Reagan administration, a colleague there would describe Thomas as "a radical, almost a black nationalist."[16] Throughout Reagan's first term, as Thomas tacked back and forth on the question of affirmative action, never quite resolving whether to support or oppose race-conscious policies as head of the EEOC, he defiantly called for criminal prosecution and jail time for violators of the nation's anti-discrimination laws.[17]

The decade that saw Thomas's ideological transformation was a peculiar moment in American politics.[18] With the hindsight of history, it's easy to plot a straight line from the reelection of Richard Nixon, whose calls for law and order and attacks on busing were welcomed by whites in the South and in the North, to the election of Reagan, who ushered in a new era of free markets and right-wing morals—with Thomas tagging along. But realignments often build on and incorporate the politics they are leaving behind. Between opposing continents of left and right run currents of shared sensibility, carrying partisans back and forth across the divide. As old orthodoxies give way to new heresies, the same thought or statement might signify a pending migration or continuing residence.

By the 1970s, there was a widespread dissatisfaction with the very idea of political transformation—and among African Americans, with the notion that the state could make a dent in America's racial hierarchies. That dissatisfaction signaled no specific trajectory; one could feel it from the left or the right.[19] After visiting sixty-six college campuses, Stokely Carmichael's co-author, the Columbia political scientist

Charles Hamilton, observed that the black students he had spoken to showed a "profound distrust of national government institutions."[20] Disillusionment with the national government went hand in hand with a waning faith in political action. Civil rights organizations suffered a massive decline in participation; none of the Black Power movements came close to achieving the popular involvement of the civil rights movement in its heyday. While activists continued to struggle in towns and cities, they lost the connective threads that once bound the local to the national. Sensing that "the marching has stopped," as one publication of black intellectuals and activists put it in 1973, organizers had a difficult time turning their smaller victories and struggles into a wider vision of forward progress.[21]

Black nationalism often gains traction when conditions for African Americans are getting worse, as was the case with the Garvey movement in the 1920s, or when the movement for multiracial democracy comes up against the hard limits of white supremacy. One of the founding texts of black nationalism—Martin Delaney's *The Condition, Elevation, Emigration, and Destiny of the Colored People of the United States*—was composed a mere two years after Congress passed the Fugitive Slave Law, effectively declaring that no black person, free or slave, would ever be safe or secure in America.[22] In the 1970s, the assassination of Martin Luther King Jr. and the reelection of Nixon produced a combination of pessimism and fatigue within the black left. "In less than a decade America has deaccelerated from a March on Washington, where hopes for the future were as high as the brilliant August sun," declared a statement of black intellectuals and activists, "to the shadows of the '70s and the depths of despair." Beneath that despair lay the widespread conviction that the freedom struggle had done little to transform the daily life of African Americans, particularly in the North and among the working class and the poor. There "are millions of blacks" whose lives are "untouched by the civil rights movement": this was a statement not of the black left but of two leaders of a mainstream civil rights group.[23]

At moments of disappointment, a withdrawal to what Delaney called "a nation within a nation" may signal less an affirmative vision of black advance than a wearying retreat to black maintenance. Delivering the keynote address at a conference of black activists in 1971, the writer Lerone Bennett Jr. set out the "Black Agenda of the Seventies." At the very top of his list was the uneasy and uncertain "question of survival."[24] Within black nationalist circles, spirits were not high. A force that had so recently exploded with impatience at the failure of mainstream black leaders and organizations to expedite the cause of African Americans was showing signs of age. While more adventurous calls for Black Power could still be heard, many nationalist-inflected efforts were settling into electoral campaigns for black candidates, winnowing a mass movement of the streets into the narrower enterprise of elite brokers, patronage clients, and urban machines.[25] The freedom struggle could no longer find expression in great legislative initiatives and policies of state, large-scale protests and demonstrations, urban riots and rebellions. Everything seemed smaller. That was the mood of the moment—and the movement.

If politics was an obstructed path, what other avenues might be pursued? The forces and factions of the freedom struggle, including Black Power, began to consider change outside the political realm, within the economy itself. While much has been made of the critiques of capitalism on the black left, less attention has been paid to the delicate dance with capitalism that black activists began to engage in—and how easy it was for a black nationalist to take this economic, even capitalist turn. As Hamilton would emphasize in his afterword to *Black Power* on the twenty-fifth anniversary of its publication, many on the left wrongly assumed that the logical terminus of Black Power was a progressive economic order, along the lines of socialism or social democracy. An equally plausible conclusion was that "blacks needed to organize their own resources, to accumulate capital, to be enabled to function better— as individuals and collectively—in a market economy."[26]

Though the term "Black Power" is often credited to Carmichael and the SNCC, Adam Clayton Powell was the first to invoke it, attaching to it a distinctive suggestion of black business ownership. More enlightened sectors of corporate America were quick to hear in the call for Black Power a voice they could do business with. The National

Conference on Black Power, held in Newark in 1967, was financed by fifty corporations. Invitations were sent out on the stationery of the Clairol Company. Tucked inside was a copy of a speech by the company's CEO, in which he defined Black Power as "ownership of apartments, ownership of homes, ownership of businesses, as well as equitable treatment for all people," and wrote, "Only business can create the economic viability for equity. And only business can make equity an acceptable social pattern in this country." Scholars and activists began to see in Booker T. Washington, the conservative avatar of black capitalism, a forerunner of Black Power.[27]

Some activists pushed for black jobs within a white-owned economy; others imagined a fleet of black proprietors and entrepreneurs competing with whites; still others called for a separate black economy altogether. Whatever the model, "taking care of business," as Carmichael and Hamilton put it in *Black Power*, was "the business of and for black people." While Carmichael had previously insisted that the economic order he envisioned was "not a capitalist one," the lines between Black Power and black capitalism were too porous for such a containment. Even as Bobby Seale was proclaiming, "Black capitalists are exploiters and oppressors," Huey Newton was admitting that "the idea of Black capitalism has come to mean to many people Black control of another one of the institutions of the community." What made the boundary between Black Power and black capitalism so blurry was the sense, shared across the spectrum, that the heroic phase of the freedom struggle was over. If African Americans were to progress, they would have to do so by inches, across the bumpy terrain of the economy.[28] In his *Autobiography*, Malcolm X wrote: "The American black man should be focusing his every effort toward building his own businesses and decent homes for himself. As other ethnic groups have done, let the black people, wherever possible, patronize their own kind, hire their own kind, and start in those ways to build up the black race's ability to do for itself. That's the only way the American black man is ever going to get respect." Two decades after he had read these lines, Thomas still remembered them.[29]

Simply turning to economic questions or engaging with capitalism did not have to signal an abandonment of politics, much less an embrace of conservatism. Sooner or later, the whole freedom struggle had to confront the question of economics and capitalism: any notion of democratic sovereignty, of a people's collective control over the institutions that governed their lives, led there. As Richard Hatcher, the first black mayor of Gary, Indiana, said to black activists in 1972: "There is much talk about control of the ghetto. What does that mean? I am a mayor of a city of roughly 90,000 black people, but we do not control the possibilities of jobs for them, of money for their schools or state-funded social services. These things are in the hands of the United States Steel Corporation and the County Department of Welfare of the State of Indiana."[30] Throughout these decades, there was a robust discussion of political economy that resisted the simple binary of politics versus economics. Activists who traversed the byways of civil rights and Black Power understood the intimate connections between state and market, particularly in a capitalist society, and knew that the struggle for freedom would have to be waged on multiple fronts.[31]

What marked someone as conservative in this moment was the belief, made possible and plausible by the defeats of the freedom struggle, that black agency would find a more hospitable environment under capitalism, idealized as a sphere of consensual exchanges and transactions, than under democracy, conceived as a terrain of collective struggle in which conflicting interests were corralled through compromise, deliberation, or force. Nixon had a keen perception of these longings for a different path within black nationalist circles and saw how they might be exploited by the right. "Much of the black militant talk these days is actually in terms far closer to the doctrines of free enterprise than to those of the welfarist thirties," Nixon observed in one of his most important broadcasts of the 1968 presidential campaign. "What most of the militants are asking is to be included as owners, as entrepreneurs, to have a share of the wealth and a piece of the action." At his acceptance address at the Republican National Convention that year, Nixon pointedly stated, "Black Americans don't want to be a colony in a nation. They want the pride and self-respect and the dignity that can only come if they have an equal chance to own their own homes, to own their own business, to be managers and executives as well as workers, to have a piece of the action in the exciting ventures of private enterprise." A campaign advertisement that ran in the black magazine *Jet* declared, "Richard Nixon believes strongly in black capitalism. Because black capitalism is black power in the best sense of the word."[32] That kind of rhetoric earned Republicans not only the temporary allegiance of Jesse Jackson but also plaudits from the *Liberator* magazine, home of some of the most vital currents of the black radical left. "The conservative is the natural ally of the moment for the black man," declared the magazine.[33] (Years later, at the Fairmont Conference, Chuck Stone, a black editor, reported that Reagan had said to him during the 1980 campaign, "If you live in a ghetto and you need to buy a toothbrush, there's no reason you shouldn't buy it from a black-owned drugstore." Stone exclaimed, "Governor, you sound like a black nationalist!" According to Stone, Reagan "smiled and . . . blushed.")[34]

"DURING THE 60's upsurge of the Black Liberation Movement," there "were pods growing in the cellars of our politics," Amiri Baraka said of black conservatism.[35] That was certainly true of Thomas, whose growing conservatism was inflected by the very ethos that once had put him on the radical left: namely, disaffection with black liberalism and the mainstream civil rights movement. As Thomas said, one of the sources of his initial attraction to the black nationalist left had been his premonition, in the wake of the assassinations of Martin Luther King Jr. and Robert F. Kennedy, that "no one was going to take care of me or any other black person in America."[36] (Thomas was not alone in this; as Kathleen Cleaver later said, the assassination of King was "probably the single most significant event in terms of how the Panthers were perceived by the black community.")[37] Though Thomas intended here to explain his initial break from the civil rights movement, his formulation reveals just how far he already had traveled from the movement's promises and aims. The animating spirit of the movement, after all, was not that the state or politicians would voluntarily take care of black people but that black people would force the state to include them in its deliberations and concerns. With their voices and their feet, African Americans would create a democratic polity in which they could legislate on their own behalf. Concessions from the state followed from black demands on the state. But Thomas was already too distant in time and mental space to see the Civil Rights Act of 1964 or the Voting Rights Act of 1965 as expressions of black agency. Late to the movement, he saw those laws as the overflow of white liberal noblesse—now slowed to a trickle.

Years later, Thomas would warn younger generations against the impulse to slight the struggles of the 1960s: "There is a tendency among young upwardly mobile, intelligent minorities today to forget. We *forget* the sweat of our forefathers. We *forget* the blood of the marchers, the prayers and hope of our race. We *forget* who brought us into this world."[38] Yet that insight would never disrupt his sense that the civil rights movement had achieved little—"Certainly I think there was a feeling of euphoria. A feeling that if those doors opened we would suddenly move into the ranks of the employed and the ranks of those who had the better jobs in society. Well, that was not to be true. There were a lot of other problems that had to be remedied. There were systems in place that had to be torn down"—and that what little it achieved was due to the actions of people who weren't black.[39]

Though Thomas initially made these claims from the left, the argument that the gains of the 1960s were paltry and the work of white liberal elites was also heard from the right.[40] Eventually, Thomas became persuaded that the same argument about paltry gains and white elites applied to the black left itself. By the mid-1970s, the whole repertoire of black politics—from mainstream activism to Black Power radicalism and beyond—seemed pointless to him. "I marched. I protested. I asked the government to help black people," Thomas said. "I did all those things. But it hasn't worked. It isn't working. And someone needs to say that."[41] It wasn't simply the radicalism of the left that pushed Thomas away from the left. It was the failure of the left to change things, at least quickly enough, and the dawning recognition that the kind of political power that would be required to change things was vastly more than African Americans were capable of mustering. "People were realizing that the major civil rights legislation of the 60's were not getting results fast enough to right the injustice of centuries of discrimination," Thomas said in 1983. "Civil rights advocates wanted more government action; action that would result in drastic change in perhaps a decade, and rid the country of racial prejudice. Needless to say, such drastic change takes drastic measures."[42]

Up until the mid-1970s, in other words, Thomas made his disaffection with civil rights activism into a narrative of black nationalism from the left. Beginning in the mid-1970s, that disaffection realigned for him as a story of black nationalism from the right.[43] What's remarkable about the transformation is how simple and small it proved to be.

LIKE MANY CONSERVATIVES, Thomas now believed that the government's involvement in the economy had a negative effect on the lives of ordinary people. Unlike most conservatives, Thomas grounded that argument in the African American experience. One example he cited was the issuance of occupational licenses. Through the licensing system, the state decides who gets to work in an occupation. Licensed work—whether as a pharmacist, librarian, social worker, or physical therapist—is a ticket to the middle class. But acquiring a license requires levels of time and money that poor people, particularly people of color, lack. The state's occupational licensing systems, Thomas would claim, effectively operate in a racially discriminatory fashion, affording opportunity to white people who already have it, denying it to black people who need it.[44] Licensing systems were one of the many ways, Thomas said, that state actions negatively affect African Americans. It was difficult to overlook "how frequently governmental regulations, despite their authors' intentions, operate against the economic interests of blacks and other racial minorities." It was impossible to avoid the conclusion that "government was and is one of the major culprits in the problems of black Americans." That was a knowledge that Thomas claimed to derive from African American history. He had witnessed how African Americans had been stifled by licensing systems in the South, he said. It was "from this experience" of Jim Crow that he had learned to be "deeply suspicious of laws and decrees."[45]

But Thomas came to believe more than that regulation harmed African Americans; his most corrosive criticism was that state action could never do anything for African Americans at all. While many conservatives argued that the state could not remedy social inequality, Thomas thought that this skepticism applied with special force to African Americans. Problems of racial inequality "cannot be solved by law—even civil rights law," he told an audience at Clark College, a historically black college in Atlanta. "Massive federal involvement still left us at the bottom rung of the economic ladder. Clearly then, the answer does not lie in more government intervention." In a 1983 interview in the *Washington Post*, he told William Raspberry, "I don't think that there's much that we can do to make it [society] fair in that sense."[46] (On the Court, Thomas's sense of futility has only increased. In 1996, he wrote that "the idea that government can be the primary instrument for the elimination of misfortune is a fundamental misunderstanding of the human condition.")[47]

American capitalism is built on centuries of slavery and Jim Crow, Thomas argued, which have led to deep structural inequities in contemporary society.[48] That was the reality African Americans confronted when they entered the market. But while liberals and leftists saw that inequality as an argument for state intervention and redress, Thomas now believed that that inequality only exposed the limitations of the state, how insufficient were its tools, how unlikely was the prospect of overcoming this social disrepair through government action. "You've got this conglomeration of factors that make it impossible for people from different groups to compete against each other fairly. Some people inherit a lot of money. You can't compete against that. Some people have six generations of educated people in their family. It's difficult to compete against that if you come from Anacostia."[49] Centuries of oppression had left black America with both economic deficits and cultural deficits: broken families, failing schools, an absence of internalized norms like hard work and deferred gratification.

The comprehensiveness of that social knowledge once pressed a younger Clarence Thomas to a more radical vision of social transformation. Indeed, if one listens carefully to that *Washington Post* interview with Raspberry, one still hears a fading echo of the Great Society. "If you run over somebody," Thomas told Raspberry, "you don't just back off of 'em and expect that they are cured."[50] That statement recalls Lyndon Johnson's famous speech at Howard University in 1965: "You do not wipe away the scars of centuries by saying: Now you are free to go where you want, and do as you desire, and choose the leaders you please. You do not take a person who, for years, has been hobbled by chains and liberate him, bring him up to the starting line of a race and then say, 'you are free to compete with all the others,' and still justly believe that you have been completely fair."[51] But in 1983, that same comprehensive understanding of black inequality inspired in Thomas only a wearying sense of the impotence of state action: "You can't compensate for all those deficiencies. [Civil rights law] cannot correct for all those years. Nor can it correct all the inequities that existed at the employment level for 400 years. We're kidding ourselves if we think it can."[52] The once radical disdain for the limited toolkit of piecemeal reforms now provoked a conservative disdain for the same reforms.[53]

Throughout his time in the Reagan administration, Thomas reiterated the claim that liberal policies were not making headway against racial stratification. Even in cases of seeming success, where African Americans were hired to managerial positions in corporate America in order to diversify the upper echelons of the economy, the deep seams of a racist society were still visible. Blacks were seldom able "to reach top positions," Thomas noted. Instead, they had their "credentials questioned" and were consigned to "staff administrative positions rather than line positions." Thomas firmly believed that blacks were "fully qualified to manage departments with bottom-line functions." Yet they were consistently packed off to "departments like community relations," which "became the depository for blacks hired as quota-fillers." In times of economic distress, theirs were the first positions cut.[54]

This wasn't just a sociological point for Thomas; it was also a moral point. The extent of the damage the United States had inflicted upon African Americans was so massive, nothing could ever make up for it. "I don't think you could ever compensate our race for what has happened," Thomas observed at a symposium of black conservatives in 1985. Two years later, Juan Williams described Thomas's position thus: "Thomas believes that government simply cannot make amends, and therefore should not try. The best it can do is to deal a clean deck and let the game resume, enforcing the rules as they have now come to be understood."[55]

AGAINST THIS BACKDROP of skepticism about politics and the state, and the larger rethinking of capitalism on the black left, it wasn't a leap for a nation-minded young man like Thomas to imagine that African Americans might find a greater sense of autonomy and efficacy, even sovereignty, in the marketplace. As Thomas explained, politics and government were spheres "you don't have any control over." The economy was different. It was one of the few realms of social life in which the individual could find his freedom: "You want to be free, you want to leave your parents' house? Then you've got to earn your own living, you've got to pay your own mortgage, pay your own rent, buy your own car, and pay for your own food. You've got to learn how to take care of yourself, learn how to raise your kids, how to go to school and prepare for a job and take risks like everybody else."[56] African Americans, he felt, should abandon protest in the streets and the pursuit of political power in favor of economic visions of development. As Williams would describe Thomas's mature vision: "It is unlikely that whites will ever fully accept blacks as equals . . . so blacks should prepare to do for themselves: by making black schools into rigorous training grounds, by investing in black businesses, by working for black corporations, and by living in black neighborhoods. Forget the traditional pressure tactics—demonstrations, boycotts, lobbying by civil-rights groups—that are meant to gain a share of power, wealth, and influence in white American institutions."[57]

Given what Thomas claimed about the pervasiveness of racism, it's difficult to see how he could believe that the economy was untouched by the forces of race that he said structure the state. If one reads Thomas carefully, however, it's clear that he didn't imagine the economy as a space of untrammeled black sovereignty. What Thomas saw in the capitalist economy was a space for partial or constrained black sovereignty: a sphere in which African Americans could carve out at least some measure of autonomy over their lives, independent of the power and reach of white people; a sphere in which white people didn't have an entirely free hand over black people. Black people had survived Jim Crow "because there was at least some economic liberty, some economic freedom, even though political and social freedom were denied."[58] While the ability of markets to provide a haven or a refuge from oppression was a truth of social systems in general, Thomas believed, that truth applied with special force to black people in the United States.

In making his argument about capitalism, Thomas would draw heavily on the example of his grandfather Myers Anderson. Through an extraordinary act of will, Anderson rose from poverty to become a successful businessman, owning a fuel-delivery company and several rental properties—"during the most repressive period of Jim Crow law and racial bigotry," as Thomas liked to point out. A pillar of the black community, Anderson was able to leverage his wealth on behalf of the NAACP, financially supporting its efforts to desegregate Savannah.[59] With his wife, Tina, Anderson raised Thomas and his brother after their mother could no longer take care of her sons. When Thomas spoke of the constrained sovereignty that capitalism afforded to black people, how markets carved out a space of liberty in even the most white-dominated worlds, it was Anderson's story that he was telling: "He worked hard to provide for his family. He was a deeply religious man who lived by the Christian virtues. He was a man who believed in responsibility and self-help. And though this could not bring him freedom in a segregated society, it at least gave him independence from its daily demeaning clutches."[60]

Defending capitalism, Thomas did not celebrate the wage economy of the black laborer. Though Thomas had come to believe in the importance of hard work, working for someone else was a different matter.[61] Given the structures of white ownership, wage labor was likely to bring black people into contact with whites in ways that were all too reminiscent of politics itself, as black subordinates dependent on their white patrons. The wage economy also meant racist white co-workers and employers. Thomas later told a story about Anderson, whom he called Daddy:

> Once, I'd asked him why he had decided to start his own business instead of working for someone else. He told me that before daybreak one morning in the late forties, he had been delivering ice when a white man had walked up behind him, startling him. "What're you doing, boy?" the man asked. "None of your business," Daddy replied, clutching the handle of the ice pick he kept in a holster on his belt. "Something boiled up in me," he told me, adding that if the man had made one move toward him, he would have stabbed him to death. After that, Daddy said, he decided he could never work for a white man again.[62]

Thomas's preference was for the entrepreneurial economy, the world of black-owned business—not because there was greater profit to be had there but because, unlike the wage economy, black business offered opportunities for autonomy and control. Anderson's example again proved instructive.

> A few years before he died, I asked my grandfather why he insisted on working for himself. It all seemed so pointless. There was not much money to be made, and it required him to work all the time, rather than just forty or fifty hours per week. It seemed to me that there was more security in having a job rather than owning an ever declining business. His response was simple: It's mine. That trumped security. Secretly, I think he just could not stand the idea of anyone telling him what to do or where to go. For that, he was willing to

accept the anxiety and the work. In fact, he seemed to relish the challenge of being successfully independent and, thus, free.[63]

Only two generations removed from slavery—and raised by his grandmother, a former slave—Anderson saw working for himself as not only a counterpoint to slavery but also as a shield from the racist stigmas and symbols of white supremacy. "To be protected from some of the effects of bigotry" under Jim Crow, it was necessary for Anderson to be "free to produce and free to keep what he produced, to be self-sufficient," said Thomas. "To my grandfather, self-sufficiency in an otherwise hostile world, was freedom."[64] The black entrepreneur may have been buffeted by the instability of a capitalist economy, but he was insulated from the meddling hand of racism. No matter how unforgiving it was, the market's impersonality was vastly preferable to the punishments and preferments doled out by whites.

Anderson did not see his entrepreneurial activity as benefiting only him. He saw it as a legacy for his grandsons. "I'm doin' this for y'all," Anderson would claim, "so y'all don't have to work for the white man, so y'all don't take what I had to take."[65] That legacy was deeply imprinted on Thomas, who would consistently eschew the celebration of a separate and isolated self that one often hears on the libertarian right. No believer in atomistic individualism, Thomas always maintained that one's success in life was a function of familial, communal, and institutional bonds.[66] Thomas's grandfather "was extremely generous with all that he had." Such generosity should be the general rule, Thomas has declared. Successful individuals should assume "responsibility for the community in which [they have] lived." They should "help those who [can] not help themselves."[67]

While Thomas's brief for the obligations owed to the community might be seen as a religious or cultural counter to the self-interested market actor, the underlying vision was not communitarian or Catholic. It was patriarchal. Thomas's aim was not to counter the taint of selfishness but to valorize the black male provider. At the very first conference of the Black Power movement, held in Newark in 1967, the general consensus, according to one observer, "was that we need to transfer the economic power wielded by white men in the Black ghettoes of America to Black men."[68] As in the black nationalism of his youth, so in the black nationalism of his maturity: the successful black man would remain the key figure of Thomas's vision, a leader of the community upon whom other African Americans depended. This was not an egalitarian vision; it was an elitist vision of black men with money offering sustenance to their flock. "My grandfather," Thomas wrote, "was especially fond of saying that because he was so fortunate to have produced more than he needed, he could now provide for those who could not do for themselves."[69]

DURING HIS SENATE confirmation hearings, Thomas frequently told—and the media frequently repeated—his grandfather's story as evidence of Thomas's humble origins and his hard work. Yet the fact that Anderson was a businessman, a homeowner and landlord with multiple properties, that Anderson was able to put his grandsons through private Catholic schools, to provide them with new clothes and pocket money—all this marked Thomas as middle class rather than poor.[70] It fell to a skeptical Toni Morrison to point out the disjuncture. Scarcely able to contain her irritation at how easily the Senate and the media had been taken in by Thomas's story, she criticized both institutions for their ignorance of the conditions of black life. "The nominee was required to shuck," she wrote, "to convince white men in power that operating a trucking business was lowly work in a Georgia where most blacks would have blessed dirt for such work. It wasn't a hard shuck. Because race and class—that is, black equals poor—is an equation that functions usefully if unexamined, it is possible to advance exclusionary and elitist programs by the careful use of race *as* class."[71] The benefits of conservatism, which emphasizes deregulated markets and low taxes, have always fallen, on the whole, to wealthy white people. But in his Senate testimony, Thomas the conservative was able to evade that reality by appealing to the widespread if wrongheaded perception among white Americans that all African Americans are poor. When Thomas spoke, he wasn't just speaking as an African American for

African Americans. To his white listeners, he was speaking as a member of the poor on behalf of the poor.

Morrison's observation holds not only for Thomas's testimony before the Senate. It also explains how Thomas, on and off the Court, has consistently leveraged his grandfather's story and the politics of race on behalf of capitalism. One such occasion occurred in 1987, four years before he joined the Court, when Thomas, in a remarkable speech, set out his case for capitalism. The setting was the Pacific Research Institute, a think tank in San Francisco devoted to "advancing free-market policy solutions."[72] Thomas opened his speech by taking aim at figures like Franklin Delano Roosevelt and John Kenneth Galbraith, whose attacks on wealthy elites used to define the common sense of New Deal liberalism. In launching those attacks, Thomas claimed, New Deal liberals were really attacking "people like my grandfather."[73] Anderson, he noted, had had all "the means to acquire wealth: hard work, intelligence, and purposefulness." Rich people also had the means to acquire wealth. Even though their means were not the same as Anderson's, they and Anderson belonged to the same category. Instead of separating his grandfather from the white men of wealth, Thomas used his grandfather—and the backstory of race—as a stand-in for all men with money. Any "attack on wealth"—no matter how that wealth was acquired—was "really an attack on the means to acquire wealth." In attacking the rich, liberals were attacking Anderson. "These critics of 'the rich' really do mean to destroy people like my grandfather."[74]

As Morrison suggested, Thomas knew how to use race to moralize moneymaking, to lend the market a legitimacy it had been denied by New Deal liberalism, to shield money and the market from political critique. In Thomas's hands, the inequality created by the market, where some succeeded and others failed, was not merely the price of freedom. It was the guarantor of precisely the kind of freedom upon which the black community depended. "As James Madison put it in his famous *Federalist* Paper Number 10: The first object of government is the 'protection of different and unequal faculties of acquiring property,'" declared Thomas. "Notice he does not say that government should protect an already existing, unequal distribution of property. Madison looks forward to a dynamic economy which would unleash human capabilities, destroying old aristocracies, and erecting new ones, which in turn would be supplanted."[75] Capitalism unregulated, in other words, made possible a new aristocracy, an aristocracy of black men, freeing blacks from white supremacy.

Thomas's strongest counter to those who would diminish the importance of capitalism to African Americans has always been to pose a simple rhetorical question: "Do you think this man [Myers Anderson] would raise his grandsons to ignore economic freedom as a major part of their lives?"[76] The defense of capitalism is not abstract for Thomas. It is personal, the telling and retelling of a family story in a political idiom. At his confirmation hearings, Thomas did the reverse, telling a political story in a familial idiom. But whichever way the translation goes, from the personal to the political or the political to the personal, Morrison's observation holds: when it comes to Thomas's ideology of black capitalism, race is being used as a sleight of hand, as a stand-in for class.

5

Against Politics

Marcus Garvey claimed that a black person should not "depend on the ballot" or "resort to the government for protection" because the government "will be in the hands of the majority of the people who are prejudiced against him."[1] Thomas agrees. As he sees it, the combination of white racism, racial inequality, and the small size of the black electorate make it impossible for African Americans, acting as a self-conscious, self-identified, coherent group, to achieve a foothold, much less win any concrete or permanent gains, in the political sphere. "Blacks are the least favored group in this society," Thomas has said. "Suppose we did band together, group against group—which group do you think would win? We're breaking down everything, ten percent for the blacks, twenty-five percent for the women, two percent for the aged, everything broken out according to groups. Which group always winds up with the least? Which group always seems to get the hell kicked out of it? Blacks, and maybe American Indians."[2] The goal of Thomas's conservative black nationalist jurisprudence is to limit the involvement of black people with the white state, to persuade black people to give up their illusion that politics can positively affect their condition and perhaps to abandon politics altogether.

On the Court, Thomas pursues this project in three ways. The first is to deemphasize and diminish the power of voting. African Americans, he believes, should cease to look to electoral politics as a means of bettering their situation; any involvement in electoral politics will only confirm white power and reinforce black powerlessness. The second way is to show that the state is unable to improve the lot of African Americans, or even actively undermines it. The third is to deprive the state of legislative and regulatory tools to intervene in the life of African Americans. The upshot of these three moves is to usher African Americans off the political stage altogether, making it possible, indeed necessary, for them to focus their attention and energy only on the economic realm.

THE JURISPRUDENCE OF voting rights divides into two areas. One concerns access to the ballot, which is a question of rights; the other deals with the ability of a group to elect representatives of its choosing, which is a question of power. Though Thomas has addressed ballot access in several cases, his opinions in those cases are unremarkable, following a familiar conservative script: we should defer to the states to determine voter qualifications, so long as those qualifications are not explicitly about race; and since the era of denials or abridgments of the right to vote for reasons of race is over, no federal action is now needed.[3] While Thomas's opinions in these cases fit with his overall critique of black participation in the political sphere, they don't speak directly to that issue.

It is in the latter area, the question of voting power, that Thomas addresses the matter of black political participation directly. His first—and, to date, most important—voting rights opinion, a concurrence in *Holder v. Hall* (1994), offers a detailed analysis of whether African Americans can or should elect black candidates. It is an extended meditation on black political agency, what Thomas variously calls the "voting strength," "fully 'effective' voting strength," "undiluted . . . voting strength," "voting power," "undiluted voting power," "effective voting power," "group voting power," and "electoral success" of African

Americans—African Americans conceived, that is, not as individuals or even as a community but as a politicized collective.[4]

In Georgia's Bleckley County, whites are the overwhelming majority, and a single elected county commissioner holds all the legislative and executive power. In 1985, six black voters and the NAACP sued county commissioner Jackie Holder. They claimed that the single commissioner system violated the Voting Rights Act, which not only stops states from denying anyone the right to vote based on race but also prohibits measures that dilute the votes of a racial group. The suit against Holder claimed that the combination of a white majority and a single seat of power made it impossible for black voters in Bleckley County to elect a candidate of their choosing: they were consistently outvoted. If the number of commissioners were expanded to five, the suit argued, one for each school district in the county, black voters would be able to elect at least one representative of their choosing, since one of the school districts had a black majority.

Writing for the Court, Justice Kennedy ruled against the plaintiffs. The single-commissioner system did not violate the Voting Rights Act, he wrote, because there was no objective way to establish the proper number of commissioners. Basing the number of commissioners on the number of school districts was entirely arbitrary, in Kennedy's view. And without an agreed-upon benchmark for how many commissioners there should be, there was no way to determine that the black vote had been impermissibly diluted by Bleckley's arrangement.[5]

Though Thomas concurred with the Court's judgment, his opinion went much further. Breaking with Kennedy (as well as Rehnquist and O'Connor), Thomas argued that the Voting Rights Act did not make voter dilution a proper or legitimate object for Supreme Court review at all. More important, Thomas used *Holder* to develop a political theory of black power in the electoral realm—really, of the absence of black power in the electoral realm—that set the template for his subsequent voting rights decisions.[6] His opinion targeted what he saw as the fundamental illusion about voting: that blacks could ever find their collective interests satisfied or addressed through electoral action, even if they were granted the ability to secure representatives of their choosing. In his concurrence, Thomas not only rejected the claim that "the 'black representative's' function . . . is to represent the 'black interest'" but challenged the notion that the "black interest" could or should be translated into the political realm at all.[7]

Throughout *Holder*, Thomas took aim at what he saw as the "pernicious" assumption that African Americans are "not merely a racial or ethnic group, but a group having distinct political interests as well."[8] The emphasis falls on the "political" in that "distinct political interests": Thomas did not express any doubt that blacks share a common experience of low social standing and electoral weakness, that they are a socially despised and politically small minority. His problem was less racial essentialism—only once in *Holder* did Thomas come near the claim that there is something wrongheaded about the notion that "members of the racial group must think alike"[9]—than its political corollary: the belief that being black should translate into some kind of particular political interest that would find an outlet in electoral politics or the state, that the "interests" of African Americans "are so distinct" that they "must be provided a separate body of representatives in the legislature to voice [their] unique point of view."[10]

The notion of a world in which African Americans might find and exercise power in the political realm, Thomas implied, is a terrible illusion. If black people think of themselves as a political collective, if they believe that they are empowered by the vote to pursue their interests and goals as a group, they will be led to believe that they can "control" or "influence" political outcomes in their favor.[11] The two words are dangerously suggestive of the kind of sovereignty that Thomas believes blacks can never achieve through politics.

Those words also have particular resonance because one of the questions Thomas explored at length in *Holder* was whether the goal of African Americans or another such constituency should be "*control* over a lesser number*" of elected offices or "*influence* over a greater number*" of elected offices. When control is the goal, district lines are drawn in order to create black majorities in a few districts, enabling African Americans to directly determine the electoral outcome in those districts. When influence is the goal, district lines are drawn to create black pluralities in many districts instead. Under that model, African Americans may not be able to control the outcome of any one election, but they can, as a "potential 'swing' group of voters," affect the outcome of several elections at once.[12] Under the control model, African Americans have more concentrated power in fewer districts; under the influence model, they have less concentrated power across more districts.[13]

For a moment in the 1980s, Thomas had suggested that African Americans should be more open to the Republican Party, on the ground that if Republicans believed they could win black votes, they would compete for those votes. Republican competition for black votes would then force Democrats to also compete for black votes rather than just take them for granted, and African Americans would become a sought-after constituency—the proverbial swing vote. (Jesse Jackson made a similar argument in a direct pitch to the Republican National Committee in 1978.)[14] In *Holder,* Thomas seemed initially to be reprising that argument, favoring the influence model over the control model. But ultimately he rejected both models. Control "is not inherent in the concept of representative democracy," he wrote, and influence is not "a necessary component of the definition of the 'effective' vote." Nothing in the right to vote "encompasses a concern for the 'weight' or 'influence' of votes."[15]

The fact that African Americans are "unable to control seats," that they cannot translate their vote into political power, was to Thomas a simple matter of arithmetic: "in a majoritarian system, numerical minorities lose elections."[16] Without race-conscious assistance from the state, African Americans will always be the losers in American politics. That is a brute fact they should come to terms with, Thomas suggested, not by accepting that assistance but by accepting their weakness, perhaps even vacating the political sphere altogether. Any effort by the state to overcome the limits of black political agency will only confirm, even augment, those limits—because if district lines are redrawn by court order to maximize the black vote, if state legislatures engage in racial gerrymandering to create black-majority districts, if the size of a government authority is increased in order to give African Americans a chance to elect a candidate of their choosing, it is white elites who are engineering those changes. If the white state acts for the sake of black interests, it is white elites acting on behalf of African Americans. That is why, in describing these efforts, Thomas consistently deploys either the passive voice or other constructions that accentuate African Americans' status as objects rather than agents. "Blacks *are drawn* into 'black districts' and *given* 'black representatives,'" he writes. District lines are drawn "*to capture* minority populations." There is a "proportional *allocation* of political power according to race." A "quota of seats *are set aside* for members of a minority group."[17]

The language gives the game away: embedded in the syntax of that discourse is a black community dependent on the goodwill of white people. The problem with that dependence is that it is as precarious as the white will upon which it is predicated. Since it is whites, in these scenarios, who cede their power to blacks, how can blacks be assured that whites won't take that power back? The goodwill of whites can always be revoked. That is what it means to be a powerless and despised minority. Blacks must forever remain vulnerable and insecure in the political sphere, the dependents of their white benefactors. If agency is what African Americans want, they should look for it elsewhere, outside the political sphere.

EVEN IF AFRICAN Americans achieve power in the electoral realm, Thomas says, the state cannot deliver the transformation they seek. The disparity between the extent of black problems and the paucity of liberal solutions is too great. This claim of Thomas's follows the conservative logic of what social theorist Albert Hirschman calls "the futility thesis," which holds that any political attempt to alter a specific social condition will be "largely surface, façade, cosmetic, hence illusory, as the 'deep' structures of society remain wholly untouched." As Hirschman points out, futilitarian arguments on the right often resemble structural arguments on the left. The latter are meant to portray reformist efforts as insufficiently radical, mere salves to social wounds that cannot be healed without a revolutionary transformation. It's no surprise, then, that Thomas's critique on the Court sounds similar to the critiques he deployed as a younger man. The difference is that the claim from the right is made not on behalf of a change that has yet to occur but against a change that already has been tried.[18] The futility thesis preys upon the disappointment that so often comes in the wake of a large effort, the feeling that the change is not great enough, the transformation not deep enough, to justify all the sacrifice that went into its making. As we've seen, Thomas's conservative critique also speaks to the pervasive sense that nothing much was achieved through the black freedom struggle. The disrepair was—is—too great for the state to fix.

Thomas's futilitarian turn can be seen in the evolution of his views regarding the doctrine of disparate impact. Unlike "disparate treatment," which involves explicit discrimination, "disparate impact" focuses on policies that are formally neutral but may adversely affect a group when they are implemented. Even if non-discriminatory in intent, such rules and policies may still be judged illegal if they are discriminatory in their effects.

The topic of disparate impact is an old one for Thomas. During his first term at the EEOC, he had expressed some support for the doctrine. In a 1983 speech, he remarked that while the traditional form of racial discrimination—"overt conscious acts of ill-will or bias"—had been reduced, that reduction only revealed that racism "has taken on a new and more complex form." Now, he said, racism appeared as "otherwise neutral practices and policies—employment systems which have highly discriminatory effects and which can perpetuate the effects of past discrimination."[19] This was the language of disparate impact.

Interestingly, while Thomas expressed willingness to consider disparate impact in the context of race, he dismissed the same philosophy in the context of gender.[20] He was a firm opponent of the principle of comparable worth, for example, which holds that because certain jobs are historically associated with women, they pay less than do male-identified jobs, and that the government should intervene in the market to increase the pay of those women-identified jobs in order to remedy the effects of such gender discrimination. Writing against comparable worth, Thomas stated that while job segregation based on gender "is recognized as a statistically provable fact of life, it is grounded in marketplace realities which the courts perceive that Title VII [of the Civil Rights Act] was not intended to reach."[21] He showed little concern for the sex discrimination that resulted from "nondiscriminatory decisions of individual employees and employers expressed through the marketplace."[22] Those realities—that simple market transactions not based on an intention to discriminate may lead to discriminatory results—belong to the family of problems that disparate impact was meant to challenge. But in the context of gender, Thomas was largely untroubled by them. He seemed to draw a fundamental distinction between the historical experience of women versus that of African Americans, between the ongoing effects of gender oppression versus those of racial oppression: "Women cannot be understood as though they were a *racial* minority group, or any kind of minority at all."[23]

Despite his initial sympathies for disparate impact in the context of race, Thomas swung hard against the doctrine in his second term at the EEOC, most likely for reasons of expedience. The reelection of Reagan emboldened conservatives in the administration to push harder to the right, particularly on race. Thinking about his future and his career, Thomas got in line and revised his positions.[24] He began to claim that disparate impact relied upon dubious statistical methods, that its critique of neutral policies and standards was based on the assumption that people of color were inferior and could not compete with white people, and that it should be applied, if at all, only to low-skilled occupations. Thomas's switch did not go unnoticed; many of his critics remarked upon it at his confirmation hearings.[25] By the time he ascended to the Court, he was ready to abandon any attempt to bolster race-neutral outcomes, portraying the effort as misguided and useless.

Thomas's dissent in *Texas Department of Housing and Community Affairs v. Inclusive Communities Project* (2015) shows him in full futilitarian mode on the subject of disparate impact. Under the Fair Housing Act, state agencies give federally funded tax credits to developers who build low-income housing. Inclusive Communities Project, a nonprofit that assists low-income families, claimed that Texas used those tax credits to site low-income housing in urban black neighborhoods rather than in suburban white neighborhoods, thereby furthering racial segregation. While Texas's criteria for allocating tax credits made no reference to race (proposed projects were evaluated largely on the basis of their finances), and the suit did not allege intentional discrimination, Inclusive Communities claimed that those criteria worked in practice to cause racial segregation. The question for the Court was whether the Fair Housing Act, which outlaws racial discrimination in housing, encompassed the doctrine of disparate impact, prohibiting policies that are "fair in form, but discriminatory in operation." Writing for the Court, Justice Kennedy held that it did. Writing for the conservative dissent, Justice Samuel Alito held that it did not.[26]

In a separate dissent, Thomas took an even harder line against disparate impact. Reaching further than Alito and the other conservatives, Thomas dismissed the entire doctrine as "made of sand."[27] Not only does disparate impact have no place in housing law, he argued, but it has no place in any part of the law. What's remarkable about Thomas's opinion is that while the overt argument is a 180-degree turn from the pro-disparate-impact position he held during his first term at the EEOC, the social vision underlying it was just the same. (That may be why no conservative justice joined him.) Thomas did not reject the claim that racial inequalities still exist or the notion that such inequalities can be sustained by seemingly neutral rules. But where once he claimed that it was conservative opponents of disparate impact who failed to understand the extent of racial inequalities in society, now he argued that it was liberal proponents of disparate impact who lacked that understanding.

In this view, advocates of disparate impact—eager to hold a specific institution accountable for acts of discrimination—overlook the fact that it is not the institution or its rules and policies that are producing the inequity. The inequity is embedded in society, with its decades and centuries of accumulated racial inequalities. The institution is merely reflecting that reality.[28] While the overt thrust of Thomas's opinion is to divest the liberal state of a tool to remedy discrimination, its deeper cuts inflict a more grievous wound, exposing the inability of the liberal state to overcome the racial inequality that is part and parcel of society itself.[29]

THOMAS'S CLAIM THAT the state cannot do anything for African Americans seems at odds with his claim that the state will make things worse for African Americans. Such contradiction is not his alone. As Hirschman points out, conservatives often invoke two other theses, in addition to futility, against reformist or radical political action. One is the "perversity thesis," which holds that "the attempt to push society in a certain direction will result in its moving . . . in the opposite direction": "any purposive action to improve some feature of the political, social, or economic order only serves to exacerbate the condition one wishes to remedy." The other is the "jeopardy thesis," which holds that "the cost of the proposed change or reform is too high as it endangers some previous, precious accomplishment." Unlike the futility thesis, the theses of perversity and jeopardy assume that state action can have an impact, albeit a negative one. Though making a simultaneous case for futility and perversity, or futility and jeopardy, seems like a challenge—affirming the state's potency and impotence in the same breath—an agonized conscience of consistency does not seem to trouble opponents of political transformation. Whenever futilitarians are not "quite comfortable with their own argument," says Hirschman, "they look to the perverse effect for reinforcement, adornment, and closure."[30] That is certainly the case with Thomas's dissent in *Kelo v. City of New London* (2005), which used arguments of both perversity and jeopardy to oppose state projects of social reform.

In its underlying facts, *Kelo* didn't involve the question of race at all. It concerned a plan by Connecticut and New London, a small city in the southeastern corner of the state, to develop New London's downtown waterfront area. After the federal government closed a naval facility in New London that employed more than 1,500 people, the city fell on hard times. Government officials moved to purchase an area in the city known as Fort Trumbull for the purpose of development. They planned to build there a new waterfront, conference center, museum, residences, office and retail buildings, and a river walk. The goal was jobs, an expanded tax base, and a revitalized downtown. Most real estate owners in Fort Trumbull sold their properties to the city; nine, including Susette Kelo, did not. The city then moved to take their property, arguing that its redevelopment would serve the public.[31]

The Fifth Amendment states that the government shall not take private property "for public use, without just compensation." Known as the Takings Clause, the provision leaves the state able to acquire private property on two conditions: it must provide "just compensation" to the property's owner, and the purpose of the acquisition must be a "public use." In practice, this means either that the public will utilize the property directly, as in the case of building a road or a courthouse, or that the property will serve some broader public purpose. Municipal governments, for example, often acquire blighted properties in rundown neighborhoods in order to develop those neighborhoods. This power of eminent domain, as it is called, has long been a bête noire of conservatives. Not only does it threaten the rights of private property, but it has also been used to construct the infrastructure of the liberal state: railroads and highways, parks and hospitals, affordable housing, and more.[32]

In *Kelo*, the Court's four liberals, joined by Justice Kennedy, upheld the government's actions: by turning the private property of Fort Trumbull into something more valuable and economically beneficial to the city, they wrote, the government had taken the properties for "public use." The Court's remaining four conservatives disagreed. Their dissent, written by Justice O'Connor, argued that the majority's definition of public use was so broad as to encompass any seizure of private property that would simply increase the value of that property.[33]

In her dissent, O'Connor dedicated a quick three sentences, almost as an afterthought, to the proposition that when the government takes private property for public use, "the beneficiaries are likely to be those citizens with disproportionate influence and power" and the victims "those with fewer resources."[34] Thomas joined O'Connor's dissent. But he also wrote a separate dissent, joined by no one, in which he turned that afterthought into a sustained polemic against eminent domain as a tool of racial oppression. Suddenly, O'Connor's non-racialized abstractions—beneficiaries, disproportion, resources—were transformed into a brutal and bitter racial narrative, drawn from some of the most difficult moments of the nation's recent past.[35]

Thomas's opinion situated eminent domain in the context of the urban renewal politics of midcentury liberal America. These were programs and policies that, in the name of downtown development or slum clearance, uprooted African Americans and their families in cities across the country: Baltimore, Detroit, New Haven, New York, San Francisco, Boston, and elsewhere. Black homes were razed, worlds were flattened, all to improve the cities in which black people lived. In a widely viewed 1963 interview with the psychologist Kenneth Clark, James Baldwin famously declared that urban renewal "means Negro removal."[36] In his *Kelo* dissent, Thomas cited that very phrase (without naming Baldwin) in order to argue that "urban renewal programs have long been associated with the displacement of blacks." Thomas quoted passages from law journals and academic studies, and offered statistics like this: "Of all the families displaced by urban renewal from 1949 through 1963, 63 percent of those whose race was known were nonwhite." By the time Thomas finished his opinion, he had transformed the Court's previous rulings on the Takings Clause—beginning with the landmark decision *Berman v. Parker* (1954), which authorized urban renewal in Washington, D.C.—into a liberal jurisprudence of ethnic cleansing: "Over 97 percent of the individuals forcibly removed from their homes by the 'slum-clearance' project upheld by this Court in *Berman* were black."[37]

Urban renewal was one of liberalism's great ambitions, a vision of the government engaging in the reconstruction of America's cities for the sake of urban dwellers, including African Americans. Thomas used it to tell a racial story of jeopardy and perversity. When the state involves itself in the economic life of an African American community, he suggested, it will inevitably do what urban renewal did: "destroy[] predominantly minority communities." Though the Takings Clause requires the government to provide monetary "just compensation" to those whose property is taken, there is "no compensation" for the "subjective value" of lost homes and crushed communities and the "indignity inflicted" upon those "displaced" by urban renewal.[38]

In a final swipe at the liberal Court, Thomas invoked a famous clause from a less famous Supreme Court case: the so-called Footnote 4 of the *Carolene Products* decision of 1938. In Footnote 4, the liberal New Dealer justice Harlan Fiske Stone argued that while most citizens in a democracy can rely upon the normal political process to protect their rights, "discrete and insular minorities" cannot always do so. Because they are victims of systemic prejudice, such minorities—African Americans are the paradigmatic example—may need to turn to the courts to protect their rights.[39] Though much of the Court's New Deal jurisprudence requires the judiciary to defer to the government on matters of economic regulation, Footnote 4 authorizes the courts to carefully scrutinize the government's treatment of marginalized or oppressed groups. Conservatives loathe Footnote 4. They would like to do the reverse: strike down economic regulations while deferring to state and local governments' treatment of women and minorities.[40]

In *Kelo*, accordingly, Thomas flipped the liberal script. If the courts are truly concerned about racial minorities, he said, it is economic legislation that they should scrutinize most. Given the logic of the *Kelo* decision, which saw any conversion of private property into something more valuable as a legitimate "public use," poor people—like the black communities done in by urban renewal—would always be the primary targets of a government taking. After all, Thomas pointed out, poor people are "systematically less likely to put their lands to the highest and best social use." They "are also the least politically powerful" members of society, the citizens least able to rely on the political process to protect their rights and interests. Enter Footnote 4: "If ever there were justification for intrusive judicial review of constitutional provisions that protect 'discrete and insular minorities,'" Thomas wrote, "surely that principle would apply with great force to the powerless groups and individuals [the Takings Clause] protects."[41] African Americans evicted by urban renewal are the emblematic victims of the white racism that gets smuggled into liberal development policies, even when those policies are supposed to benefit African Americans. The Court's approval of those policies, he said, is "deeply perverse."[42]

NOT CONTENT TO argue that the liberal state will leave untouched or even worsen the racial inequalities of American society, Thomas also seeks to take away from the liberal state one of its most potent weapons in the battle against those inequalities: the Commerce Clause. The power to "regulate Commerce . . . among the Several states" is only one of the many powers the Constitution assigns to Congress, yet since the late nineteenth century it has been the keystone of American liberalism. With the authorization of a mere six words, the federal government has been empowered to abolish child labor, legislate a forty-hour work week, institute a minimum wage, and establish the right to form unions. Working conditions have a profound effect on commerce, goes the argument. If workers are not allowed to advocate collectively for higher wages, they will be paid too little; if workers are paid too little, they won't be able to buy commodities; if workers do not buy commodities, the streams of commerce will dry up. And commercial activity within one state affects commerce in another state: if workers in a Pittsburgh steel factory go on strike, firms in Ohio may not be able to buy steel to manufacture construction beams; if those firms cannot manufacture construction beams, construction companies may not be able to build office towers in Chicago; if those towers cannot be built, construction workers in Illinois can't earn wages and buy goods. Because the interstate economy is so dependent on intrastate economies, Congress must be able to impose uniform rules—including rules of a more just and humane economy—across the country. All in the name of regulating interstate commerce.

The Commerce Clause has also been used to empower the federal government to fight racial discrimination. When Congress passed the Civil Rights Act (1964), which prohibits a wide range of discrimination—by schools and private employers, courthouses and restaurants—it relied upon the Equal Protection Clause and the Commerce Clause. The Equal Protection Clause stipulates that "no state shall . . .

deny to any person within its jurisdiction the equal protection of the laws." Ever since the nineteenth century, the Court has interpreted that clause to apply only to government action, not the private actions of individuals or non-state institutions.[43] On what ground, then, could Congress regulate the hiring decisions of private employers or a res-taurant's decision to serve a customer? Racial discrimination in res-taurants and hotels, liberals claimed, discourages black people from traveling from the North to the South or within the South, and dis-suades black people from patronizing public accommodations when they do travel. Racial discrimination also dissuades businesses from relocating to the South. Discrimination, in other words, hampers inter-state commerce. That is why Congress has the power to ban it, or so Congress argued, and the Court agreed in *Heart of Atlanta Motel v. United States* (1964).[44]

There's always been something discomfiting about the reliance on the Commerce Clause to achieve racial and other forms of equality. Some might call it a sleight of hand. Why go through the rigmarole of arguing for the impact of unjust actions on interstate commerce? Does the Constitution not provide tools and instruments of a nobler purpose that could be used against racial injustice? The liberal Justice William Douglas, who supported the Civil Rights Act, thought the Fourteenth Amendment's guarantee of equality offered a sounder and simpler rationale for banning discrimination. "Though I join the Court's opin-ions," he wrote in his concurrence in *Heart of Atlanta Motel*, "I am somewhat reluctant here . . . to rest solely on the Commerce Clause. My reluctance is not due to any conviction that Congress lacks power to regulate commerce in the interests of human rights. It is, rather, my belief that the right of people to be free of" racial discrimination, a right that Douglas grounded in the Fourteenth Amendment, "'occupies a more protected position in our constitutional system than does the movement of cattle, fruit, steel and coal across state lines.'"[45]

Yet for many African Americans, there is nothing abstract or cir-cuitous about the connections between interstate commerce and racial equality, between the right to buy and the right to move. High on the list of criticisms of white supremacy that Bigger Thomas offers in

Native Son is that the market is the medium of black constraint. Contrary to the vision set out by Sowell and other conservatives, many African Americans have suffered restrictions on their movement in and through the market: the housing market, the employment market, and so on. "It's just like living in jail," Bigger says. "Why they make us live in one corner of the city? Why don't they let us fly planes and run ships. . . . I reckon we the only things in this city that can't go where we want to go."[46] In his confirmation hearings, Thomas made a similar connection between the movement of goods and the movement of black people:

> I can remember reading, I believe, the *Heart of Atlanta Motel* case, which challenged, I believe, the accommodations provisions in the Civil Rights Act of 1964, which is based on the interstate commerce powers. And one of the factors that was used there was that blacks who traveled across the country were impeded from traveling because of the lack of accommodations.
>
> What that brought to mind was that when I was a kid and we would travel occasionally—I think two or three times during my childhood—by highway from Savannah to New York, my grandfather would go through this long exercise of making sure that the car was working perfectly, that you had new tires, that we had a trunk full of food, et cetera, because there were no accommodations. And should you break down, you would be met with hostilities. That was the reality. So there was indeed some, I would consider significant, impediment on the ability of us to travel and certainly, by extension, on the flow of commerce or travel in our society.[47]

As it happens, the liberal interpretation of the Commerce Clause is rooted in a case specifically about transportation: *Gibbons v. Ogden* (1824). In *Gibbons*, Chief Justice John Marshall held that a federal law licensing ships engaged in the Atlantic coastal trade superseded New York State's grant of a monopoly to a steamboat company that ferried goods and people across the Hudson River. Though the immediate question of the case was narrow—did the term *commerce* in the Constitution include "navigation," that is, not simply the sale or trade of goods but also transportation for the sake of that sale or trade (Marshall ruled that it did)—the ambit of Marshall's opinion was not. Seeking to empower the federal government to override state regulations, to bring together the separate and discrete economies of the states into a single, integrated national economy—much the way the European Union is now doing for the separate economies of the continent's nation-states—Marshall argued for a broad interpretation of the Commerce Clause.[48] Commerce should be understood not in limited terms, he said, as only the buying and selling of goods, but as a social activity that transcends simple business transactions. "Intercourse," Marshall called it, invoking an eighteenth-century conception, popular among the Framers, of commerce as interactions between diverse people across the globe. Commerce was a way of being social, of living with others in a single civilization; it was a dialogue among strangers. Among the definitions of commerce cited in Samuel Johnson's *Dictionary* was "interchange of anything."[49] That "anything" could be commodities, texts, or opinions. Any proper reading of the term would include a great many activities beyond the buying and selling of goods.

When the 1964 Court upheld anti-discrimination laws in the name of interstate commerce, therefore, it was not conjuring an understanding out of nowhere. It was following Marshall's interpretation, arguably the original meaning of the Commerce Clause, which saw in the creation of a national economy the instrument of a great civilizing process, with people across the states brought together and improved—economically, socially, culturally—by that contact and conversation. Nor was this understanding limited to the high precincts of the (white) bench; it pervaded the black freedom struggle as well. It's no accident that so much of the civil rights movement took place in buses and over lunch counters: from the coffeehouses of eighteenth-century London to the ports of the Atlantic, our places of eating and paths of travel have been sites of communication and exchange. One need only recall Frederick Douglass's experience upon reaching Baltimore to see how interrelated these ideas of commerce and civilization can be. It was at the bustling wharfs of the global economy that Douglass, still a slave, met two white sailors from Ireland, who encouraged him to run away to the North. Douglass credits this encounter as the source of his resolution to overcome the conditions of his enslavement.[50]

Gibbons is also the source of the argument that Congress could regulate any activity within a state that affects another state. Congress is prohibited from regulating only those "concerns" that "are completely within a particular State" and that "do not affect other States." Activities within a state that have "spillover effects" onto other states are legitimate objects of congressional action, Marshall suggested.[51] Even if one did not adopt a broad definition of commerce as "interchange of anything," authorizing the national government to regulate activities inside a given state that have spillover effects onto other states has proven a potent source of federal power. When conservatives in the nineteenth and twentieth centuries tried to restrict the scope of the Commerce Clause to the sale of goods across state lines, Progressives and liberals used the spillover argument to defend the federal regulation of activities as various as the conditions of manufacturing, child labor, the growing of wheat for personal use on family farms, the mergers of firms, and violence against women. Whether or not any one of these acts is a form of commerce in itself, each of them affects commerce in another state. Since no one state can be counted upon to take care of the spillover effects in other states, Congress must be allowed to do so.

When Thomas takes aim at the Commerce Clause, therefore, he is seeking to take away a tool of the regulatory state that has exercised conservative passions for over a century. In *United States v. Lopez* (1995), Thomas confronted the entirety of Marshall's legacy from *Gibbons*. The case concerned the Gun-Free School Zones Act, which Congress passed in 1990 to prohibit the possession of guns within a thousand feet of a school zone. Gun possession leads to violent crime, argued the bill's sponsors, and gun possession near schools creates a bad learning environment. Both results hamper interstate commerce. Even though regulating guns is an activity usually left to the states, the sponsors said, Congress has the right to regulate it because of these effects on interstate commerce. Led by Chief Justice Rehnquist, conservatives on the Court were able, for the first time since the New Deal, to muster a majority to push back on this liberal use of the Commerce Clause. Congress, the Court decided, may use the Commerce Clause to regulate activities within a state that are economic in nature and that have a "substantial effect" on interstate commerce. Having a gun is not an economic activity, Rehnquist said, and claims that gun possession within one state substantially affects commerce between the states are too speculative, involve too many links in a causal chain, to be sustained. The Gun-Free School Zones Act was thus unconstitutional.[52] Rehnquist did not overturn the Court's civil rights or New Deal jurisprudence. Instead, he sent a clear signal to Congress that the Court was no longer willing to tolerate the promiscuous use of the Commerce Clause to advance liberalism's social agenda.

Claiming that Rehnquist hadn't gone far enough, Thomas wrote a separate opinion, joined by no one, in which he argued for radically restricting the definition of commerce. Commerce, he suggested, should be defined as it was at the time of the adoption of the Constitution: as "selling, buying, and bartering, as well as transporting for these purposes," and no more than that.[53] In Thomas's view, commerce does not include all economic activity, as Rehnquist had claimed. The term excludes manufacturing and agricultural production, for example—which suggests that a great deal of federal regulation, from the Progressive era through the New Deal, is unconstitutional.[54] Thomas reiterated that position ten years later in his dissent in *Gonzalez v. Raich*, which upheld a federal ban on the use of medical marijuana as a legitimate application of the Commerce Clause. Thomas, again, was unwilling to grant the federal government such power. Commerce, he wrote, should be taken to mean only "trade or exchange for value" and transportation for that purpose. Any definition of commerce must not be so wide as to include "all economic or gainful activity that has some attenuated connection to trade or exchange."[55]

In both *Lopez* and *Raich*, Thomas offered nods to *Gibbons v. Ogden* by including transportation within his otherwise narrow definition of commerce. Still, were they adopted as the Court's position, Thomas's opinions in the two cases might have had the effect of overturning *Gibbons*. In his ruling, Marshall had claimed that the term *commerce* "describes the commercial intercourse . . . in all its branches." Even though the transportation of goods does not involve trade or exchange for value, even though it is not commerce in the strictest sense, it is one of the phases of commercial intercourse. Limiting commerce to trade or exchange for value, as Thomas has done, and simply tacking on transportation, does not reflect the letter or the spirit of Marshall's decision. Marshall also insisted that the regulation of commerce could not be limited to "rules for the conduct of individuals in the actual employment of buying and selling or of barter."[56] The rules of commerce had to extend to activities significantly beyond those of buying, selling, or barter not only because this wider range of activities affected buying, selling, and barter but also because commerce itself, in all its phases, extended significantly beyond buying, selling, and barter. Against this argument, Thomas made his bottom line clear. Commerce is not nearly as expansive as liberals want it to be; not as expansive as Rehnquist's somewhat tighter interpretation would have it; and perhaps even not as expansive as Marshall conceived it in 1824.[57]

Hovering in the background of this struggle over the vocabulary of commerce is the profound question of how power gets distributed in society, whether it lies within the market or the state. Polity and economy are the yin and yang of the Commerce Clause: whenever claims for the authority of the state are advanced, claims for the autonomy of the market must give way, and vice versa. The meaning of a word is potent; definitions are destiny. "With each new locution," Thomas wrote in *Raich*, with each new meaning given to the term *commerce*, "federal power expands, but never contracts."[58] Even in *Lopez*, where Rehnquist stopped the expansion of federal power, the Court settled on a definition of commerce that in Thomas's view still legitimized exercises of federal power vastly greater than any envisioned by the Framers. The more the Court resorts to "rootless and malleable" definitions of commerce, Thomas said in another Commerce Clause case, the more power the state will have to involve itself in the affairs of citizens.[59] The same goes for the word *economic*. In a footnote in *Raich*,

Thomas took issue with the Court's definition of economic activity as "the production, distribution, and consumption of commodities." That phrasing, he wrote, is "remarkably expansive." It would authorize Congress to regulate "quilting bees, clothes drives, and potluck suppers." The proper definition, as Thomas saw it, was to be found in the third edition of *The American Heritage Dictionary*, which came out in 1992: "[o]f or relating to the production, development, and management of *material wealth*, as of a country, household, or business enterprise."[60]

FROM HIS EARLIEST days on the right, Thomas has understood the question of federal power as an especially fateful one for the black community. African Americans have long viewed the states as their enemy and the national government as their ally, or at least potential ally, in the struggle for emancipation. This is particularly true, Thomas believed, of African Americans of his generation. "Over the past two decades or so," he wrote in 1985,

> it has been the view of most black Americans that a strong involvement by the national government in the affairs of state and local governments and the private sector, has resulted in benefit to blacks. It was felt that the national government was good, and the more involvement the better, because the states didn't do what was right and businesses didn't do what was right. We felt that way, I know, in Savannah, Georgia, where I grew up.
>
> It was the federal government that got rid of Jim Crow laws, segregation, vagrancy laws, separate schools, and all those rules that said blacks couldn't walk across the park or go to the library.[61]

That backstory—the depth and resonance of this vision of federal power among African Americans—is ever present in Thomas's writing on the Commerce Clause. It explains, perhaps, why no other justice has demonstrated such zeal in undoing not only the last century of the Court's Commerce Clause jurisprudence but also the structuring premise of Marshall's vision. Borrowing from the Enlightenment, Marshall promoted an expansive understanding of commerce in order to make the national government the agent of a great civilizing process, a process of economic exchange and unification across differences. In the name of the original meaning of the Commerce Clause, Thomas seeks to put Marshall's genie back in the bottle. That's not simply because, as Thomas wrote in *Raich*, he does not want commerce to "cover the entire web of human activity."[62] Nor is it simply because he does not believe in the unification of different peoples. It is also because Thomas believes race matters. In his jurisprudence, African Americans have nothing to gain—and everything to lose—from a national government set on improving their condition.

6

Men of Money

If one half of Thomas's political economy is meant to combat African Americans' belief in politics and the state, the other half seeks to reorient African Americans toward the capitalist economy, to get black people to see in money and the market the path of their ascent. It is not enough to undermine electoral politics, as Thomas does in his voting rights jurisprudence, or to constrain the state, as he does in his Commerce Clause, Takings Clause, and disparate impact jurisprudence. The market must be emancipated from the state. This requires more than defending the market as an efficient mechanism for providing commodities or supporting innovation. The market must be rendered a moral good, worthy of the praise that is usually reserved for values such as equality or dignity. Moneymaking must be reconceived as something other than an instrument of creature comforts. It must become akin to individual fulfillment or personal expression. It must be thought of as the means by which people pursue their most fundamental purposes and deepest selves. Only if money and the market are thought of in the same way that we think of elemental rights—speech, bodily autonomy, belief, sexual intimacy—will the market be protected from the impulse to regulate and control it through the state.

In that 1987 Pacific Research Institute speech discussed earlier—where Thomas set out his theory of capitalism by way of Myers Anderson, whom he analogized to the men of wealth criticized by FDR and John Kenneth Galbraith—Thomas also gave a sense of how he would pursue this vision of a moralized black capitalism on the Court. The target of that speech was midcentury liberalism, which held money and markets in bad odor. Such a view of liberalism may be unrecognizable today, when liberals are often as enamored of entrepreneurs and bankers as those entrepreneurs and bankers are of themselves. But the midcentury liberal, whose values and beliefs dominated the worlds of academia and government when Thomas came of age, was a different animal. That liberal, said Thomas, viewed economic activity as "venal and dirty," "materialistic and crass," a grubby means to an only slightly less grubby end. Far nobler, on the liberal account, were the "idealistic professions" of the academy, law, and journalism. Because professors, lawyers, and journalists are "people who make their living by producing words," the midcentury liberal viewed speech as the true bastion of freedom, the real subject of rights. "Economic rights are considered antagonistic to civil or human rights—the former being materialistic and dirty while the latter are lofty and noble," Thomas said. "The split has evolved in such a way that some who consider themselves great champions of human rights contrast themselves with advocates of property rights or economic rights."[1]

In the liberal view, according to Thomas, words and their cognates—ideas, sentiments, beliefs—were the most vital concerns, the most intimate expression, of the self. That's why liberals believed that words should be afforded the greatest protection from government interference. Hence the emphasis in midcentury liberalism on the First Amendment's guarantee of freedom of speech, which was seen as the crown jewel of all freedoms, and the corresponding indifference to restrictions on money and its pursuit. The only concern relevant to the regulation of money and markets was pragmatic: having established the end—the dignity of persons rather than purses—one only had to figure out the means, determining whether a specific regulation advanced people's dignity. The subject of economic regulation deserved no more consideration than that.[2]

The task of conservatism, Thomas made clear, was to overcome this dichotomy between economics and morals, money and speech. It was not enough to argue that a "renewed emphasis on economic rights must play a key role" in conservatism.[3] Economic rights had to be established as human rights, economic freedom had to be treated as a constituent form of freedom. People had to be made to understand that there is a "full" and "indivisible range" of "individual rights," which are both "economic and civil."[4] Money and markets were not simply economic categories for Thomas. They were moral categories, akin to speech and belief, as deserving of rights as the sorts of rights liberals traditionally championed throughout the twentieth century.

It thus is no surprise that Thomas's most important contributions to the project of liberating the market from the state come not in cases involving property rights or anti-trust—that is, disputes directly connected to issues of money and the market—but in cases involving the First Amendment. It is there, in the guarantee of freedom of speech, that most sacred space of the constitutional imagination, that Thomas finds the greatest source of economic freedom. If the project of developing capitalism involves the moralization of money and the market, elevating them to the status of other activities that are worthy of protection as rights, it makes sense to align or equate money and the market with the individual speaking his mind. In Thomas's First Amendment jurisprudence, spending money and making money become the constitutional equivalents of artists creating art, writers writing books, journalists reporting the news, citizens arguing views, and believers expressing belief.

Thomas's First Amendment jurisprudence focuses on two areas: campaign finance and so-called commercial speech. Through his campaign finance jurisprudence, which defends the rights of the wealthy to donate unlimited sums to their favored candidates, Thomas empowers the man of money to play an outsized role in the political sphere. Through his commercial speech jurisprudence, Thomas argues that speech connected to profit-making—minimally, advertising, but maximally, any language involved in an economic transaction—should be elevated to the status of political, literary, and other kinds of protected speech. From the point of view of Thomas's First Amendment, commercial speech is as important, even more important in some cases, than many of the other kinds of speech that are protected by the First Amendment.

While Thomas's jurisprudence of monied speech is connected to moral questions, it is also instrumental. Pursuing a strategy deployed by other legal conservatives, Thomas's First Amendment opinions suggest that if economic life can be reconceived as a form of speech, it will be afforded the same sanctuary from state regulation that speech now enjoys. It will be as immune to state power as speech is.[5] As Justice Elena Kagan noted in a recent case, "Speech is everywhere—a part of every human activity (employment, health care, securities trading, you name it). For that reason, almost all economic and regulatory policy affects or touches speech." By turning economic activity into speech, she said, conservatives are "weaponizing the First Amendment," empowering the Court to strike down a great many regulations of business as infringements or abridgements of speech.[6] Kagan's point is well taken. As a recent study shows, businesses are increasingly the most important beneficiary of the Court's First Amendment rulings. Where businesses used to win First Amendment cases at a much lower rate than individuals, they now win those cases at roughly the same rate as individuals do. Once upon a time, the typical free speech case involved a student or a protester; now it's just as likely to involve a firm.[7]

Thomas's Commerce Clause jurisprudence restrains the national government by preventing it from exceeding its enumerated powers. His First Amendment jurisprudence works differently: it surrounds money and the market with a fence of rights claims, each bearing a sign that says "no trespass." Rights claims are designed to make it difficult for the government to interfere in our lives. By turning economic activity into a fundamental right of speech, Thomas secures "the liberation of commerce" that he has envisioned since his days in the Reagan administration.[8] And where Thomas's Commerce Clause jurisprudence has a potential loophole—it puts restrictions only on the national government, leaving the states with a free hand to regulate their internal economies—his First Amendment jurisprudence applies to state and local governments as well. The economy is thus doubly protected: against a meddling Congress by a narrowed Commerce Clause and against a meddling state or locality (and Congress) by an expanded First Amendment. What Thomas's rollback of the Commerce Clause began, his expansion of the First Amendment completes.[9]

Unlike most of the jurisprudence discussed in this book, Thomas's opinions on campaign finance and commercial speech make no explicit mention of race. They simply re-moralize money and the market, along the lines Thomas set out at the Pacific Research Institute. But the text of that speech (as well as Thomas's other writings and speeches) is the inescapable subtext of these opinions. Each move Thomas made in that speech—the transformation of moneymaking into self-expression, the erasure of the boundary between money and morals, the joining of economic rights to other rights, and the elevation of the man of wealth to a leadership role in society—he made on behalf of men like Myers Anderson, in whose accumulation of wealth Thomas saw the path to black freedom.

Thomas has repeated each of those moves in his jurisprudence. He may not state his destination, but it's hard not to see it all the same. In a market freed of government constraints, extraordinary black men like Myers Anderson will emerge. If Myers could succeed in the market despite Jim Crow, others can do so too. Every bit of reality would suggest that this is a fantasy on Thomas's part, that the odds are overwhelmingly against African Americans, that the market clearly privileges whites. But that's how all romance, including capitalism, works: one Cinderella will be chosen, a special someone will succeed, and that will make all the difference.

"MONEY IS A kind of poetry," wrote Wallace Stevens.[10] Thomas agrees. Money, to him, is more than just a condition of speech, a factor in speech, an aid to speech, an instrument of speech, or speech in the figurative sense. It *is* speech. It communicates. It is a "mode of expression." Not only do our financial "contributions to political campaigns generate essential political speech," he wrote in one opinion, but we also "speak through contributions" to those campaigns.[11] Minimally, we communicate our support for a candidate and his positions. If we give more money, we express the greater intensity of our support—much like the antiwar protester wearing a jacket that says "Fuck the draft," whose attire registers not merely the fact of his opposition to the draft but the vehemence of that opposition.[12] From Thomas's perspective, if liberals wish to claim that nude dancing and flag burning are modes of speech, as they often do—if the Court is willing to use the First Amendment to protect cross burning, pornography, defamation, and begging for money, as it has—then we should accord at least the same status to money that funds political expression, which lies at the core of First Amendment activity.[13]

Thomas never tells us precisely why he believes money is speech as opposed to only a resource for speech, why it is expressive and communicative rather than instrumental. But we can find an explanation for his position in a thinker whose work Thomas frequently cites and whom both Thomas and his biographers have claimed as an influence on him: the Austrian-born economist and philosopher Friedrich Hayek.[14] In *The Road to Serfdom*, Hayek argues that money is more than an instrument or resource for the pursuit of our interests; it is the medium through which we express our values and beliefs. There are no "purely economic ends," writes Hayek, "separate from the other ends of life."[15] Life is a trade-off. If I wish to devote myself to philosophy, I must forgo the violin. Acquiring a self is an act of sacrifice: of time, effort, focus, other options. That finitude—that something can be had only at the expense of something else—is part of the human condition. This needn't be a source of sadness, however. It is only through sacrifice, the relinquishing of other possibilities, that we learn what we value. If everything were had for free, if nothing cost us anything, we'd never know how much we care for the various things of the world. Material scarcity and economic constraint are occasions for moral expression and self-discovery. Indeed, says Hayek, they are the only such occasions: "Freedom to order our own conduct in the sphere where material circumstances force a choice upon us, and responsibility for the arrangement of our own life according to our own conscience, is the air in which alone moral sense grows and in which moral values are daily re-created in the free decision of the individual."[16]

All of us, says Hayek, have some things we will never part with. These are things that "stand high above the amenities or even above many of the necessities of life": the love of a child, belief in God, and the like. There are other things, however, that we will give up. These are at "the fringe, the 'margin,' of our needs"—the things we can put a price tag on. We call them "'merely' economic" because we can convert them into cash. None of us knows in advance what is marginal and what is major, which things matter a great deal to us and which matter little. We only know when we decide. Those moments of decision occur in the marketplace, when we are free to choose—and forced to choose. In the market, we must "decide what to us is more, and what less, important."[17] There we are offered a price for something: an expensive gold pocket watch, say, from a cherished grandfather. If we're willing to sell it, we learn that the watch matters less to us than the money we get for it; if we refuse to give it up for anything, we learn that it is priceless. That is why economic matters are so revelatory. What we elect to spend our money on, what we choose to put a price tag on, even if the commodity is trivial—these are matters of the greatest weight. For it is in the accumulation of such trivia, in the heap of goods that we can put a price tag on, that we reveal, if only in a negative way, what is truly of value to us, what we can't put a price tag on.[18] Acts of spending, in other words, are deeply expressive. In some cases, they are more expressive than speech itself, which is often costless. Talk is cheap; money's not.[19]

In a different age, our morals and mettle would have been measured by a different sacrifice: a sacrifice of life, whether on the battlefield, where we would have had the opportunity to show our love of God or country or king, or at the stake, where we would have had one chance to renounce our heresies. So it is now, says Hayek, with money. With each dollar we give up, we affirm its lesser value to us. As we get closer and closer to our financial limits, each dollar acquires greater and greater value. At some point, we reach a place in our accounts where we are forced to give up something else, beyond money, to secure what we wish or desire. If we refuse to part with that something else, we'll know that it is a higher good, perhaps our highest one.[20]

When it comes to political speech, Thomas proposes, men and women speak most forcefully not through the idle chatter of social media or cocktail conversation but through giving up their money as campaign donations. Donors "speak through the candidate," Thomas writes.[21] That candidate better reflects their values than whatever it is that they are forgoing to make the donation. In putting our money where our mouth is, we show a steadiness of purpose and strength of conviction that words alone cannot convey.

If the decisive moment of reckoning only arrives when we reach our financial limits, the Hayekian argument would seem to favor limitations on accumulations of wealth. How are the wealthy ever to make a moral choice if they never approach the end of their riches? How are their words to be meaningful if their money doesn't come close to running out? Only those of modest means seem to be in a position to make moral choices. Perhaps a prohibition on accumulation of wealth, or even an equalization of it, would promote the most meaningful, expressive speech. Yet that is not a question that Hayek discusses in his social thought—or that Thomas raises in his jurisprudence. If anything, his jurisprudence insistently pushes in the opposite direction.

WHILE THOMAS'S ARGUMENT for *why* money is speech may be his (and Hayek's), the underlying claim that money is speech long predates him. The widespread belief that the equation of money and speech is an innovation of the Roberts Court in *Citizens United* and that this equation is a conservative position is mistaken. The claim that money is speech was already accepted in *Buckley v. Valeo*, the 1976 case that established the framework for our modern campaign finance jurisprudence.[22] Though *Buckley* was announced as a decision of the entire Court, with no particular justice named as its author, scholars believe it was mostly the work of Justice William Brennan, the liberal titan of the second half of the twentieth century.[23] The liberal provenance of that decision is still evident today. The belief "that money is 'not speech,'" writes Yale law professor Robert Post, one of the most influential liberal scholars of the First Amendment, "is far from obvious." Distinguishing between money and speech presumes that there is a medium of speech that has nothing to do with the materiality of the world. But that is not the case, says Post. "There is no such thing as 'pure speech.' All communication requires a physical substrate." A book cannot be published without the paper upon which it is printed. A movie cannot be made without the film stock upon which it appears. Speech "is dependent upon the resources necessary to create and disseminate it." Those resources cost money. Banning or limiting those resources—or the money that can be expended upon them—is thus a ban or limit on speech. "The regulation of the substrate is not separable from the regulation of the speech."[24]

But *Buckley v. Valeo* drew a distinction between expenditures made by a campaign and contributions that donors give to a campaign—and applied the First Amendment's guarantee of freedom of speech only to the former. Since campaign expenditures enable a campaign to speak, to communicate its message, any limits on those expenditures are a limitation on speech and are prohibited by the First Amendment. But limits on donor contributions, the *Buckley* Court ruled, are permissible. Such contributions are still a form of speech, but the government has an interest in eliminating "the reality or appearance of corruption in the electoral process." As long as the goal of restricting campaign contributions is to remove the stink and stain of influence-peddling, to protect the democratic process from the sense that politicians are for sale, the *Buckley* decision held, limiting such contributions does not violate the First Amendment. The gain in electoral integrity is great; the infringement on the donor's liberty, small. "A limitation upon the amount that any one person or group may contribute to a candidate or political committee entails only a marginal restriction upon the contributor's ability to engage in free communication," the Court ruled.[25]

It is this second part of *Buckley*—that the government may, consistent with the First Amendment, put restrictions on the amount of campaign contributions—that Thomas has sought, from his earliest days on the Court, to overturn.[26] Indeed, though other conservative justices dissented at the time from the second part of *Buckley*, Thomas may be the very first justice on the post-*Buckley* Court to explicitly seek to overturn it.[27] In the process, he aims to elevate the man of money, to empower that man to determine how much and what kind of speech there will be.

In the Book of Exodus, God instructs Moses to go to Pharaoh—initially to tell him that the Israelites wish to head into the wilderness for three days of prayer, later to inform him that they intend to depart Egypt altogether. Each time, Moses begs off, complaining that he lacks the eloquence, the rhetorical fluency and lingual dexterity, to speak on God's behalf. Swatting away Moses's excuses, God finally explodes in anger and tells him to have his brother Aaron speak to Pharaoh on Moses's behalf. "I know that he can speak well," God says. "And thou shalt speak unto him, and put words in his mouth: and I will be with thy mouth, and with his mouth. . . . And he shall be thy spokesman unto the people . . . he shall be to thee instead of a mouth, and thou shalt be to him instead of God."[28] It's about as close a vision of a person as mouthpiece, a vessel for communicating and amplifying the message of another, as we're likely to get. The physicality of the text—God "will be with" Moses's mouth and Aaron's mouth; Moses will "put words" in Aaron's mouth; Aaron will be Moses's mouth—is suggestive of the kind of thinking that informs Thomas's effort to overturn the second part of *Buckley*. Having an intermediary speak on behalf of oneself is no different from speaking for oneself; the spokesman-candidate is the mouth of the self.

When a citizen donates to a candidate, writes Thomas, he is exercising his "right to speak through the candidate." Like Moses, the citizen has made the calculation that the candidate will communicate ideas better than he, and do more to make those ideas into reality. With his audience and platform, the candidate acts like a sound system, amplifying the donor's opinions. An "individual may add more to a political discourse by giving rather than spending," writes Thomas.

The decision to contribute to a campaign reflects a "practical judgment by a citizen that another person or organization can more effectively deploy funds for the good of a common cause than he can." To limit an individual's donation to a political campaign, therefore, is to consign him "to less effective modes of communication."[29]

As Thomas explains, "even in the case of a direct expenditure" by a campaign, which the Court has held cannot be limited, "there is usually some go-between that facilitates the dissemination of the spender's message."[30] No candidate simply speaks; he always speaks through advertisements, in stadiums, on commercials, all of which require intermediaries (agencies, owners, networks) and money. If we accept that campaign expenditures are a vital and protected form of political speech, we must accept that a contribution to a campaign is, too. For "a contribution is simply an indirect expenditure," writes Thomas, the equivalent of God speaking through Moses and Moses through Aaron. "Contributions and expenditures may thus differ in form" from each other, but "they do not differ in substance."[31]

If the conversion of a campaign contribution into a campaign expenditure is the transmission of the donor's words into the candidate's mouth, it stands to reason that the candidate is the mouthpiece of the donor. Thomas doesn't shy away from what seems like the plutocratic implication of that argument: the message of the donor becomes the message of the candidate. Indeed, Thomas says that the notion, found in *Buckley*, that a donation to a candidate "signals only general support for the candidate" rather than for a specific idea or policy proposal is "questionable." Contributions to a campaign, he wrote in *Colorado Republican Federal Campaign Committee v. FEC* (1996), signal a statement of "social, economic, and political beliefs" and a desire "to have those beliefs affect governmental policy."[32] In his dissent in *Nixon v. Shrink Missouri Government PAC* (2000), Thomas elaborated: "Donors seek to disseminate information by giving to an organization controlled by others. Through contributing, citizens see to it that their views on policy and politics are articulated." A contribution "helps to ensure the dissemination of the messages that the contributor wishes to convey."[33]

The import of these opinions is to make political candidates mere actors on the political stage, speaking the lines of the man of money. Thomas makes no effort to hide this fact. He approvingly cites a passage from Herbert Alexander's 1972 text *Money in Politics*: "Some views are heard only if interested individuals are willing to support financially the candidate or committee voicing the position. To be widely heard, mass communications may be necessary, and they are costly."[34] Costly communications require big donations. Big donations mean big donors. Moreover, not only are the men of means supporting an activity that is central to the First Amendment—the transmission of political views and arguments—but those views and arguments will tend to be heterodox and rare, precisely the sort of views and arguments that need to be heard. This, again, is in keeping with Hayek, who claimed that historically it was wealthy patrons who advocated and sustained unpopular and unorthodox views like abolition and penal reform.[35]

Liberal critics will claim that Thomas's model is pure influence peddling, money buying access and legislation, the essence of corruption. Thomas counters that corruption happens only if there is a simple quid pro quo, a bribe, which is illegal. Influence and access, by contrast, are what all citizens seek. Influence peddling, in other words, is the essence of citizenship. If the liberal complaint is that some citizens have more access and influence than others, their complaint moves in a direction that *Buckley* itself foreswore and declared unconstitutional: mandating equality in speech. Legislating equality in speech either lies beyond the scope of the First Amendment or would violate it by silencing some voices in order that others might be heard, the *Buckley* Court ruled. So long as money is speech, and equality is proscribed as the aim, greater access and influence by the man of means will be the form that advocacy and representation take in a capitalist democracy.[36]

Access and influence for the men of money, candidates serving as mouthpieces for the men of means: to Thomas, these are not perversions of politics; they are politics. Politics is not a sphere where pure speech, uncontaminated by materiality, reigns supreme. It is the art of persuasion, the leading of citizens or politicians from one position to another, and whenever that occurs money will be the medium, the men of money its maestros. As Thomas argued in *McConnell v. Federal Election Commission* (2003):

> The only effect, however, that the "immense aggregations" of wealth will have (in the context of independent expenditures) on an election is that they might be used to fund communications to convince voters to select certain candidates over others. In other words, the "corrosive and distorting effects" . . . are that corporations, on behalf of their shareholders, will be able to convince voters of the correctness of their ideas. Apparently, winning in the marketplace of ideas is no longer a sign that "the ultimate good" has been "reached by free trade in ideas," or that the speaker has survived "the best test of truth" by having the "thought . . . get itself accepted in the competition of the market." . . . It is now evidence of "corruption." This conclusion is antithetical to everything for which the First Amendment stands.[37]

By allowing "citizens and candidates to determine who shall speak, the means they will use, and the amount of sufficient speech to inform and persuade," the state and the courts would allow the men of means to try to influence voters as much as they wish. That, says Thomas, is how it should be.[38]

Though the overt thrust of Thomas's opinions is to authorize men of means to dominate the political realm—in keeping with the agenda of the Republican Party and the conservative movement, Thomas is one of the foremost defenders of plutocracy on the Court—his opinions also compel a more corrosive deflation of politics. If the currency of politics is money, if the primary movers of politics are men of means, what better argument could there be for African Americans of few means to withdraw from politics? Why not concentrate instead, at least for the time being, on accumulating wealth in the market? That way, African Americans might return to politics one day, only this time as men of money rather than as a movement of masses. Or perhaps African Americans might vacate the political realm altogether and develop their own institutions of wealth, much as Booker T. Washington recommended during Jim Crow: their law firms, banks, corporations, chambers of commerce, and so on. These institutions might serve as a platform for a different mode of politics, one that looks less like politics as it has traditionally been understood and more like the economic action that Thomas has long sought to valorize.[39]

ON THE COURT, Thomas is one of the leading and most forceful proponents of the claim that the First Amendment protects commercial speech—communication we use in pursuit of profit—from government regulation. According to one estimate, more than a quarter of Thomas's freedom of speech opinions concern commercial speech.[40] A relatively new category of jurisprudence, commercial speech includes advertising, but it can also encompass, as Justice Kagan suggested, all economic transactions that involve speech: from contracts to consultations, from buying and selling to hiring and firing.[41] While the scope and implications of Thomas's commercial speech jurisprudence remain unclear, it's not difficult to see how that jurisprudence, in the name of protecting freedom of speech, might authorize the courts to overturn multiple economic regulations.[42]

What has consistently distinguished Thomas's commercial speech jurisprudence from that of his colleagues is that where they have focused on the contributions of commercial speech to the marketplace, on the importance of the free flow of information to consumer decisions, Thomas has pressed the notion that commercial speech is like political speech, indeed, may be better thought of as political speech.[43] Read closely and carefully, Thomas's opinions suggest that the commercial marketplace may best be understood as a kind of political sphere, full of activities traditionally understood to be political: persuasion, action, and advocacy. It is in the market, Thomas intimates, that the leadership customarily associated with politics is to be found. It is in the market where black men like Myers Anderson stride atop the world, where we find the world that Thomas first glimpsed in those tantalizing passages of Sowell's *Race and Economics*.

Here again, a return to Hayek's argument is helpful. Throughout history, Hayek argues, it has been the great men of money and property who have advanced the cause of civilization—not just by using their wealth to advocate unorthodox political causes, but also by developing mass commodities, turning what previously had been luxury items for an elite few into products for the many. Through these material improvements to the human estate, men of wealth shape the culture, crafting and constructing the everyday sensibilities of men and women, anticipating and designing popular desires. These improvements are not only economic; as we've seen, Hayek does not believe the economic can be hived off from the moral or the cultural. All of economic life is fraught with moral, cultural, even spiritual concerns.

> The important point is not merely that we gradually learn to make cheaply on a large scale what we already know how to make expensively in small quantities but that only from an advanced position does the next range of desires and possibilities become visible, so that the selection of new goals and the effort toward their achievement will begin long before the majority can strive for them. If what they will want after their present goals are realized is soon to be made available, it is necessary that the developments that will bear fruit for the masses in twenty or fifty years' time should be guided by the views of people who are already in the position of enjoying them.[44]

In their ability to design the desires of the masses, the men of money are like the great political and spiritual leaders of old. When they deploy wealth—whether in the conventionally defined economic sphere or through their patronage of the arts or their support of unpopular causes—they are engaging in modes of action that have marked political activity since the Greeks: shaping how people conceive the pursuit and cultivation of the good life. "It is only natural that the development of the art of living and of the non-materialistic values should have profited most from the activities of those who had no material worries," Hayek writes.[45]

In his opinions on commercial speech, Thomas makes a similar set of moves as Hayek. Minimally, he argues that political and commercial speech are intertwined and inextricably linked. "Severing 'commercial' speech from speech necessary to democratic decisionmaking," he writes, is a "near impossibility." Freedom of the press, for example, prohibits government bans not only on newspapers or on specific newspaper articles but also on the advertisements that newspapers rely upon to sustain themselves. From the dawn of the republic, "commercial life and advertising were" thought to be "integral" to the life of the polity. The Framers "equated liberty and property and did not distinguish between commercial and noncommercial messages." Thomas also draws comparisons between commercial and political speech, demonstrating their likeness, even equivalence. In the same way that political speech—on behalf of "totalitarian dogmas," for example—can lure people to acts of political harm, so can commercial speech—on behalf of smoking cigarettes—lure people to acts of biological harm. Commercial speech and political speech are of equivalent value, and laws that regulate them deserve the strictest scrutiny from the Court: "I do not see a philosophical or historical basis for asserting that 'commercial' speech is of 'lower value' than 'noncommercial' speech."[46]

But Thomas's grander claim is that moneyed men and political actors are engaged in an analogous enterprise of advocacy and persuasion. Ever since Machiavelli, political writers have understood that political action straddles that elusive space between what is and what might be, between truth and fiction. Politics, Hannah Arendt argued, is a stage where we seek to persuade each other through artful speech. Political actors are akin to liars—and vice versa. The liar is an actor in the theatrical sense, creating a fictitious world through speech, and he is an actor in the political sense, seeking to introduce new things into the world and thereby to change it. Arraying himself against the given world, the known world, the liar claims for himself the same freedom that the politician claims when he brings something new into that world: the freedom to say no to the world as it is.[47]

Not only does Thomas make a similar set of claims about the commercial man, but in the course of doing so, he explicitly analogizes advertising to political advocacy and action. In *Lorillard Tobacco*

Company v. Reilly (2011), the State of Massachusetts claimed that "the simple existence of tobacco advertisements misleads people into believing that tobacco use is more pervasive than it is." But such deception, Thomas argued, is as critical to the art of advertising as it is to the art of politics.

> The State misunderstands the purpose of advertising: Promoting a product that is not yet pervasively used (or a cause that is not yet widely supported) is a primary purpose of advertising. Tobacco advertisements would be no more misleading for suggesting pervasive use of tobacco products than are any other advertisements that attempt to expand a market for a product, or to rally support for a political movement. Any inference from the advertisements that business would like for tobacco use to be pervasive is entirely reasonable, and advertising that gives rise to that inference is in no way deceptive.[48]

In the same way that the political actor seeks to turn an unpopular cause into a mass movement, so does the commercial man seek to turn a niche product into a mass commodity. And both of them use the instruments of illusion. The very reason a political actor seeks to turn his particular concern into a political cause is that not enough people care about it and he needs their support in order to see his concerns addressed. Part of the way he will generate that support is by arguing for the merits of his position. But he will also suggest that, however barren the public square may currently seem, supporters of his position are on their way there. Lots of people already back his position, he'll tell his potential supporters. All that these potential supporters need to do is show up at the commons and see for themselves. What they will see, of course, is the support that they themselves have created. They are the performance of the promise, the materialization of the myth.[49]

The commercial man operates in a similar realm between truth and illusion, a realm protected by the First Amendment. (Indeed, the First Amendment even protects political speech that is outright false.) In making the advertiser, or the commercial man more generally, analogous to the political actor, Thomas inches us considerably closer to his view that the men of money should be given free rein to preside over these various spheres of persuasion. Not men of money considered as a class or conglomerate—in Thomas's opinions on both commercial speech and campaign finance, he takes pains to emphasize that he is not talking about collectives or corporations—but men of money considered as individuals, as singular and heroic figures in society.[50]

More than a straightforward assault on the New Deal regulatory state or an effort to empower already privileged economic actors to control that state, Thomas's commercial speech opinions set out a vision of society in which politics need not transpire in the conventionally defined political sphere at all—in the sphere, that is, of campaigns and elections, administrative policy and congressional legislation. Politics may occur within the economic realm itself: through entrepreneurs who shape our tastes and desires, transform our everyday forms of life, or use their wealth to create and support alternative institutions such as charter schools. And to the extent that politics still does occur in the conventionally defined political realm, Thomas's campaign finance opinions argue that it is better understood through economic considerations than traditional political ones, through categories in which a wealthy few rather than an activist many preside.

At the heart of Thomas's thinking about the First Amendment is the notion that the economy has displaced the state as the primary locus of political values and concerns and that money is the preeminent medium through which moral and political values and concerns get expressed. The kinds of elements one used to look for in the world of elections and government—heroic action of an elite few, the arts of persuasion, the mobilization and transformation of popular belief—are to be found in the economy. Not, coming back full circle to Sowell, in the state, which favors whites, but in the market, which is at least open to blacks.

PART III

CONSTITUTION

7

Grandfathers and Sons

In the second half of the 1980s, well into Ronald Reagan's second term, Clarence Thomas began to think about his future. He recently had been reappointed chair of the EEOC. His tenure there was controversial. His shoddy record as the enforcer of the nation's employment and anti-discrimination laws provoked constant criticism from liberals and Democrats, as well as from labor unions, feminist organizations, and civil rights groups. Yet few doubted that he had brought some semblance of order to an agency suffering from an ancient computer system, erratic budgets, errant management, and crumbling infrastructure. On his first day at the EEOC, Thomas had been unable to find any pencils or pads in his office. "But that was alright," he observed, "because there was no chair on which to sit down to write." By his last days in office, the *Washington Post* exulted that "the EEOC is thriving."[1] Despite such plaudits, Thomas's ambitions lay elsewhere. As far back as 1981, perhaps earlier, he had expressed a desire for a seat on the Supreme Court. With Republicans making plans for George H. W. Bush's presidency as, essentially, Reagan's third term, and conservatives casting about for successors to the aging liberal Justices William Brennan and Thurgood Marshall, Thomas set out to turn his aspiration into reality.[2]

There was one catch: Thomas had no view on the Constitution. He decided to get one. He hired two conservative scholars, Ken Masugi and John Marini, as advisors. Masugi and Marini had been schooled in the teachings of the political philosopher Leo Strauss, a Jewish émigré from Germany who sought to infuse American institutions with principles of natural law derived from ancient Greece. Several of Strauss's conservative students—most notably Harry Jaffa, who had a great influence over Masugi and Marini, and Herbert Storing—were interested in questions of race, slavery, and segregation. Storing even showed a partiality for the work of Malcolm X.[3] Masugi and Marini gave Thomas a crash course on the nation's founding text and its philosophical underpinnings. Thomas worked his way through an eclectic syllabus of readings, a mix of the canon (John Locke, the Framers, Alexis de Tocqueville, Abraham Lincoln) and a counter-canon of African American thinkers that included Frederick Douglass, Booker T. Washington, and Martin Luther King Jr. His reading was guided by an overarching question: How could one reconcile the facts of slavery with a faith in the Constitution as the nation's most sacred legal text?[4]

Of the Constitution's original eighty-four clauses, eleven pertain to slavery, ten of those to protecting it. "Considering all circumstances," declared a South Carolina delegate to the 1787 convention in Philadelphia, "we have made the best terms for the security of this species of property it was in our power to make." How was it possible to find a path out of bondage from the words of a text so manifestly dedicated to its protection? Before Lincoln's election in 1860, he and his fellow Republicans had constructed a plan for ending slavery from the text alone. Armed with the power to regulate territories that is granted to the legislature by Article IV of the Constitution, Congress would ban the introduction of slavery in new territories. Quarantined to one region of an ever-expanding nation, slavery would die a slow but steady death. Or, in the event of a civil war that many Republicans anticipated, the president would use his Article II powers as commander in chief to abolish slavery as a military necessity.[5]

Thomas and his tutors, by contrast, found their answer outside the text. The Constitution, they said, should be read in the context of the Declaration of Independence's opening statement of universal equality: "We hold these truths to be self-evident, that all men are created equal." That preamble, Thomas argued, is grounded in an extra-constitutional tradition of higher law, which derives from nature, reason, or God. Even if some of the Constitution's passages defend slavery, the purpose of the document is to enact the freedom and equality of all human beings that is stated in the Declaration. That is a principle of natural law, which rises above the text of the Constitution.[6]

Before the revelation that Anita Hill had accused him of sexual harassment, the most contentious discussion at Thomas's Supreme Court confirmation hearings concerned this interest of his in natural law. To his liberal critics, Thomas's claim that he had been looking for a principle of equality to authorize the abolition of slavery seemed like a ruse. His real agenda, they said, was to use natural law, and its corollary notion of natural rights, as an extra-constitutional stratagem to promote laissez-faire economics and prohibit abortion—to import into the Constitution conservative positions (the unconditional right to property, the fetus's right to life) that simply aren't there. Harvard law professor Laurence Tribe sounded the alarm in the *New York Times*, claiming that Thomas was "the first Supreme Court nominee in 50 years to maintain that natural law should be readily consulted in constitutional interpretation." In the *New York Review of Books*, legal philosopher Ronald Dworkin warned that natural law was code for "an objective moral reality which endows people with fundamental rights that are not created by custom or convention or legislation, but rather exist as an independent body of moral principle"—i.e., outside the Constitution. Dworkin worried about that independent body of moral principle, for it was grounded on "an explicitly theological explanation" (natural law had been passed down from the ancients via the Catholic theologian Thomas Aquinas) "of the source of the conservative view of moral rights." Thomas's ultimate purpose, suggested Delaware Democrat Joseph Biden, who was chair of the Senate Judiciary Committee, was to "place 'natural law above the Constitution.'"[7]

With the passage of more than a quarter century, it's clear that liberal concerns about Thomas's interest in natural law were misplaced. Despite what some of Thomas's conservative admirers claim, natural law plays almost no role in his jurisprudence.[8] Thomas, as we've seen, has sought to strike down economic laws and regulations; he's also made clear his opposition to *Roe v. Wade*.[9] But those opinions rest upon claims that have nothing to do with natural law.

In his abortion jurisprudence, for example, Thomas makes little attempt to hide his revulsion for the act itself, some instances of which he likens to infanticide. Nor does he soften that revulsion with any acknowledgment of a woman's right to bodily autonomy. He expresses a great deal of skepticism, bordering on contempt, for the Court's declared concern in protecting the health of a pregnant woman, which he sees as little more than a pretext for advancing the cause of abortion. He invokes as a basis for his opposition to *Roe* one of the dissenting opinions from that case, in which Justice Byron White characterized a woman's decision to have an abortion as reflecting the "convenience, whim, or caprice of the putative mother." Yet while those beliefs about women and abortion are evident throughout Thomas's jurisprudence, as a judicial matter his opinions rest upon the proposition that "although a State *may* permit abortion, nothing in the Constitution dictates that a State *must* do so." His case against abortion, in other words, is less that it is prohibited by the Constitution than that it is not a right that can be found in or discerned from the text of the Constitution—just as Justice Rehnquist claimed in his dissent in *Roe*, which Thomas also cites on behalf of his position.[10] One can find misogyny in Thomas's abortion opinions. One can find warnings of judicial overreach and invocations of constitutional text, precedent, and history. What one cannot find is natural law.

Thomas's natural law episode remains salient, however, for what it tells us about his grappling with the Constitution. When Thomas began to think about the Constitution, the question of race, of slavery and its long aftermath, was uppermost in his mind. This was not just a story Thomas and his handlers in the Bush administration concocted to get him through his confirmation. As the relevant writings and speeches from that moment in the 1980s reveal, the reason Thomas was attracted to natural law was that it helped shine a light on how deeply the Constitution was embedded in the institutions of and struggles over white supremacy throughout American history, from slavery to Jim Crow.[11]

But if the Constitution is bound up with white supremacy, why remain faithful to it? For liberals of a certain generation—justices like Brennan and Marshall, whose jurisprudence Thomas came on to the Court to displace—the answer was simple. The Constitution, they said, is a living document, adaptable to changing manners and mores. It is a conveyance to a more perfect union—if the Court is willing to poke or push it along.[12] Thomas's jurisprudence, by contrast, invokes a Constitution frozen in time, its meaning fixed at the moment of its adoption.[13] That meaning may be gleaned from the intentions of the authors of the document ("original intent"), the understandings of the men who ratified the document in state conventions ("original understanding"), the sense of the words in the document that was applicable at the time of its adoption ("original public meaning"), or some combination of those. Whatever iteration of originalism Thomas opts for, the original Constitution is the one he reads.[14]

Or claims to read. In truth, Thomas's originalism is at best episodic. Sometimes he relies upon the original meaning of the text; sometimes he distorts or ignores it. The fact that when he's in the mood he can choose from a grab bag of originalisms—intention, understanding, public meaning, or a mix of all three—gives Thomas ample resources to reach the often-conservative judgment he would have come to anyway. The Constitution's text alone, in other words, seldom dictates where he comes down in any given case.[15] (Even one of Thomas's staunchest defenders concedes that on some critical issues Thomas departs from originalist canons.)[16]

There is little doubt, however, that the originalist Constitution, the vision of the text as it was written and understood at a distant point in time, plays an outsized role in Thomas's imagination. The originalist Constitution functions as an organizing myth, a holy fire Thomas is forever nearing, an idea more important for its "expressive function"—what it says to Thomas and what he means to say by invoking it—than for its regulatory role in his jurisprudence.[17] While that originalist Constitution does not compel or oblige Thomas to take the positions he takes, it is a fixture of his thinking. If he abandons it in the decision time of a noonday ruling, he'll circle back to it in the shadow time of an evening's reflection.

In Thomas's jurisprudence, though, that Constitution is not a single document. Rather, there are two different Constitutions Thomas has in mind when he speaks of taking an originalist approach to the text. In some cases—very few, as it turns out, but nonetheless important ones—Thomas's Constitution is not the Constitution that was adopted in 1789 but the Constitution that was revolutionized in and by the struggle against slavery. This is the Constitution of the Thirteenth, Fourteenth, and Fifteenth Amendments—the so-called Reconstruction amendments that abolished slavery, established the full citizenship of African Americans, and gave African American men the right to vote. This is Thomas's Black Constitution, which takes its bearings from the abolitionist imperative of the Civil War and Reconstruction. According to Thomas, that imperative profoundly transformed the American government and brought African Americans into the American polity.[18] In Thomas's Black Constitution, the African American question remains paramount, as it was in those ten clauses that buttressed slavery in the original Constitution, but it can no longer be strictly answered by the practice of white supremacy.

Yet Thomas also frequently invokes and returns to a Constitution that predates abolition, a Constitution that is understood much as the slaveholders and their white supremacist heirs under Jim Crow understood it, as a compact of sovereign states rather than as a national charter of a unified people.[19] This is Clarence Thomas's other, more unsettling, Constitution, the White Constitution. Thomas sees something of value in the social worlds of slavery and Jim Crow that justifies a recurrence to that Constitution: the Constitution as it was before being transformed by emancipation, the Constitution that returned with Jim Crow. This is not because slavery or Jim Crow are social models he now seeks to resurrect, but because he believes that under those regimes African Americans developed virtues of independence and habits of responsibility, practices of self-control and institutions of patriarchal self-help, that enabled them to survive and sometimes flourish. In returning to the White Constitution of slavery and Jim Crow, Thomas hopes to find the resources for African American renewal today.

AT THE HEART of Clarence Thomas's two Constitutions is the black man. But it is not the black man of Thomas's political economy, the provider for his family and community. This black man is a figure of authority whose word is law for the women and children under his care. In the story offered by the Black Constitution, as we'll see, the black man is a protective presence, wielding a gun to guard his family from marauding white supremacists. In the White Constitution story, he's an absent figure, abandoning his family for the pleasures of drugs, crime, and sex, leaving his children in the care of weak-willed black women who cannot supply the authority children need to grow up into the sturdy, proud folk their ancestors once were. The purpose of Thomas's Black Constitution is to support the black patriarch where he exists; the purpose of Thomas's White Constitution is to create that patriarch where he does not exist. In both cases, the project of the Constitution, as Thomas understands it, is the construction of black male authority—at the level not of the state but of society, in the private world of the black family and the public world of the black community.

The absent father and present patriarch are the bookends of Thomas's own biography. Thomas is the biological child of Leola Anderson, who was the daughter of Myers Anderson, and M. C. Thomas, a fifth-grade dropout. Leola's mother died when she was five, and Myers then left her to be raised by her aunt Annie in Pin Point. Leola and "C.," as Thomas and his brother called their biological father, met as teenagers, just after the Second World War. Within four years, they had three children: Emma Mae, born in 1946; Clarence, born in 1948; and Myers, born in 1949. While Leola was pregnant with

Myers, C. deserted the family and headed north for Philadelphia. Ulti-mately fathering three different sets of children, C. was never again a presence in the lives of Clarence Thomas and his siblings.[20] "In every way that you think of a father, what a father gives you, the way a father requires you to do things, everyone here who's had a strong father or an uncle or a coach, there are certain things that they leave you"—Thomas got none of that from C.[21] What he got was this:

> I saw him only twice when I was young. The first time was when my mother called her parents, with whom my brother Myers and I then lived, and told them that someone at her place wanted to see us. They called a cab and sent us to her housing-project apart-ment, where my father was waiting. "I am your daddy," he told us in a firm, shameless voice that carried no hint of remorse for his inexplicable absence from our lives. He said nothing about loving or missing us, and we didn't say much in return—it was as though we were meeting a total stranger—but he treated us politely enough, and even promised to send us a pair of Elgin watches with flexible bands, which were popular at the time. Though we watched the mail every day, the watches never came, and when a year or so had gone by, my grandparents bought them for us instead. My father had bro-ken the only promise he ever made to us. After that we heard noth-ing more from him, not even a Christmas or birthday card. For years my brother and I would ask ourselves how a man could show no interest in his own children. I still wonder.[22]

In the 1980s, as he began narrating his biography to conservative and black audiences, Thomas never shied from talking about his absent father. He returned to that theme repeatedly, sometimes as a personal story, sometimes as a depersonalized object of critique. "We procre-ate with pleasure and retreat from the responsibilities of the babies we produce," he told the students of Savannah State College in 1985. "We subdue, we seduce, but we don't respect ourselves, our women, our babies." In refusing to take care of their children and their partners, black men have abandoned their responsibilities not simply as caregivers and husbands but also as figures of authority in the family and the community.[23]

Myers Anderson, by contrast, emerges in Thomas's telling as a true figure of authority, as hard and unforgiving as the poverty he was born into and the racism he had to overcome. Myers had an "iron will," says Thomas, which he used "to control every aspect of our lives." Myers commanded his grandchildren to work at their chores in the early morning and late afternoon during the school year, and all day during the summers, with a simple injunction: "If you don't work, you don't eat." He required them to perform well in school. He insisted that they steer clear of any behavior that might earn them the attention of the law—and any friends whose behavior might earn them the attention of the law. He set up "guardrails," says Thomas, which "kept us well within the bounds of the criminal law" and "did not permit us to wander into that gray zone of impropriety not governed by the criminal law." Beyond those guardrails lay an "inexorable downward spiral of conduct." Myers Anderson expected his grandchildren to obey authority, above all his. He "loomed over us like a dark behemoth, instilling fear and demanding absolute adherence to all his edicts, however arbitrary they might appear to be."[24]

Thomas and his brother were fortunate to have their grandfather. Their sister Emma was not so lucky. After Leola decided she could no longer take care of her three children, she put the two boys with Myers, and Emma with Leola's aunt Annie. It was at that point, Thomas explained in 1983, that Emma's life went careening in a different direction from his: "AFDC (welfare). Four kids. She's a good person, a super person. But she's different from us. She isn't educated. She works in the crab factory, picking crabs, just like my mother did. My brother is a comptroller of a Sheraton Hotel in Chicago. He's got an accounting degree. And my grandfather is responsible for that."[25]

Having been pilloried in the media over his earlier comment in 1980 about Emma getting angry with the mailman for being late with her welfare check, Thomas now took care to sound empathetic. Yet the gendered quality of his vision of authority could not be contained: the effects of being raised by a woman versus a man were devastating, he believed. (The same went for how Thomas described the brief period when Leola raised him and his siblings, after C. had fled but before Myers took over: in Thomas's telling, Leola, whom he called Pigeon, was a disaster, unable to provide the structure, the hard rules and firm authority, that Myers would eventually supply.)[26] At the same time, as feminist scholars such as Nell Painter, Kimberlé Crenshaw, and Christine Stansell pointed out after his confirmation, nowhere in Thomas's account of Emma's life did he acknowledge the truly gendered quality of their opposing fates. It was his gender that ensured he got a private school education and the attentions of his grandfather; it was her gender that consigned her to a life of caregiving for her children after her husband deserted the family (much as M. C. Thomas had deserted his family and Myers Anderson had deserted his), of caregiving for her aunt after she had a stroke, of minimum-wage jobs, sometimes two at a time.[27] Instead, Emma's story was reduced to one of welfare dependency, even though her time on welfare was actually brief—and Thomas's to the redemptive power of the black patriarch.

Despite his family history of black men, including his sainted grandfather, not living up to Thomas's ideal, despite his sister's care for her extended family and the role of black women in the ongoing care of the black community, Thomas refused to abandon the belief that "the salvation of our race" depends upon "the strength and the will of black men."[28] That belief was not purely personal. It was also political—not in the sense of the state, elections, or policy but in the sense of politics as the sphere of power and authority. In a Father's Day speech he delivered in the 1980s, Thomas defined the father as "the founder, the originator, the leader." Originating and founding a new order or society are the most important roles that political theorists since the Romans have attributed to the political leader. Such a leader, in the tradition Thomas would have imbibed from his Straussian tutors, has the divine powers of creation and control. The father, Thomas declared, is "a setter of standards," "a setter of direction," and "the setter of rules." In political theory, these are the attributes of the supreme lawgiver, whether that lawgiver is a deity like Zeus or the God of the Israelites, or a man like Solon and Moses.

In Thomas's telling, the father's law does not simply establish boundaries and impose constraints; it gives shape and direction. The father is not just a man of prohibitions and interdictions, forever saying no. His no is also a yes, pressing his children toward choices and behaviors that help them thrive. As a setter of standards, the father is "a demander of . . . the *best* his child can do." As a setter of directions, the father "helps put the first steps on the way." The firm hand of authority, in other words, is a hand that nurtures—not by softening its blow but by directing the blow to its proper end. Concentrating all power in the hands of the father ensures that he will be "the lion of children's safety" and "the sheep of their peace." As with a king or a duke, *father* is "a title," Thomas says, using a term of political art that derives its meaning and definition from the law. But unlike with kings and lords, it is "not a hereditary title, but a title that must be earned."[29]

IT WOULD BE a mistake, however, to reduce the two men—the black patriarch and the errant father—of Thomas's two Constitutions to displaced biography, a retelling of what Thomas never got from C. or believes he got from Myers. Whatever the personal experiences behind Thomas's constitution of authority—and there are many—his understanding of authority also reflects the politics of the last third of the twentieth century.

In the 1970s and 1980s, there was a widely shared sense across the spectrum, from Spiro Agnew to Bruno Bettelheim to Ted Kennedy, that American society was suffering from a glut of rights and a crisis of authority: in the schools, the streets, the family, in every institution of common life.[30] Confronting urban riots, rising crime, student protest, draft-dodging, and a pervasive feeling of decadence and decay, influential writers and politicians came to believe that America needed a restoration of old-fashioned authority, a will to discipline and punish of the sort that Thomas would identify with Myers Anderson. The United States, the *National Review* editorialized, had been seized by "a sentimentalized hyperfastidiousness that seeks to expunge from the society all that appears harsh and suppressive." Countering its effects required "sufficient strength of character and will to do the unpleasant."[31] The New York intellectual Midge Decter spoke for a generation of older liberals and leftists mugged by reality when, in a 1975 issue of the *Atlantic*, she declared to the younger generation that her generation had made a terrible mistake in how they had raised their children:

> We refused to assume, partly on ideological grounds, but partly also, I think, on aesthetic grounds, one of the central obligations of parenthood: to make ourselves the final authority on good and bad, right and wrong, and to take the consequences of what might turn out to be a lifelong battle. . . . We allowed you a charade of trivial freedoms in order to avoid making those impositions on you that are in the end both the training ground and the proving ground for true independence. We pronounced you strong when you were still weak in order to avoid the struggles with you that would have fed your true strength. We proclaimed you sound when you were foolish in order to avoid taking part in the long, slow, slogging effort that is the only route to genuine maturity of mind and feeling.[32]

On the left, the claim was less that authority was declining and more that it was being cloaked in a therapeutic language of help and compassion that allowed parents, teachers, managers, social workers, psychiatrists, lawyers, and judges to maintain a façade of benevolence while exercising power in a more insidious fashion.[33] The consensus was clear: "a little more deliberate discipline and a little less freedom of expression would make the world a better place."[34] And bipartisan: "Ronald Reagan made us realize that in lots of things, we went too far," declared an influential liberal economist in 1985. "Permissiveness is the key word. We gave up on old-fashioned standards like punishment for crime, and family values."[35]

This was the background conversation when Thomas began thinking about authority and the Constitution in the 1980s. As a constitutional idea, that conversation took the form of opposition to what

Thomas and others would eventually call "the rights revolution."[36] They were referring to a series of liberal Court decisions between the New Deal and the Great Society that effectively sent laissez-faire economics and social conservatism into exile. For Thomas, the idea of the rights revolution spoke to a wider dispensation concerning authority: the project of removing the fetters that bound children to parents, students to teachers, women to men, and men to the communities and families for which they were responsible. The rights revolution toppled long-standing orders of rule, ranging from the most obviously political (the authority of the police, for example) to the most intensely personal (the authority of fathers). The critique of the rights revolution allowed Thomas to render the story of Myers and C. in a more explicitly political vein: how one black man, born before liberalism's demolitions, assumed his responsibilities and rightful authority; and how the other black man, lured by liberalism's false promise, abandoned those responsibilities—and with them, his standing and place in society.

With time, Thomas would come to focus on three elements of the rights revolution: liberalization of criminal law, sexual freedom, and the welfare state. The first involved the campaign to transform the criminal justice system, expanding the rights of individuals at the expense of the most punitive sectors of the state: prisons, courts, and police. Throughout the 1960s and 1970s, liberals on and off the Court sought to enhance the protections of the Bill of Rights and thereby diminish the government's power to police and punish American citizens. Among other things, liberals strengthened the Fourth Amendment's stricture against unreasonable searches and seizures. They declared that the Fifth Amendment ban on self-incrimination and the Sixth Amendment guarantee of a right to counsel required the police to notify men and women of their rights upon arrest. They said that the Eighth Amendment's ban on cruel and unusual punishment meant that prison conditions should be humane and that the death penalty should be suspended if not eliminated. Most important, they argued that the constitutional guarantee of habeas corpus should ensure that if any of these rights were violated, the affected individuals would have the right to seek repeated redress from the federal courts. According to Thomas, this first part of the rights revolution "worked a fundamental transformation in our criminal law."[37] And not to the good.

Since Richard Nixon, conservatives have made the threat to law-abiding citizens (coded as white) from untamed lawbreakers (coded as black) the centerpiece of their attack on liberalism and liberal courts. The law-abiding citizens Thomas has in mind, however, are not whites in flight from the cities but black inner-city residents—in particular, black women who are victimized by crime. The threat to black women from this new approach to criminal law is a topic that recurs through-out Thomas's writings.[38] "The people who will suffer from our lofty pronouncements," Thomas declared of one liberal Court opinion defending the rights of gang members, "are people like Ms. Susan Mary Jackson; people who have seen their neighborhoods literally destroyed by gangs and violence and drugs." These black women are "our most vulnerable citizens," he wrote.[39] It is no coincidence that they are the very constituency the black patriarch is meant to protect.

In criticizing this first aspect of the rights revolution—and in these gendered terms—Thomas reprises a move that black activists and poli-ticians made in the 1970s. As white liberals began pushing for the decriminalization of drugs, African Americans, particularly black nation-alists, mounted a countermobilization against what they perceived to be an effort to cripple black neighborhoods in cities like Washing-ton, D.C. Reeling from the heroin epidemic, which had done terrible damage to black communities across the country, black leaders—and black journalists like William Raspberry and Juan Williams, both of whom helped launch Thomas's career—demanded more aggres-sive prosecution and harsher sentencing of criminals. Getting tough on crime was only one element of their vision, which also included a Marshall Plan–type strategy of economic development and urban renewal. But it was an element with a distinct racial charge. Reform of the criminal justice system was associated with white liberalism, so white liberalism was increasingly perceived as an existential threat to the black community. The staunchest opponents of decriminalization were "committed race men" who saw themselves as promoting not a "politics of respectability"—that is, putting on a bourgeois black face for the white middle class—but a "politics of responsibility." They felt they were acting in the best interests of the black community, particularly black women and children, against a white liberalism in league with traitorous black drug dealers and users.[40]

The second strand of the rights revolution of the 1960s involved sexual freedom and personal expression—in the eyes of its opponents, cultivating a society of the libertine and the licentious. An "orgy of self indulgence," Thomas complained in 1986, "is running rampant in our society." The rights revolution encouraged men and women to flout the rules of traditional morality in pursuit of pleasure and desire. "We have a free-for-all society," Thomas wrote, "where everything is all right as long as it makes you feel good." Like the rights of criminal defendants, the sexual revolution is a topic of long-standing conservative complaint. Yet Thomas once again distinguishes himself from other conservatives by locating its worst effects in the black community. Black men are the focus of the immoralism Thomas denounces: it was they, he argues, who most succumbed to the lure of sexual emancipation, and their wives, girlfriends, and children who paid the price.[41]

The third aspect of the rights revolution goes back to the 1930s and the New Deal. Where the rights championed by the 1960s Warren Court were the due process rights of criminal defendants and the expressive rights of individualists—that is, negative rights against government constraint and social sanction—the rights of the New Deal were positive rights to material provision from the government. In his 1944 State of the Union Address, Franklin Roosevelt set out a "second Bill of Rights"—to employment, housing, healthcare, retirement, and education—on the grounds that "necessitous men are not free men." FDR's vision, Thomas came to believe, encouraged men and women to expect things from the state and society, to believe that the world owed them something beyond the protection of a few essential rights. The New Deal fostered the illusion of a society free of obstacles, a society in which people did not merely possess the right to pursue happiness but were entitled to happiness itself. Assuming "that suffering and adversity" could "be eliminated," and that it was "the role of the state" to do that eliminating, an entire culture was created in which the things men and women traditionally had to struggle and work for were now considered goods owed to them by society.[42]

That culture of welfare and entitlement, Thomas believes, undermined the independence and autonomy that come to those who provide for themselves, whether as individuals or through their immediate communities of care. "Once you accept" aid from the government, Thomas claims Myers told him, "they can ask you whatever they want to. They can tell you whatever they want to. They can come into your home whenever they want to. They can tell you who can come and who can go, and I'd prefer to starve to death first." The historical backdrop to Myers's vision is not lost on Thomas: "Are we going from a state of slavery to a more deceptive, but equally destructive, state of dependency?" Nor is the gendered connotation of that vision: dependent men are emasculated men. "I never took a penny from the government," Myers told Thomas, "because it takes your manhood away." Sapping black men of their will and vitality, welfare deprives them of their ability and drive to provide for themselves and their families. With that deprivation, black men lose their standing and authority in society. According to Thomas, the architects of the welfare state did not simply undermine people's work ethic and create generations of poor people who need a government handout, as most conservatives claim. Rather, white liberals had set out "to destroy people like my grandfather and declare his manliness to be foolishness and wasted effort."[43] So targeted, black men no longer could shield their women and children from the predations of white America.

Beyond the question of slavery and natural law, these apprehensions about black men and authority, about the triple threat of the rights revolution to the gendered order of the black community, lay at the heart of Thomas's thinking about the Constitution on the eve of his ascension to the Supreme Court. Some of these ideas he struggled to articulate to the Senate Judiciary Committee. Others he steered clear of. But somehow, he got through the hearings. Most people were disappointed by his performance. Instead of a spirited defense of conservative principles, his supporters got canned answers and a stilted delivery.

Instead of a genuine commitment to Thurgood Marshall's legacy, his critics got evasiveness and double-talk. But Thomas's performance was deemed by a majority of the Senate, including some Senate Democrats, to be good enough. After five grueling days of testimony—the second longest of any Supreme Court nominee in American history—and an additional three days of testimony from other witnesses, the hearings came to a close. Thomas and his allies readied themselves for a robust Senate vote in favor of his confirmation.[44]

Then came Anita Hill.

IF IT WASN'T clear to everyone at the time, it's since become clear that Thomas lied to the Judiciary Committee when he stated that he never sexually harassed Anita Hill. The evidence amassed by investigative journalists over the years is simply too great to claim otherwise.[45] It's also clear that when Thomas elected not to rebut or refute Hill's accusations but rather to repulse them—claiming that he was the victim of a "high-tech lynching for uppity blacks," that he had been "hung from a tree," that he had been brought down by an "assassin's bullet," that the Senate and liberal interest groups were like the Ku Klux Klan and the Knights of the White Camelia—he was telling, if not the truth, then at least his truth.[46] The people who know Thomas best say that his reaction to Hill's accusations was authentic, the moment when he revealed himself, as he understood himself, to the world. Even Kendall Thomas, one of Thomas's sharpest critics in the legal academy, does not deny "the depth of . . . feeling" behind the vivid and violent metaphors Thomas used against his accusers. Nor does he question Clarence Thomas's "conviction that, but for the color of his skin, he would never have been asked to answer these questions about the content of his character."[47]

With the passage of time, the intensity of Thomas's feelings about the hearings has only grown. After five years on the Court, he described the hearings as "just a whipping . . . a plain whipping." His 2008 memoir contains references to himself as Bigger Thomas of *Native Son*, who is unjustly accused of raping and intentionally murdering a white woman (Bigger Thomas does accidentally kill the woman; he also deliberately rapes and kills a black woman), and Tom Robinson of *To Kill a Mockingbird*, who is likewise unjustly accused of raping a white woman. Thomas's memoir also compares liberals and Democrats to slaveholders and the KKK.[48]

Anita Hill was an overdetermined figure for Thomas, so laden with political and social meaning he could not but respond to her accusations as he did. For years, he had been explaining that black men—stolid, moral, responsible, authoritative, upstanding black men—were the key to the fate of the black community. For years, he had been narrating his family story, extracting from the examples of Myers and C. a larger political truth about the toxic effects of liberalism on African Americans. For years, he had been constructing in his head a constitutional order founded upon the power and example of black men. There never was any room in this dreamscape for black women. At best, they were victims of black male criminals and ne'er-do-wells empowered by the rights revolution to abandon their responsibilities. At worst, they were like his mother or sister, treacherous sources of dependency and dissolution.[49] One way or another, black women would fail to provide the firm authority that black boys needed if they were to grow up to be responsible and powerful black men, able to protect their families from a threatening white world. One way or another, black women would hurt black men.

However unprepared he was for Hill's accusation, Thomas was immediately ready with his response. Indeed, he had been preparing it for over a decade, in essay after essay, in speech after speech. Hill did not simply threaten to undo Thomas's nomination to the Supreme Court, though she did threaten that. She did not simply threaten his reputation and career, though she threatened those too. With her white liberal allies, Hill threatened to undo the black male presence upon which, according to Thomas, the entire African American community, from slavery through Jim Crow, had depended. She was the consummation of liberalism's half century's assault on black male authority. Ironically, it was a cynical operation, the African-American Freedom Alliance, organized by a cynical white operative, the religious conservative Gary Bauer, that put the matter, as Thomas saw it, most plainly. Targeting black voters across the South, the organization ran ads throughout the confirmation hearings that compared the liberal groups opposing Thomas to the infamous enforcer of segregation in Birmingham, Alabama: "Like Bull Connor, they are siccing the dogs on an innocent man."[50]

The skein of truth and lies that Thomas presented to the Senate Judiciary Committee—about natural law, slavery, Anita Hill, sexual harassment, and high-tech lynching—was organized by a deeper truth about what Thomas saw as the centrality of African America to the constitutional order and the place of black men in that order. If the rights revolution had undermined black male authority, and with that the black community, then a counterrevolution, grounded in some originalist vision of the Constitution, would restore that authority and that community. The darkest hours of the African American past would provide the resources for, if not a brighter future then at least not a worse future. "It has been said that I would turn the clock back," Thomas declared several years before the hearings. "That's true—I would turn it back *in time* but forward in progress."[51] Whether that past involved the Black Constitution or the White Constitution, Thomas was certain that in some version of the Constitution's text, and in some idea of the black patriarch, he would find the way forward for African Americans.

8

The Black Constitution

The Constitution that was forged in the struggle against slavery is not the same Constitution that was ratified in 1789. Before emancipation, people of African descent had virtually no standing in the American polity, even if they were free, even if they were citizens of the states in which they resided. As Chief Justice Roger Taney notoriously declared in *Dred Scott v. Sandford* (1857) on the eve of the Civil War, black people were not "constituent members" of the United States. At the time of the nation's founding, he wrote, black people had been "considered as a subordinate and inferior class of beings who had been subjugated by the dominant race." Enslaved or not, they were "subject" to the "authority" of white people, with "no rights or privileges but such as those who held the power and the Government might choose to grant them." That remained true in 1857, Taney said, and it would remain true, he implied, into the future.[1]

The Civil War and Reconstruction—and the three amendments Reconstruction produced—changed all that, transforming American society. The Thirteenth Amendment not only emancipated black people; it also revolutionized property relations, stripping whites of their most valuable asset besides land. (Aside from the taking of Native

American lands, abolition is the largest expropriation of property the country has ever seen.) The Fourteenth and Fifteenth Amendments, which established black citizenship and black male suffrage, recast political and social relationships between whites and blacks. And beyond these changes, the Reconstruction amendments reconfigured the American state itself. Before emancipation, the states were thought of as asylums of freedom, under constant threat from a distant, potentially tyrannical federal government. That's why the Bill of Rights was phrased as limiting the powers of the national government rather than those of the states. With the abolition of slavery, the national government stepped forward as freedom's protector. For the first time in American history, it was empowered to secure the freedom and equality of its citizenry—now defined as anyone born on American soil, including people of African descent—against whatever abridgments the state governments might impose on them.[2]

When most conservatives think of the original Constitution, their minds drift back to 1789, to the Constitution that was made for and by white men. As political cartoonist Herblock put it in a cartoon featuring Chief Justice William Rehnquist, Justice Antonin Scalia, and other white conservatives, "They revere the Constitution, it's just some of the Amendments they don't like."[3] But when Clarence Thomas speaks of the "original" Constitution, the Constitution that he is referring to, at least some of the time, is this Constitution of the Civil War and Reconstruction, the Black Constitution, revolutionized by the struggle over slavery and emancipation. More than most conservatives, and certainly more than other conservatives on the Court, Thomas sees a break between the Constitution of 1789 and the Constitution that was transformed by emancipation. The first, he says, "was tainted by a deeply rooted history of prejudice."[4] But the Reconstruction amendments "brought blacks within the existing American political community." In doing so, he declares, the amendments "significantly altered our system of government."[5] Reconstruction transformed the American regime.

The left had its own political vision that came out of emancipation. That vision built on the egalitarian ethos and collective spirit of the institutions African Americans created or supported after the Civil War, such as the Union Leagues, in which African Americans educated each other about their rights, mobilized for elections, helped laborers negotiate contracts and challenge their employers, organized strikes, and armed themselves against the racial terrorism of whites. African Americans also joined the Republican Party, where they found opportunities to run for office and interact with white people as fellow citizens in state conventions and state governments. Meanwhile, the Freedmen's Bureau of the national government provided public education and made efforts to redistribute land.[6] All of these institutions of collective provision contributed to the left's idea of an alternative political order—one that was both bottom-up and top-down, with tight links between a strong and vibrant democracy at the local level and an equally strong and vibrant government at the national level. This vision underlay progressive projects such as the New Deal and the Great Society, which also featured linkages between the local and the national, between a grassroots democracy and the federal government.

That progressive political vision gave rise to the twentieth-century idea that the Constitution empowers the federal government to overthrow entrenched hierarchies of race and class (and ultimately of gender as well). These hierarchies were thought to be supported not only by state governments but also by employers and other private actors, as well as by the failure of state governments to take action against those private actors.[7] To counteract all of these, the federal government was authorized to step in and attack the entrenched hierarchies at the local level. The constitutional keystones of that project were the Commerce Clause, as we have seen, and the Fourteenth Amendment.

Thomas's Black Constitution looks nothing like that progressive enterprise. Far from making the United States racially egalitarian and humane, far from creating a multiracial democracy, the Black Constitution features a society that is violent, racist, and regressive, a mix of *Mad Max* and *Do the Right Thing*. The centerpiece of that Constitution is the Second Amendment, reinterpreted—via the Fourteenth Amendment—as applying not just to the federal government but also to the states. The individual's right to bear arms is what Thomas sees as the black man's main protection against a rampaging white supremacy, the critical right that the new constitutional order provides. There are no cooperative institutions of racial equality and democratic mutuality in Thomas's political vision. There are no Union Leagues, no Freedmen's Bureau, no interracial politics and parties. There is only the defiant black man, reliant upon his constitutional right to arm himself and to defend his family against white marauders. For Thomas, the broadened Second Amendment, with its attendant vision of a racialized society armed to the teeth, is the keystone of the constitutional transformation that emancipation has wrought.

A SINGLE SENTENCE of the Fourteenth Amendment sets out the constitutional revolution that the authors of the Reconstruction amendments hoped to achieve: "No State shall make or enforce any law which shall abridge the privileges or immunities of citizens of the United States; nor shall any State deprive any person of life, liberty, or property, without due process of law; nor deny to any person within its jurisdiction the equal protection of the laws." These three clauses have come to be known, respectively, as the Privileges or Immunities Clause, the Due Process Clause, and the Equal Protection Clause. Today, the latter two are the more celebrated: the Equal Protection Clause is the foundation of claims for equality by people of color, women, and other oppressed groups; the Due Process Clause protects us against a police state and grounds our right to privacy and other goods. Though it has been eclipsed by its two more famous siblings, the Privileges or Immunities Clause was originally supposed to be the Fourteenth Amendment's true charter of freedom, securing the fundamental rights and liberties (that's what "privileges or immunities" mean) of free people.

Before the Privileges or Immunities Clause, it was unclear whether state citizenship gave the citizens of a state the same fundamental rights—habeas corpus, freedom of speech, freedom of religion, and so on—as national citizenship gave to American citizens. Did the Constitution's restrictions on the power of the national government apply to state governments? Did the First Amendment bind only the federal government, for example, so that a state government was still allowed to suppress the speech of the citizens of that state? In *Dred Scott*, Justice Taney insisted that regardless of the citizenship a black person might acquire in his state of residence, there was no possibility that he ever would enjoy citizenship at the national level. This revealed a deep truth about the antebellum Constitution: in it, the rights of state and national citizenship were not the same. While citizens could claim a great many protections against the federal government, they enjoyed little protection against their state governments (unless those states decided to give it to them). After the Privileges or Immunities Clause, though, the rights of state citizenship were supposed to include all the rights of national citizenship, which were conceived as fundamental freedoms. That was the main point of the clause and of the Fourteenth Amendment as a whole.

Each of the three Reconstruction amendments also includes an enforcement clause. It appears in slightly different phrasing in each one, with the version in the Thirteenth Amendment the plainest: "Congress shall have power to enforce this article by appropriate legislation." In addition to abolishing slavery, establishing birthright citizenship, setting out the rights and guarantees of national citizenship, and establishing the right to vote, the Reconstruction amendments empower the national government to take whatever steps are deemed necessary to achieve those goals. The language of the amendments' enforcement clauses is sweeping, deliberately so. Previously the national government had been confined to a specific set of enumerated powers, which limited what Congress could do, and further restrained by the Bill of Rights. Now the national government was authorized to use a vast set of new and undefined powers with great latitude, so long as those powers were directed to the ends of equal citizenship for all. The combination of these broad enforcement clauses and the Privileges or Immunities Clause produced nothing short of "a constitutional revolution": a new vision of the federal government, with a new set of broad powers to achieve a new promise of democratic citizenship.[8]

It was not to be. Against the backdrop of growing white terror in the South and flagging commitment in the North, the Supreme Court began to interpret the Reconstruction amendments in ever narrower, more limited ways. The first step was to gut the Privileges or Immunities Clause of almost all meaning. In the *Slaughter-House Cases* (1873), the Court restored the distinction between the rights of national citizenship and the rights of state citizenship that the Privileges or Immunities Clause was supposed to overcome, ruling that the clause protected only the former, not the latter. Placing great weight upon the fact that the clause prohibits states from abridging only the rights "of citizens of the United States," the Court reasoned that the Fourteenth Amendment did not eliminate the distinction between state and national citizenship, or the difference between the rights that attach to those modes of citizenship. It still remained up to the states to protect the rights of state citizenship, the federal government to protect the rights of national citizenship. Though the amendment does not specify what those latter rights are, the Court drew upon a series of antebellum cases to argue that those rights were limited in nature, covering only such matters as the freedom to travel between states. All other rights, including "fundamental civil rights," remained the domain of state governments alone.[9] (This is not considered the Court's finest hour. As one legal scholar put it, exaggerating only slightly, "everyone agrees the Court incorrectly interpreted the Privileges or Immunities Clause" in *Slaughter-House*.)[10]

Leaving the question of basic rights and liberties to the states—letting them define those rights, no matter how meagerly, and enforce those rights, no matter how listlessly—was a far cry from the position abolitionists and radical Republicans had adopted on the eve of Reconstruction: "No general assertion of human rights can be of any practical value," Frederick Douglass declared in 1866, while "there remains such an idea as the right of each State to control its own local affairs." Deprived by *Slaughter-House* and other cases (not to mention the end of Reconstruction and onset of Jim Crow) of federal guarantees of the most basic freedoms of citizenship, African Americans in many parts of the South were rendered essentially rightless. State governments and white racists could do with them what they wished. The result, as one writer put it, was "slavery by another name."[11]

After *Slaughter-House*, all that African Americans had left were the Equal Protection Clause and the Due Process Clause; both proved to be hardly any protection at all. In the *Civil Rights Cases* (1883), for example, the Court held that the only acts of racial discrimination the Equal Protection Clause prohibited were those of the state; private actors and institutions such as restaurants and hotels could discriminate freely. Because Jim Crow was such a comprehensive institution, structuring not only the state but also society, the *Civil Rights Cases* almost did to the Equal Protection Clause what *Slaughter-House* did to the Privileges or Immunities Clause, narrowing it nearly to oblivion. Then, in *Plessy v. Ferguson* (1896), the Court rendered moot even that distinction between public and private discrimination. According to the Court, the state was in fact allowed to discriminate against African Americans, to treat them differently and keep them apart from whites, so long as their treatment was nominally "equal"—a qualifier that meant nothing in practice.

But in the twentieth century, the Equal Protection Clause and the Due Process Clause would be resurrected. When *Brown v. Board of Education of Topeka* finally overturned *Plessy* in 1954, it was a victory for the Equal Protection Clause, which would also serve as the basis for subsequent desegregation decisions. When the Court began holding that the crime and punishment amendments of the Bill of Rights applied not only to the federal government but also to the states, it was a victory for the Due Process Clause, which would serve as the basis for protecting African Americans from racist policing and punishment. The Equal Protection Clause and the Due Process Clause were key to the hard-won gains of the civil rights movement.

Even before he joined the Court, however, Thomas had expressed dissatisfaction with the way the Court reached those decisions. He regretted that the *Brown* decision had not used the Privileges or Immunities Clause to overturn segregation, and intimated that he might be open to revisiting the Court's ruling in *Slaughter-House*. Bringing back the Privileges or Immunities Clause, he stated, "gives us a foundation for interpreting not only cases involving race, but the entire Constitution and its scheme of protecting rights."[12] The Privileges or Immunities Clause, in other words, might provide the basis for the kind of constitutional order Reconstruction was meant to create.

Thomas fully understood the explosions he was setting off. To suggest an entirely new track for the protection of basic rights and liberties, a track with little case law or precedent, was unorthodox and outré. Since the onset of Jim Crow, the only Supreme Court justice who had been willing to pursue this track was John Marshall Harlan, whose dissent in *Plessy v. Ferguson* suggested that the Privileges or Immunities Clause offered the surest foundation for the declaration of racial discrimination as unconstitutional. No other justice had ventured down this path in nearly a century.[13] Yet this is precisely what Thomas's Black Constitution proposes: to revive the Privileges or Immunities Clause and abandon the Equal Protection and Due Process clauses.[14] Doing so would allow Thomas to radically limit the scope of rights provided by the Constitution, while placing racial violence firmly at the center of his constitutional vision.

ON THE COURT, Thomas first pursued this argument about the Privileges or Immunities Clause in *Saenz v. Roe* (1999).[15] At issue was a 1992 California law that gave poor people who moved into the state lower welfare benefits, essentially limiting it to whatever amount the newcomers would have received in the states they had left behind. (At the time, California had one of the highest benefit levels in the country.) Two new arrivals to California—one from Oklahoma, the other from Washington, D.C.—claimed that California had discriminated against them by granting them a lower level of benefits than that received by native-born residents of the state. Ruling in their favor, Justice Stevens made the rare move of invoking the Privileges or Immunities Clause as the basis for his decision. The right to travel from one state to the other, Stevens argued, was one of the few rights of national citizenship that the Privileges or Immunities Clause protected even according to the narrow interpretation of that clause in *Slaughter-House*. And because that "right to travel embraces the citizen's right to be treated equally in her new State of residence," Stevens concluded, granting lower benefits to new residents violated the Privileges or Immunities Clause. He further concluded that the related provision in Bill Clinton's 1996 welfare reform bill, which authorized states to limit the amount of welfare benefits new arrivals received, violated the Equal Protection Clause.[16]

In his dissent, Thomas pursued two different tacks. The first was to announce his willingness to broadly review the role of the Privileges or Immunities Clause in the Court's jurisprudence, instead of just invoking the *Slaughter-House* precedent as Stevens did. Complaining of the "near-talismanic status" that the Equal Protection Clause and Due Process Clause had assumed "in modern constitutional law," Thomas lamented the fact that "the Court all but read the Privileges or Immunities Clause out of the Constitution in the *Slaughter-House Cases*." Because the "demise" of the Clause had wrongly elevated the Equal Protection Clause and Due Process Clause, Thomas declared, he was not only "open to reevaluating" the "meaning" of the Privileges or Immunities Clause but also wanted to "consider whether the Clause should displace, rather than augment, portions of our equal protection and substantive due process jurisprudence." Taking direct issue with one of *Slaughter-House*'s key claims, he argued that "at the time of the founding, the terms 'privileges' and 'immunities' . . . were understood to refer to those fundamental rights and liberties" enjoyed by everyone. The upshot of this, Thomas said, is that the Privileges or Immunities Clause is the real foundation of the "fundamental rights that belong to all citizens of the United States"—realer and surer than the Equal Protection or Due Process Clauses.[17]

This first line of argument suggested an expansive reading of the Privileges or Immunities Clause and its place in the constitutional order created by Reconstruction. The rest of Thomas's dissent, though, revealed a dramatically narrow interpretation of the clause. Justice Stevens's majority opinion made equal access to state benefits into one of the defining elements of the clause. Thomas, by contrast, used every opportunity to insist that the clause protects only a limited set of rights, such as habeas corpus, the right to property, and the right to sue in court. Those rights, he said, have nothing to do with any broader notion of state or collective provision, such as the liberal idea of welfare rights. Because welfare and material provision are not among the fundamental rights protected by the clause, Thomas wrote, a state doesn't violate the clause when it denies those benefits to new arrivals.[18]

The combined effect of Thomas's claims in *Saenz* was to suggest a new basis, drawn from Reconstruction, for the defense of constitutional rights, including the constitutional rights of African Americans—but with a radically diminished sense of what those rights entail, completely stripping them of the solidaristic elements of state and social provision, as well as popular politics, that Reconstruction helped inspire.

ELEVEN YEARS LATER, in *McDonald v. Chicago* (2010), Thomas again raised the Privileges or Immunities Clause, but in a much more extensive fashion. Where Thomas's *Saenz* opinion had a rushed quality to it, touching on a few notes of constitutional history in seven pages and twenty-five hundred words, Thomas's opinion in *McDonald* consumed fifty-six pages and took up eighteen thousand words. It was Thomas's most sustained and detailed inquiry into the Privileges or Immunities Clause, delving into the full question of Reconstruction, its transformation of the constitutional order, the place of African Americans in that order, and their role in creating it. This time, the fundamental right protected by the Clause was not habeas corpus or the right to property but the right to bear arms.

Before *McDonald*, Thomas had already distinguished himself as the first justice of the contemporary Court to claim that the right to bear arms was not a reference to state militias, which is how the Second Amendment had been interpreted for decades. The right to bear arms, Thomas insisted in the 1997 case *Printz v. United States*, is "a *personal* right" of individuals.[19] Though footnoted with an impressive list of the most up-to-date scholarship on the Second Amendment, Thomas's brief mention of an individual right to bear arms received little notice at the time. More than a decade later, however, Thomas's position was picked up by Justice Scalia's decision in *District of Columbia v. Heller* (2008), which struck down a federal handgun ban on the same grounds Thomas had set out in *Printz*: the Second Amendment protects the individual's right to bear arms. Left unresolved in *Heller* was whether the Second Amendment applied only to the federal government (the District of Columbia falls under the purview of Congress) or to the states as well. Two years later, Chicago's ban on the possession of handguns—the ordinance under question in *McDonald v. Chicago*—offered the Court the opportunity to decide this question.

Writing for a conservative plurality in *McDonald*, Justice Samuel Alito argued that because the Court had decided in *Heller* that the right to bear arms was a fundamental individual right, the Second Amendment should now apply to the states via the Due Process Clause of the Fourteenth Amendment.[20] This argument made the kind of move that had long been practiced by the left. To conservatives, the Due Process Clause—no state government may "deprive any person of life, liberty, or property, without due process"—had traditionally meant only that the state must undertake certain steps before depriving someone of any of these goods: publicly deliberate and declare its laws, stipulate the punishments for their violation, formally charge suspects with a violation of those laws, try defendants in court, and so on. Liberals, on the other hand, had insisted that the Due Process Clause is so fastidious about the deprivation of rights because certain rights are fundamental to what it means to be free, and thus may not be abridged without a vital reason. On the liberal account, the point is not that the government should dot all its *i*'s and cross its *t*'s before it takes such rights away—it's that they should not be taken away at all, unless the government has to. "No amount of process can legitimate some deprivations" of liberty, as Justice Stevens wrote.[21]

Throughout much of the twentieth century, conservatives rejected this move as a sleight of hand. Under the guise of due process, they said, liberals smuggled into the Constitution a set of rights they happened to favor (such as the right to privacy, contraception, abortion, the intimacy of the bedroom, and so on), rights that appear nowhere in the text. In more recent years, however, savvy-minded legal conservatives have made their peace with this approach.[22] As Alito's opinion suggests, conservatives now include their favored rights under the banner of the Due Process Clause.

Had Thomas wished simply to ensure that the Second Amendment applies to state governments, he could have joined Alito in adding the right to bear arms to the list of fundamental rights protected by the Due Process Clause. Thomas, however, refused that path. While he agreed with Alito and other conservatives on the Court that the Second Amendment protects an individual right to bear arms and applies to the states, he took great exception to Alito's method of getting there. One cannot find a substantive right to bear arms in "a clause that speaks only to 'process,'" Thomas wrote. "The notion that a constitutional provision that guarantees only 'process' before a person is deprived of life, liberty, or property could define the substance of those rights strains credulity for even the most casual user of words." The individual right to bear arms should not be smuggled into the Constitution through an embarrassing "legal fiction," he proclaimed.[23] Instead, wrote Thomas, the Court should ground the application of the right to bear arms to the states precisely where the Fourteenth Amendment grounds it: "in the minimum baseline of federal rights that the Privileges or Immunities Clause established in the wake of the war over slavery."[24]

Why did Thomas take this route? One possibility, mooted by many of his admirers, is that Thomas is a constitutional purist, a judge who takes the original words and meaning of the Constitution seriously. Yet Thomas is not an especially fastidious jurist; he can cut constitutional corners with the best of them. Another possibility is that Thomas demands consistency and disdains hypocrisy. For decades the right criticized the left's use of the Due Process Clause; perhaps he believed that it would be too much of a scandal for the right to turn around now and use it in the same way, a hypocrisy that Justice Stevens in his dissent could not help tweaking his conservative brethren for.[25] Yet inconsistency—either his own or the right's—has seldom held Thomas back in other cases.

Thomas's position in *McDonald* raises a deeper question: If his goal is to revive the Privileges or Immunities Clause in general, why did he choose to do so in this case, for the sake of this right—a right, as Justice Breyer pointed out in his dissent, that does not command a popular consensus, that so profoundly divides the country?[26] Why make the right to bear arms the emblematic instance of the kind of freedom that the Privileges or Immunities Clause is meant to secure? As Thomas made clear in this and other opinions, he believes the Privileges or Immunities Clause may underwrite a great many of the rights stipulated in the Bill of Rights.[27] Why not pursue his campaign for the Privileges or Immunities Clause in a case involving more popular rights such as freedom of speech or assembly?

The answer, it becomes clear, is that the right to bear arms allows Thomas to tell a version of American history—from the revolution against slavery to the counterrevolution of Jim Crow—in which racial violence has been the motor of change and African American men have at times taken the wheel. When white conservatives think of the right to bear arms, they imagine sturdy white colonials firing their muskets at redcoats and then mustering in militias, or modern-day whites guarding their doorways against government tyranny and black criminals. Thomas sees black slaves arming themselves against their masters; black freedmen defending their rights against white terrorists; and black men protecting their families from a residual and regnant white supremacy. Thomas's *McDonald* opinion returns repeatedly to scenes of white terror and black revolt.[28] No other justice in *McDonald* devoted nearly as much attention to the violence of the black struggle against slavery and the violence of the white struggle to restore slavery.[29] But in Thomas's story of the Second Amendment, black actors and black violence are central both to the making of freedom and to its unmaking.

THE STORY OF the Second Amendment and the Black Constitution that Thomas told in *McDonald* opened on a note of ambiguity. Before the question of abolition seized the country, the Constitution was a list of equivocations rather than a manifesto of affirmations. Who was the guarantor of rights: the national government or the states? What rights attached to national or state citizenship? Did the Bill of Rights apply to the states? The declarative verve often seen in Thomas's writings was absent here, and for good reason. Before emancipation, these questions had no clear answer. Most Americans did what they always do in the face of constitutional unsettlement: they wished it away or pretended the facts were other than what they were. All of "that changed," wrote Thomas, "with the national conflict over slavery."[30] The movement to emancipate the slaves put the question of rights on the national agenda as it has never been put before: Would the promise of liberty and equality be uniformly guaranteed throughout the country, and would the federal government be its guarantor?

One of the reasons black people set off such a profound debate about the nationalization of rights was that the actions they took on behalf of their freedom were so disruptive and the response they provoked so vehement. In the decades leading up to the Civil War, black slaves began organizing armed rebellions against their masters. (Thomas's account here relied on the work of Communist historian Herbert Aptheker, whose pioneering history of slave rebellions helped inspire decades of academic research.)[31] Thomas focused on the violent uprisings of Denmark Vesey and Nat Turner, "although there were others," he drily noted. These uprisings generated in the master class a fear so panicked and profound it would be "difficult to overstate the extent" of it. That fear, Thomas added, "was not unfounded." It was grounded in the reality of abolitionist sentiment making its way through the South, inspiring black slaves to take up arms. Across the South, that fear incited the master class to divest free blacks and white abolitionists of the most basic rights and liberties of citizenship.[32] The defense of slavery, in other words, rapidly morphed into an assault on liberal democracy itself. That, in turn, reinforced the abolitionist idea of turning the Constitution into a guarantor of freedom everywhere; the document was not just to be a limited compact of states but a national charter of basic rights and liberties. That idea came to be embodied in the Reconstruction amendments, which, Thomas argued, via the Privi-

leges or Immunities Clause critically included—and for the sake of the black freedman, protected—the right to bear arms.

The struggle between black violence and white terror didn't come to an end with emancipation. "After the Civil War," Thomas noted, "Southern anxiety about an uprising among the newly freed slaves peaked." The revanchist master class and their white supremacist allies sought immediately to take all guns away from the black freedmen, particularly anyone who had fought in the Union Army. This they did, state by state, with devastating effectiveness. Whites went rampaging throughout black communities, "waging a campaign of terror against the very people the Fourteenth Amendment had just made citizens."[33] After a racially explosive election in Louisiana in 1872, for instance, both parties, Republican and Democrat, claimed victory and the right to rule throughout the state. In the town of Colfax, African Americans gathered to defend the county seat, by arms if necessary, from white supremacist Democrats seeking to take it over. On Easter Sunday, the African Americans were killed by the whites. Estimates of the number of victims range as high as three hundred; to this day the exact tally is unknown, so wholesale was the slaughter.[34]

Louisiana state authorities were not about to prosecute whites for the murder of blacks, but the federal government brought civil rights charges against roughly a hundred perpetrators of the Colfax Massacre, as it came to be called. Three of them were convicted of depriving African Americans of their privileges or immunities, specifically of their Second Amendment right to bear arms and their First Amendment right to assemble. In *United States v. Cruikshank*, the Supreme Court overturned the convictions, holding that neither the First nor the Second Amendment—indeed, none of the Bill of Rights—applied to state governments or to private individuals. The amendments applied only to the federal government. The three whites were set free. *Cruikshank* became a landmark ruling: before *McDonald* reached the Supreme Court, a lower court had upheld the Chicago handgun ban on the ground that the Second Amendment did not apply to the states, citing *Cruikshank* as its precedent.[35]

After the Court held in *Cruikshank* that state governments could take away people's guns, the die was cast against African Americans and the project of black freedom and interracial democracy. Possessing the means of violence was the keystone of black freedom, Thomas wrote; without it, African Americans were doomed. The black revolution came to an end. The consequence was nothing short of "an effective return to slavery" for African Americans, even though many white Americans believe this institution had ended with the stroke of Abraham Lincoln's pen.[36]

Throughout his opinion, Thomas repeatedly returned to the two-pronged assault on "the rights of free blacks and slaves to speak or to keep and bear arms for their defense." It is these twinned powers—black speech and black arms—that the slaveholders and their successors feared most and sought to crush. In pairing these powers so consistently, Thomas was doing more than elevating the right to bear arms to the status of free speech, although he was indeed doing that. In the same way that Thomas turned buying and selling into an expression of self, so did he make violence—black violence—the emblem of black liberty. Most African Americans after the Civil War were terrorized into humiliating submission, Thomas wrote. The ability to fight back, to wield the weapons of violence against their oppressors, was the keystone of their freedom. Sounding notes often heard only in the outer reaches of the black radical tradition, Thomas concluded with a resonant image of a black father as seen through the eyes of his black son. "One man recalled the night during his childhood when his father stood armed at a jail until morning to ward off lynchers. . . . The experience left him with a sense, 'not "of powerlessness, but of the 'possibilities of salvation'"' that came from standing up to intimidation." Here, the right to bear arms was not the white kitsch of suburban right-wingers. It was a deep source of black pride, a monument to the heroism of black men, to the promise of Reconstruction and the tragedy of its end. It was "essential to the preservation of liberty" of the black man.[37]

Though Thomas's position may sound alien to white liberal ears, "the list of African Americans who invoked gun ownership as a tool of racial self-defense reads like a Who's Who of black America," writes Yale law professor James Forman Jr.[38] Arming blacks not only played a central role during Reconstruction; "the black tradition of arms" continued well into the twentieth century. At the time of Thomas's coming of political age, that position spanned the spectrum of black politics—from Stokely Carmichael declaring, the day after the assassination of Martin Luther King Jr., "Black people know that they have to get guns," to Detroit mayor Coleman Young opposing gun control in the 1970s on the grounds, as he later explained, that "I'll be damned if I'll let them collect guns in the city of Detroit while we're surrounded by hostile suburbs and the whole rest of the state . . . where you have vigilantes practicing in the wilderness with automatic weapons."[39]

Guns were central to the iconography of the Black Panthers, who saw an intimate relationship between arms and the man. In keeping with Eldridge Cleaver's dictum that "the Black Panther Party supplies very badly needed standards of manhood," the Panthers made sure to circulate photographs of Huey Newton and other Panther leaders holding guns. A friend of Cleaver's from prison who founded the southern California chapter of the party insisted, "The only thing that will deal with the Man is the gun, and men who are willing to use the gun." If black men ever hoped "to call ourselves men," they could not "allow the pig's armed forces to come into our communities and kill our young men and disrespect our Sisters." The police could not send in their "occupying army to maraud and maim our communities, without suffering grave consequences." That kind of talk and the imagery associated with it earned the Panthers a following not only among black men but also among black women. Elaine Brown, who eventually would lead the party in the 1970s, noted: "Here were men who were saying, 'Listen, we are willing to take charge of our lives. We are willing to stand up.'" Such men appealed to Brown's "emotional need to say, 'Yes, there were men in this world—black men—who cared about the community, wanted to do something and were willing to take it to the last degree.'"[40]

In Europe and the United States, there is also a tradition of the republican citizen-soldier, the man who cares about and helps take care of the polity to which he belongs, as evidenced by his willingness to bear arms on its behalf, to fight tyrants and defend freedom. That vision was concretized in the Second Amendment's solicitude for local militias.[41] But in recent years, as we've seen, that vision has been complicated by jurists and scholars—not all of them on the right—who claim that the right to bear arms belongs not only to state militias but also to individual citizens.[42] Even Barack Obama felt the impress of that argument, declaring the day after a mass shooting in 2008: "I believe that the Second Amendment means something. I do think it speaks to an individual right. There's been a long-standing argument among constitutional scholars about whether the Second Amendment referred simply to militias or whether it spoke to an individual right to possess arms. I think the latter is the better argument."[43]

Thomas's treatment of the Second Amendment combines and transforms these collectivist and individualist accounts of the right to bear arms. On the one hand, Thomas's black man of arms is no libertarian individual. He is a member of a community. The scene of a black man warding off a lynch mob, placed at the end of Thomas's lengthy *McDonald* opinion, is freighted with social and political context, without which it would not attain its aura of salvation, its triumph of black manhood over powerlessness and intimidation. On the other hand, the reason arms and self-defense are so critical to the black man is that there is no polity to protect him: "The use of firearms for self-defense was often the only way black citizens could protect themselves from mob violence."[44] Without a polity to protect him, there is no polity for him to protect. There is no government to which he owes his allegiance, much less his arms and speech. Indeed, once Thomas reached the post–Civil War era in his *McDonald* opinion, the emphasis on speech dropped out entirely, suggesting that the political element of this vision has been eliminated. We are left simply with arms and the black man. That man is an outcast from white government and racist society; he is a refugee from politics. His guns are no longer the tools of a world-building project; they are the emblems of a fugitive black patriarchy.

ACCORDING TO THOMAS, the fading promise of the Privileges or Immunities Clause was last heard on the Court in Justice Harlan's dissent in *Plessy v. Ferguson*, where Harlan famously declared: "Our Constitution is color-blind, and neither knows nor tolerates classes among citizens." Not only does Thomas champion this dissent as the foundation for civil rights, but he also casts himself as Harlan's inheritor on the Court. In an essay on *Plessy* that he wrote after joining the Court, Thomas fixes on the elements of Harlan's biography that are similar to his own. He emphasizes that Harlan was frequently a lone dissenter, as is Thomas. He praises Harlan for his "moral certainty," which "allowed him to endure the solitary position in which he often found himself" and "allowed his words to speak to future generations." In the same way that Harlan's visionary attack on segregation in 1896 was vindicated by the Court's decision to strike down segregation in 1954, so, Thomas believes, will his opinions one day be vindicated by a future Court.[45]

It is no small irony that Thomas would style himself and his jurisprudence on the example of Harlan, a southern white man, former slaveholder, and, prior to his ascension to the Court, firm opponent of abolition. As Thomas notes, even after emancipation Harlan opposed black suffrage and federal intervention on behalf of former slaves. He supported segregation as a politician, spoke against the Civil Rights Act of 1875, and told racist jokes. There was little in Harlan's biography, writes Thomas, to suggest that he would ever be the "natural defender of equal rights for blacks" on the Court.[46]

But though Thomas is forthright about Harlan's racism, he never acknowledges the most notorious instance of that racism: the very same dissent in *Plessy v. Ferguson*. Just before the "our Constitution is color-blind" passage, Harlan wrote: "The white race deems itself to be the dominant race in this country. And so it is in prestige, in achievements, in education, in wealth and in power. So, I doubt not, it will continue to be for all time if it remains true to its great heritage and holds fast to the principles of constitutional liberty."[47] There may be a reason why Thomas passes over this statement: it shows just how easily a color-blind Constitution can sit beside, or rest atop, the facts of a racially unequal society.

Thomas is often held up, and occasionally styles himself, as a proponent of the color-blind Constitution.[48] But that phrase conceals more than it reveals. As we've seen, Thomas does not believe in a color-blind society. Even the phrase "color-blind Constitution" appears in only a handful of his more than seven hundred opinions—and in one of those opinions, Thomas is careful to point out that such a Constitution "does not bar the government from taking measures to remedy past state-sponsored discrimination." There is room, in other words, for race-conscious measures within Thomas's color-blind Constitution. The Fourteenth Amendment, after all, was a race-conscious measure that, Thomas says, sought "to bring former slaves into American society as full members."[49] Despite his celebration of Harlan's dissent in *Plessy*, Thomas is quick to add that its affirmation of color-blindness has "been overused by opponents of affirmative action."[50]

Conservatives believe a color-blind Constitution disposes of the political question of race: a good society requires only a government and laws that do not distinguish between white and black citizens. Liberals counter that a color-blind Constitution is not enough: precisely because it stops at the government and its laws, it will not reach and reconstruct racial inequalities throughout society. What has marked Thomas's thinking about the Constitution from the beginning is his insistence on the juxtaposition, the necessary collision, between a color-blind Constitution and a race-conscious society. Asked during his confirmation hearings about Harlan's statement about color-blindness in *Plessy*, Thomas replied, "We have to remember that, even though the Constitution is color blind, our society is not, and that we will continue to have that tension."[51]

Harlan's dissent, particularly the lines Thomas has omitted, thus emerges as a more telling revelation of Thomas's convictions than he may realize. The window of a color-blind Constitution opens out onto a racial landscape that is anything but color-blind. That landscape is drawn from the dystopian images of Thomas's Black Constitution: one marked by considerable race consciousness and group identification among blacks and whites, and enormous suspicion and violent enmity between them.

In the end, however, neither the color-blind Constitution, with its focus on race-neutral rules of the game, nor the Black Constitution, with its focus on arms and the black man, is enough for Thomas.[52] Neither vision is sufficiently attentive to the context or culture, the deep soil and social space, that are necessary to create the type of black man Thomas wishes to champion, the black man who can protect his family and community. For that, we need a different sort of Constitution, a more menacing Constitution of harsh rules and authoritarian strictures. We need the White Constitution, which will produce the kinds of black men who led their families and communities during the dark night of slavery and Jim Crow, and which may do so again in the dark night of the post–civil rights era that has been Thomas's reality since he first came to political consciousness.

9

The White Constitution

The Black Constitution is the story of rights gained in the struggle for emancipation and rights taken away in the counterrevolution of Jim Crow. That conflict between rights won and rights stolen creates a space, in Thomas's telling, for the emergence of the armed black patriarch. For such a patriarch to exist, however, society must remain in a permanent state of tension, forever suspended between promise and betrayal. As soon as that tension slackens, the conditions for his emergence will cease. Liberalism, Thomas believes, has dissolved that tension. Liberalism makes life more tractable. There's freedom, but it's frictionless: no one ever encounters an obstacle to his will. It's also costless: no one confronts the negative consequences of his actions; everyone is protected from loss and harm. People get assistance, and if they fail, more assistance. There's no exigency. All is permitted, all is provided. Society is an open space.[1]

What liberalism fails to confront, says Thomas, is the necessary interdependence of the individual and authority, selfhood and punishment. Liberals wish to cultivate the former while avoiding the latter. They "prefer the ideal of self-expression without much attention to the ideal of self-discipline or self-control."[2] But there can be no self without self-discipline or self-control. And there can be no self-discipline or self-control without the firm hand of authority and punishment. "There is much that we do to order our lives that results, to some extent, from the penalty of the consequences for violating certain rules," Thomas says. Sometimes those consequences are part of the natural order. "The laws of nature are quite exacting: defy nature, die."[3] But most of life's lessons, particularly those of morals and politics, do not come to us that way. We cannot leave it to nature to take its course. The punishing figure of authority must stand in for nature. That figure must have power, his rules must be authoritative, his edicts unyielding.

Before liberalism became the public sense and private sensibility of American culture, Thomas believes, rules of personal conduct were enforced through social sanction and state punishment. The point was less to deter lawbreakers than to inculcate within the self the rules and norms of decent society, developing the inner resources and restraints that made for better lives. Far from threatening the self, discipline and punishment were instruments of the self: "I am convinced that there can be no freedom and opportunity for many in our society if our criminal law loses sight of the importance of individual responsibility," Thomas explains. "Indeed, in my mind, the principal reason for a criminal justice system is to hold people accountable for the consequences of their actions."[4] Punishment, in other words, was less a question of law and order than a condition of self-development. Its chief beneficiary was not society but the self in formation, forever tempted by the indulgence that threatened its undoing.

These are universal social truths, Thomas believes, but they apply with special force to the black community. Because of their vulnerable position, African Americans have the greatest need of the personal will and individual effort that are necessary for survival and success. They are the most harmed by the loss of authority and discipline: "It is the urban poor," Thomas writes with uncharacteristic euphemism about African Americans, "whose lives are being destroyed the most by this loss of moral sense."[5] Living a life without consequences under liberalism, African Americans lose the skills and virtues, the muscle and memory, that made it possible for them to survive, even thrive, under

Jim Crow—and that they still need to survive today. As white society slackens, so do black people, only more so. The result of the liberal culture of rights is the dissolution of the black self, particularly the self of the black man who once led his people to freedom or at least protected them from its abridgments.[6]

In this view, the harm of Jim Crow is that it denied rights; the harm of the end of Jim Crow is that it granted them. Thomas does not shrink from the implications of his argument: black people must look for the key to their survival in the social worlds of slavery and Jim Crow. The "road of hope and opportunity," he says, "is the road—the old fashioned road—travelled by those who endured slavery—who endured Jim Crowism." Before the civil rights movement, he points out, black people managed the miraculous feat of surviving the cruelest and most oppressive forms of white supremacy. Consigned to social death, they "refused to accept" that social death "as inevitable." They resolved not to succumb. "They endured—they survived," Thomas says. Their descendants should "learn the values which made their survival possible." One of the great failures of contemporary black politics, he feels, is that it forsakes the hard-won knowledge of the black past for a false promise of the black future. "We prefer the speculations of seers and clairvoyants to the certainty of past experience. We ignore what has permitted Blacks in this country to survive the brutality of slavery and the bitter rejection of segregation." When Thomas insists that African Americans "draw on that great lesson and those positive role models who have gone down this road before us," he is not indulging in nostalgia for better days.[7] He is self-consciously averring that African Americans need to go back to the years of their greatest degradation and despair and to retrieve from that darkness the habits and virtues that enabled their ancestors to survive.

The task of Thomas's White Constitution is to re-create the conditions that made for black survival, to undo the culture of rights and replace it with a state of exigency. That exigency is to be found in the harsh rules of the penal state. Thomas's aim, therefore, is to restore the "moral authority for the state to punish."[8] Even if punishment is implemented in a racist fashion—especially if it is implemented in a racist fashion—it holds out the promise of a life of constraint and transcendence, of obstacles and overcoming. Where the liberal state, as Thomas sees it, achieves its poisonous ends by helping black people, the White Constitution makes black freedom possible through the instruments of policing, punishment, and prison. With the help of these instruments, black people, particularly black men, are restored to a world of harsh consequences from which they can learn the virtues of responsibility. They are given a chance to develop intentional selves and assume the role once played by the elders of the black community. The errant fathers created by the rights revolution can give way to the armed black patriarchs of Jim Crow.

Like the Black Constitution, the White Constitution requires a constitutional reordering of the American state. Despite the rise of the national government under the New Deal, crime and punishment still remain, on the whole, the responsibility of the state governments. Since the rights revolution, however, the Supreme Court has sought to bring those punitive powers of the states under the scrutiny—and sometimes regulation—of the federal courts. The result, according to Thomas and a great many other conservatives, has been a defanging of the states. If the soft despotism of liberalism is to give way to the White Constitution, the states must be restored to their full punitive glory. A return to federalism, which privileges the sovereignty of the states over that of the national government, is thus for Thomas a keystone of black recovery. Where the Black Constitution centers on the nationalization of the individual's right to bear arms, the White Constitution hinges upon the devolution of power back to the states.

THE TENSION BETWEEN the absent father and present patriarch is felt throughout Thomas's White Constitution. Thomas opened his opinion in *Brumfield v. Cain* (2015), for example—putatively about whether prisoners with intellectual disabilities are entitled to a hearing about whether those disabilities disqualify them from receiving the death penalty—with the claim that "this case is a study in contrasts" between two types of black men. One man, Kevan Brumfield, was a criminal who had been abandoned by his father as a child. The other, Warrick Dunn, had also been abandoned by his father, and was being raised by his mother, police officer Betty Smothers. When Dunn was eighteen years old, Brumfield murdered Smothers during an armed robbery. Left without parents, Dunn managed to raise not only himself but also his five younger brothers and sisters, providing them with the fathering that he and Brumfield never got; he eventually became a star player in the NFL. "Unlike Brumfield," Thomas noted, Dunn "did not use the absence of a father figure as a justification for murder." So jarring and explosive was Thomas's extended juxtaposition of the two black men—the case, after all, was about Brumfield's sentence, not about the life of the victim's son—that Justice Alito, joined by Chief Justice John Roberts, made a concerted move to absent himself from that part of Thomas's opinion. "The story recounted," Alito wrote in a separate dissent, "is inspiring and will serve a very beneficial purpose if widely read, but I do not want to suggest that it is essential to the legal analysis in this case."[9] For Thomas, however, it was indeed essential to the legal analysis. At the heart of his White Constitution is a vision of two different kinds of black men: one who wills himself to become a patriarch, and another who wastes life—his own and others'—in the absence of that patriarch. The liberal state, Thomas believes, would protect the second; his White Constitution would help to produce the first.

Dunn's example notwithstanding, the actively involved father is mostly a fantasy figure in Thomas's jurisprudence. A stern man of no particular racial identity, Thomas's patriarch once helmed the republic, instructing, chastising, and punishing his children in the interest of their development as moral beings and good citizens. In the beginning, Thomas proposes in one opinion, "fathers ruled families with absolute authority." That authority was critical to "the moral health of the nation," for it fostered children who learned the virtues and values of the republic. And despite changes in the polity and parenting styles over the years, Thomas says, people still believe that parents—Thomas alternatively depicts the authority figure as paternal and parental—"have authority over their children." The father is "the head of the household," Thomas writes in another opinion (quoting from an earlier precedent), and has "the responsibility and the authority for the discipline, training and control of his children." That authority is "based on the 'societal understanding of superior and inferior.'"[10] In cases about the rights of minors, Thomas freely drops phrases like "continued subjection to the parental will" and "total parental control over children's lives."[11]

This vision of complete authority comes through most clearly in Thomas's statements about the power of schoolteachers. That power, Thomas reminds us, is "*in loco parentis*," delegated by the parent to the teacher, who now stands in for the parent.[12] When the teacher acts, in other words, he is exercising parental power. Throughout the history of the republic, Thomas says approvingly, teachers have wielded an "iron hand" in the expectation of "absolute obedience" from their charges. That kind of power helps the child develop his capacity for deferred gratification, to internalize the rules and norms of proper behavior. Citing a nineteenth-century case, Thomas writes that the teacher must "quicken the slothful, spur the indolent, restrain the impetuous, and control the stubborn." Educational sentimentalists might like to think of the teacher's methods as intellectual or inspirational, but Thomas takes almost perverse glee in emphasizing the role of coercion in instruction. "In the earliest public schools, teachers taught, and students listened. Teachers commanded, and students obeyed. Teachers did not rely solely on the power of ideas to persuade; they relied on discipline to maintain order." Thomas even compares the power of the teacher—and by implication, the father—to that of the police.[13]

That is the fantasy father of Thomas's idealized history, active and present in his children's lives. But there is "a rising incidence of out-of-wedlock births," Thomas says, giving rise to a division "between two different categories of men: fathers who support their children born out of wedlock and fathers who do not." The "social consequences" of the latter are "dire." Children of such fathers experience higher rates of infant mortality and other health problems, and are at greater risk of cognitive and other disabilities, poverty, lower rates of educational achievement, and a host of assorted social ills, including crime.[14] "When fathers fail in their duty to pay child support," Thomas concludes in another case, "children suffer." Their mothers do too, for they are left to raise children on their own, with no financial support. Even fathers who are financially able to provide for their children may opt for the role of the "deadbeat dad," hiding their wages from the state through a variety of measures.[15]

These absent fathers did not arise from nowhere. Before the rights revolution, Thomas says, the laws "supported parental authority with the coercive power of the state." That view still "persists" in some traditional quarters, he suggests, but it has fallen on hard times.[16] It can be resurrected both by enhancing the rights of parents (and teachers) over the children in their charge, and by punishing—with penalties ranging up to imprisonment—those absent fathers who refuse to live up to their responsibilities. "The mere threat of imprisonment is often quite effective," writes Thomas, in persuading fathers to pay their child support.[17]

Enhancing the state's power to punish disengaged fathers is about more than getting deadbeat dads to pay up, however. It's about creating the type of black men who will take their full responsibilities— to their children, wives, and communities—seriously, much as Myers Anderson did with his grandsons. Enhancing the punitive power of government is essential to bringing back the patriarch of old.

THOMAS'S STRATEGY FOR restoring the state's moral authority to punish is a complex of seeming contradictions, containing ostensibly liberal elements that protect some of the rights of individuals and conservative elements that enhance the discretionary power of prisons and police. The first set of those has led some commentators to wrongly describe Thomas as a champion of the rights of individuals against the punitive state, a scrupulous devotee of originalist tenets, or both.[18] The truth is that there is a unifying line running through all of Thomas's crime and punishment decisions, which seek not only to enhance the state's power to punish but also to ensure that those powers are used in response to activity that is worthy of punishment or sanction or scrutiny. What Thomas wants is a world in which criminal and anti-social behavior are met with the full force of social censure and state sanction, a world in which there is an obvious connection, tight and clear to all, between the harm that one does and the harm that is visited upon one as a result. The point of this convergence is to create a world in which malignant action and punitive consequence align.

Given the number of state actors who are involved in the act of punishment (the police, the prosecutor, the bailiff, the judge, the jury, the jailer), and the number of steps that lead to the imposition of punishment (from stopping a suspect to sentencing him to prison and everything in between), the task of aligning crime and consequence is no simple feat. For Thomas, it entails distinguishing those elements of the state's actions that constitute punishment from those that do not. If there is to be an "intimate connection between crime and punishment," as Thomas writes, if "the relationship between crime and punishment" is to be "clear," there must be a demarcation of moments, an identification of specific actions to which society can point and say to the lawbreaker: there was your crime, here is your punishment, this is the consequence of the wrong you have done.[19]

On the front end, Thomas seeks to ensure that each detail of a defendant's crimes is specified in advance of prosecution and that defendants are charged, tried, convicted, and sentenced only for those details. Legislatures, he says, must itemize all the facts or elements of a crime that make it a crime and that may incur or increase punishment for that crime.[20] Prosecutors must provide a fully itemized list of the facts of the crime of which a defendant has been accused; that list must set out each incident that may contribute to or enhance the defendant's punishment. Judges and juries must try and sentence defendants only for those incidents; they cannot mete out harsher punishments because of facts learned in the course of a trial.[21]

Thomas's constant insistence that charges, trials, and sentences must reflect the exact facts of a crime has less to do with the rights of the accused than with the preservation of the purity of punishment. When Thomas speaks of a "clear" and "intimate connection between crime and punishment," the protagonist of his solicitude is not the offender or the victim. It is not even the need for proportionality between crime and consequence; indeed, Thomas rejects the liberal notion that proportionality constitutes any part of the Constitution's stipulations about criminal law.[22] The protagonist is the pellucid quality of punishment itself.[23] The reason all the facts or elements of a crime must be specified in advance, the reason each of them must be tried and proved beyond a reasonable doubt, is that the punishment imposed by a court of law must publicly disclose the entirety of the crime. If authority is to be restored, the sentence must speak.

On the back end, therefore, Thomas seeks to close off much of what happens after sentencing from any review by the courts. If a punishment were thought to include not only what is imposed at sentencing (say, ten years in prison) but also all the unknowable and uncontrollable events that occur while that sentence is being carried out (for instance, abusive treatment by the prison's guards), society would not be able to announce a punishment that fully discloses the crime that's been committed. The sentence would no longer speak. Whatever may happen to a criminal in a prison, no matter how foul or unfair, cannot be taken to constitute any element of the punishment. Any injuries and injustices that a prisoner may suffer are incidental details of what it means to have been convicted and sentenced for a crime. They are not part of the punishment itself.

This need to associate the act of punishment only with a public court of law—and to read out of that act whatever may happen in the dark and discretionary space of the prison—helps explain the more overtly punitive cast of thinking in Thomas's jurisprudence, which earned him, just months into his tenure on the Court, the moniker "the youngest, cruelest justice" from the *New York Times*.[24] In his opinions, Thomas regularly refuses to deem brutal prison conditions—whether the sadism of guards, a tolerance by guards of the sadism of other prisoners, or other gratuitous or abusive deprivations and indifference—a violation of the Eighth Amendment's ban on cruel and unusual punishment. When it comes to crime and punishment, Thomas is proudly indelicate about the rights of individuals, and broadly deferential to the police, prison officials, and the criminal justice apparatus more generally. He wants to enhance rather than diminish the state's powers to police and punish, and is generally eager to get the federal courts out of the business of protecting the rights of individuals and reviewing state decisions regarding crime and punishment.[25]

It may seem that Thomas's opinions in these cases can be explained by a belief that punishment should impose real costs on a lawbreaker; that those costs include a diminution in one's quality of life and the assumptions of decency one can expect from that life; and that the Constitution should not be viewed as an instrument to "address all ills in our society," including prison conditions that shock the conscience.[26] There is certainly much in these opinions to support that conclusion. In *Hudson v. McMillian* (1992), for example, a prison guard had put Keith Hudson, a black inmate, in shackles. While leading him to lockdown, the guard beat Hudson repeatedly in the face, chest, and stomach. A second guard held Hudson from behind, kicking and punching him in the back. The beating left Hudson with "facial swelling, loosened teeth, and a cracked dental plate." All this was done under the watch of a supervisor whose only intervention was to remind the guards "not to have too much fun" with their charge. Though Thomas called the guards' actions "abusive behavior" and "deplorable conduct that properly evokes outrage and contempt," he refused to claim that their actions violated the Eighth Amendment's ban on cruel and unusual punishment. Among other reasons, Thomas cited the fact that the guards had inflicted "concededly 'minor' injuries" that did not require medical attention—this was a fact accepted by both parties to the case—and the fact that "harsh treatment" and "harsh conditions" had been features of prison life from "the early years of the Republic" when "surely prison was not a more congenial place . . . than it is today."[27]

Thomas's later opinions showed even greater equanimity in the face of the barbarities of prison life. In *Farmer v. Brennan* (1994), prison officials had placed Dee Farmer, a transgender woman convicted of credit card fraud, among male prisoners, who beat and raped her. Thomas opened his opinion thus: "Prisons are necessarily dangerous places; they house society's most antisocial and violent people in close proximity with one another." He went on, citing a lower court opinion: "Regrettably, '[s]ome level of brutality and sexual aggression among [prisoners] is inevitable no matter what the guards do.'" And in *Baze and Bowling v. Rees* (2008), a case about the death penalty, Thomas once again expressed a shrugging indifference to gratuitous suffering and pain inflicted upon criminals. Quoting from a 1947 opinion, he noted "the necessary suffering involved in any method employed to extinguish life humanely," and proceeded to remark that on no understanding of "cruel and unusual" could a method of execution be struck down "simply because it involves a risk of pain—whether 'substantial,' 'unnecessary,' or 'untoward'—that could be reduced by adopting alternative procedures."[28]

Yet for all the abusiveness and cruelty Thomas is willing to tolerate, the driving force in these decisions is less a conviction that punishment should be as grievous as possible than a desire to sequester the act of punishment itself. Simply put, Thomas does not believe that the quality of prison life is any part of the act of punishment: "conditions of confinement are not punishment in any recognized sense of the term, unless imposed as part of a sentence."[29] From his first year on the Court, Thomas has taken the position—one not even Justice Scalia was willing initially to adopt, though eventually he was brought around to it, by Thomas no less—that punishment does not "apply at all to deprivations that were not inflicted as part of the sentence for a crime" or "to any hardship that might befall a prisoner during incarceration." Punishment should be understood to apply only to what is "meted out by statutes or sentencing judges."[30] Thomas reiterated that position even more forcefully the following year: "Judges or juries—but not jailers—impose 'punishment.'" To claim that a practice constitutes cruel and unusual punishment, he said, one must show that the practice "constitutes *punishment*." A "prison deprivation that is not inflicted as part of a sentence" does not.[31]

Thomas thus performs a double move. On the one hand, he confines the imposition of punishment to the moment of sentencing, thereby preserving the public qualities of punishment and the alignment between crime and consequence that he believes is critical to authority. On the other hand, by refusing to consider much that occurs in prisons and in the administration of the death penalty, he removes those occurrences from the reach of any constitutional claim about punishment. He thus allows for a considerable degree of harshness and cruelty to obtain in any experience of punishment without having to itemize the specific facts and elements of a crime that would warrant those acts of harshness and cruelty. When Thomas writes that "the Eighth Amendment is not, and should not be turned into, a National Code of Prison Regulation," he can sound as if he is issuing a standard conservative apologia: arguing that much of the criminal justice system is run by the states and that federal courts should stay out of it, leaving the job of administering prisons to prison officials and the job of reviewing the system's operations to state courts and legislatures.[32] But the more profound meaning of Thomas's position is that he is attempting to establish a system of punishment in which crime and consequence are aligned without admitting what he knows to be true: that no specified litany of a crime's elements and facts could ever result in a public sentence that includes each and every harm that might befall lawbreakers once they enter the state's matrix of punishment. What facts of her crime earned Dee Farmer the punishment of being raped and beaten by her fellow prisoners? What element of Keith Hudson's offense justified a jailer allowing his guards to crack Hudson's dental plate? The only way to answer those questions is to exclude, ex ante, those horrors from the definition of punishment. The terribleness of the prisons remains, but isolated from punishment's official definition.

Perhaps, then, this is the belief that underlies Thomas's penal jurisprudence: no state, no matter how fervent its belief in the moral right to punish, would ever be willing to publicly and formally sentence a convicted criminal to the actual harms and abuses that are routinely meted out to inmates as they make their way through the nation's prison archipelago.[33] By delimiting the act of punishment to what happens in a court of law—and declaring that what happens in jail stays in jail—Thomas, so eager to rehabilitate the state's moral right to punish, so eager to establish the "intimate connection between crime and punish-ment," is able to have his cake and eat it too.

THE MOST OBVIOUS objection to Thomas's exaltation of punishment is the one he himself has raised against the liberal state. No matter how well intentioned or well designed, the American state is the handiwork of white people whose interests are not aligned with those of black people—indeed, whose interests are resolutely opposed to those of black people. Why should the white punitive state, of all things, be less liable to racist implementation and racist effects than the white liberal state? For every one of Thomas's defenses of prisons and police, for every one of his claims about the value of punishment, one could easily cite, as a counterargument, Thomas's many statements—on affirmative action, integration, eminent domain, and more—about the enduring power and poison of white racial animus, particularly as it is manifested in the actions of the state. Given the intricate connections between racism and policing in this country, why should the carceral elements of white state power be exempt from what Thomas claims are the intrinsically racist elements of liberal state power? Why should black people welcome such racism as advancing their lot?

Thomas is not unaware of this objection. Indeed, he highlighted it in one of his early speeches after he joined the Court. Many have ques-tioned, he noted in 1994, "how we could tell blacks in our inner cities to face the consequences for breaking the law when the very legal sys-tem and society which will judge their conduct perpetuated years of racism and unequal treatment under the law."[34] And though he never responded to this objection in that speech, Thomas has provided some clues about his thinking on the matter in his other speeches, writ-ings, and opinions. What's most striking about his reasoning on the matter is that, with a few exceptions, Thomas doesn't work actively to rebut what once would have been perceived as a scandal of the car-ceral state: that it is laden with racism.[35] Instead, he either minimizes the significance of that claim, quietly conceding its truth, or ignores it altogether.[36] This may be because Thomas believes such a carceral state, even if it's racist, serves a vital function: it provides African Americans with every reason they need to steer clear of trouble. That is a foundation not only for law-abiding behavior but also for the market-based activity that, as we've seen, Thomas regards as critical to the African American community. The carceral state re-creates the kind of adversity African Americans once suffered under Jim Crow, the kind of adversity that produced Myers Anderson. In other words, though Thomas owns up to the racist dimensions of the carceral state, he believes it is beneficial to African Americans—despite that racism, or perhaps even because of it.

In the 2016 search and seizure case *Utah v. Strieff*, a policeman conducting surveillance of a suspected drug house in South Salt Lake saw Edward Strieff exit the house. Though he didn't suspect Strieff of wrongdoing, the officer stopped Strieff anyway, ran a check on his ID, and discovered an outstanding warrant for his arrest due to a minor traffic violation. The officer arrested Strieff, searched him, and found drugs in his pocket. Charged with unlawful possession, Strieff claimed that the drugs were inadmissible as evidence because they were discovered through an unlawful stop. The state essentially conceded that the stop was unlawful; the police officer did not have a reasonable basis for stopping Strieff in the first place. Nevertheless, it insisted, the outstanding warrant gave the officer all the reason he needed for the subsequent arrest and search, and the drugs were thus admissible. In a 5–3 ruling authored by Thomas, the Court ruled for the state.

Much of the case hinged on technical legal questions, but what stands out in Thomas's opinion is his exoneration of the police through a recitation of extenuating circumstances. Thomas conceded that the officer lacked a reason to stop Strieff and to demand that Strieff speak to him. But Thomas softened the significance of the stop, claiming it was one of two "good-faith mistakes"—the other being that the officer did not note how long Strieff had been in the house, so had no way of knowing whether he was there for quick drug-related business or a lengthier personal visit. These were "errors in judgment," Thomas wrote, "isolated instance[s] of negligence." They did not reflect any "systemic or recurrent police misconduct."[37]

In a dissent joined only by Justice Ruth Bader Ginsburg, Justice Sonia Sotomayor made quick dispatch of that argument. She cited multiple studies showing that outstanding warrants for harmless crimes are pervasive, and are frequently used as pretexts for searches occasioned by baseless police stops. What Thomas dismissed as isolated and innocent, Sotomayor described as systemic and patterned. "Respectfully," she wrote, "nothing about this case is isolated."[38]

In the last part of Sotomayor's dissent, Ginsburg took her exit, leaving Sotomayor to speak "only for myself."[39] Strieff was white, but the topic under consideration now moved to the question of policing and race. The dramatic appositeness of one justice of color, arguably the most liberal on the Court, speaking directly to the Court's only other justice of color, easily the most conservative on the Court, is hard to ignore. "This case involves a *suspicionless* stop," wrote Sotomayor,

one in which the officer initiated this chain of events without justification. As the Justice Department notes . . . many innocent people are subjected to the humiliations of these unconstitutional searches. The white defendant in this case shows that anyone's dignity can be violated in this manner. . . . But it is no secret that people of color are disproportionate victims of this type of scrutiny. See M. Alexander, The New Jim Crow 95–136 (2010). For generations, black and brown parents have given their children "the talk"—instructing them never to run down the street; always keep your hands where they can be seen; do not even think of talking back to a stranger— all out of fear of how an officer with a gun will react to them. See, *e.g.*, W. E. B. Du Bois, The Souls of Black Folk (1903); J. Baldwin, The Fire Next Time (1963); T. Coates, Between the World and Me (2015).

By legitimizing the conduct that produces this double consciousness, this case . . . implies that you are not a citizen of a democracy but the subject of a carceral state, just waiting to be cataloged.[40]

Thomas did not respond in his ruling to this moment in Sotomayor's dissent. Elsewhere, though, he has offered his own version of "the talk" that he thinks black parents should be giving their children. And in that talk, we find the worldview that separates him from Sotomayor and that explains the mitigating thrusts of his treatment of the police.

Where Sotomayor's version of the talk focuses strictly on the rules of the street, on how black and brown children should conduct themselves in the presence or shadow of the cops, Thomas's talk is more expansive. A combination of moral uplift and slippery slopes, freely mixing capitalist norms and carceral rules, Thomas's talk exposes just how critical he thinks policing, even racist policing, is to the development of black life. Children should always act in such a way as not to attract the attention of the police, he says. On that he and Sotomayor agree, though she would like it to be otherwise. But avoiding criminal trespass is the bare minimum of what Thomas expects from children. "On an individual basis, rules of personal conduct allow us to confront difficulties constructively, and they provide guardrails down what is an often dangerous and precarious road of life," he told a group of Georgia law students, before offering up the example of his own childhood:

> These guardrails, of course, kept us well within the bounds of the criminal laws. My grandfather made it very clear that a man did not keep his good name merely by not breaking the criminal law. Our family laws required much more of us and did not permit us to wander into that gray zone of impropriety not governed by the criminal law. So not only were we not to do bad things or engage in mischief, we were not to associate with those who did, because as my grandparents would say, "They were up to no good." Somehow, with the benefit of little formal education, my grandparents recognized the inexorable downward spiral of conduct outside the guardrails: If you lie, you will cheat; if you cheat, you will steal; if you steal, you will kill.[41]

In addition to avoiding any criminal behavior, Thomas proclaimed, children should observe the rules and norms of propriety: "Yes, we were, as they said, to be 'mannerable'—period. We did not dare . . .

walk down the street without saying 'Good morning' to Miss Gladys, Miss Moriah, Miss Beck, and especially Miss Gertrude. . . . We would never think of addressing an adult only by his or her first name, or as the adults would say, without a 'handle' on that name. We would never refuse to make a trip to the store for an adult who asked."[42] For Thomas, learning the rules of propriety is not just about enforcing bourgeois norms of respectability. Impropriety is fraught with the very sorts of dangers Sotomayor would highlight in her version of the talk. "Raised to survive in spite of the dark oppressive cloud of governmentally sanctioned bigotry," says Thomas, he learned that any sort of impropriety, no matter how trivial, "made the difference between freedom and incarceration; life and death; alcoholism and sobriety."[43] It's not just a matter of the attentions of the police; Thomas sees a wide range of improprieties leading black people to tumble down the rabbit hole. Impropriety might lead directly to criminal behavior, from lying to cheating to stealing to killing, but it might also just bring one into contact with the wrong sort of person—the kind of person who wouldn't mind his manners, who wouldn't heed the word of an adult, who would lie or cheat or steal or kill. The kind of person who would lead to unwelcome contact with the police.

Thomas's stance here is reminiscent of Burtell Jefferson, the legendary first black chief of police of Washington, D.C., who did so much to diversify the police force there during the 1980s. Jefferson liked to tell a story from his youth about how he had been tossing around a football near some black boys who were shooting dice. All of them, Jefferson and the other boys, were rounded up by a white police officer. Rather than focusing on the racism of the officer who refused to distinguish between black boys shooting dice and a black boy playing ball, Jefferson proffered a different lesson: "I've always been taught that if you yourself are not actually engaged in some wrongdoing, if you're with a crowd you're just as guilty."[44]

WHERE SOTOMAYOR SEES unbounded police power as a grim reality around which black and brown people have to navigate and negotiate for their very lives, Thomas sees that same police presence as a structuring force that helps African Americans organize, even improve, their lives in several distinct and positive ways. First, repeating a long-standing complaint within the African American community, Thomas reminds those who criticize the police that black people are often the victims of black criminals. Black people, he suggests, suffer less from overpolicing than from police indifference to crimes committed against them.[45] In other words, where liberals and leftists locate police racism in the discriminatory treatment or profiling that officers dole out to black suspects, Thomas locates it in the refusal of the police—and white society more generally—to do anything to protect black victims of crime. Glenn Loury, the black economist at Brown who was once a friend of Thomas's, reports that the last time they spoke, Thomas said, "Look at these young brothers dying in the street—the drive-by shootings, the violence. If dogs were being struck down at the same rate and in the same way, and left bleeding in the gutter, there would be a society of blue-haired women to save our canine friends. But these are young black men bleeding in the gutter, and no one seems to give a damn."[46] In his memoir, Thomas traces his realization of the centrality of black-on-black crime to the start of his work in John Danforth's office in Jefferson City, Missouri.

> What bothered me more was that as a criminal-appeals attorney, I would have to argue in favor of keeping blacks in jail. I still thought of most imprisoned blacks as political prisoners. I had no facts to back up this opinion, a reflex response left over from my radical days, and didn't need any: I knew that anything "the man" did to black people was oppression, pure and simple. What changed my mind was the case of a black man convicted of raping and sodomizing a black woman in Kansas City after holding a sharp can opener at the throat of her small son. He was no political prisoner—he was a vicious thug. Perhaps he and the woman he'd brutalized had both been victims of racism, but if that were so, then she'd been victimized twice, first by "the man" and then by the thug. This case, I

later learned, was far from unusual: it turned out that blacks were responsible for almost 80 percent of violent crimes committed against blacks, and killed over 90 percent of black murder victims.[47]

On the Court, Thomas has defended the discretionary elements of police power by making explicit reference to black victims of crime. In *Chicago v. Morales* (1999), he took aim at the liberal majority's decision to strike down an anti-loitering ordinance in Chicago that gave the police the power to disperse anyone gathered on the street whom they "reasonably believed" to be a gang member. Race hung heavily over the case, and much of Thomas's opinion was devoted to reversing the standard liberal script of racism and the cops. Thomas pointed out that the anti-loitering ordinance was introduced by a black alderman representing Chicago's Seventh Ward, a predominantly black neighborhood on the South Side of Chicago. The ordinance was the product of a "democratic process" in which the city council sought "to attempt to address these social ills" that plague communities like the Seventh Ward. Members of that community gave extensive testimony to the city council, documenting how beset they were by rampant criminal gangs. Quoting liberally from that testimony, Thomas populated his dissent with lengthy and vivid descriptions of the terror gang members inflicted on inner-city residents, "law-abiding citizens" who were "sentenced" to be "prisoners in their own homes."[48]

While any Supreme Court justice would defend the right of citizens to be protected by the police from the harm of criminals, Thomas went out of his way to link the interests of the black community to police officers exercising discretionary power to decide whether an individual—who, on these streets, was likely to be black—was a potential criminal or not. The people whom the police are assigned to protect, he wrote, were "good, decent people who must struggle to overcome their desperate situation, against all odds, in order to raise their families, earn a living, and remain good citizens." Those men and women constituted 98 percent of the population, but they were terrorized by a remaining 1 to 2 percent in gangs. To protect the 98 percent from the 2 percent, the police had to be empowered to make distinctions on sight, based on their experience, judgment, and above all, "discretion."[49]

Discretion is precisely where race often does its most pernicious work, whether the officer in question is white or black. (The record, at least from the early years of African Americans integrating metropolitan police forces, suggests that black officers are no less likely to make judgments of criminality based on indices of race and class than are white officers.)[50] But vesting the police with broad power that they were to exercise with "discretion" is precisely what Thomas insisted on.

> Just as we trust officers to rely on their experience and expertise in order to make spur-of-the-moment determinations about amorphous legal standards such as "probable cause" and "reasonable suspicion," so we must trust them to determine whether a group of loiterers contains individuals (in this case members of criminal street gangs) whom the city has determined threaten the public peace. . . . ("Articulating precisely what 'reasonable suspicion' and 'probable cause' mean is not possible. . . . [O]ur cases have recognized that a police officer may draw inferences based on his own experience in deciding whether probable cause exists").[51]

Thomas is not unaware of the argument that such policing measures are saturated in racism; he just chooses not to address it. In a 1994 speech, for example, after acknowledging that historically "vagrancy, loitering, and panhandling laws were challenged because the poor and minorities could be victims of discrimination under the guise of broad discretion to ensure public safety," he simply moved on, without attempting to rebut the challenge.[52] In *Morales*, he resorted to defensive temporizing, relying on formulations so laced with circumlocutions and double negatives as to be almost unreadable: "Nor do I overlook the *possibility* that a police officer, acting in bad faith, might enforce the ordinance in an arbitrary or discriminatory way. But our decisions should not turn on the proposition that such an event will be anything but rare. Instances of arbitrary or discriminatory enforcement of the ordinance, like any other law, are best addressed when (and if) they arise, rather than prophylactically through the disfavored mechanism of a facial challenge on vagueness grounds."[53]

Protecting black neighborhoods from crime is not the only reason why Thomas is willing to tolerate and even embrace harsh policing. As we've seen, he believes that adversity helps the black community develop its inner virtue and resolve. Nostalgia usually burnishes the past in sunlight; Thomas's nostalgia is bathed in darkness. Here is just a smattering of the phrases he has used to describe the African American past: "the totalitarianism of segregation," "a hostile environment," "the dark oppressive cloud of governmentally sanctioned bigotry," "the hot, humid climate of segregation," "a *system* designed to keep a race ignorant—a *system* bent on establishing racial dominance." But for every mountain of hardship Thomas cites, he has a matching story of overcoming. Indeed, the entire point of these mentions of past adversity is to narrate an attendant tale of mastery.[54] The power of adversity, he proclaims, is that it "reinforces those principles and rules without which a society based upon freedom and liberty cannot function."[55] If the rights revolution's elimination of adversity was a social disaster, re-creating adversity can undo the disaster. Reauthorizing discretionary police power is a way to do just that.

In his *Morales* dissent, Thomas repeatedly takes on the idea that Chicago's anti-loitering measure is "anachronistic." "The ordinance merely enables police officers to fulfill one of their traditional functions," he wrote. "Police officers are not, and have never been, simply enforcers of the criminal law. . . . Nor is the idea that the police are also *peace officers* simply a quaint anachronism."[56] What's odd about Thomas's move here is that anachronism is a notion that the liberal majority opinion never invokes. The self-imposed obligation to rebut a charge that no one has made suggests that Thomas recognizes that the police telling young black men on the street to "move along" may in fact be anachronistic, all too redolent of the world of Jim Crow. Then again, Jim Crow adversity is what he believes produced great black men like his grandfather. "My grandfather," Thomas once wrote, "would be an anachronism in today's world. He would be looked upon as an insensitive brute." Myers Anderson is no longer here. But Thomas is, so it has fallen to him to declare, "I am proudly and unapologetically irrelevant and anachronistic."[57] Arming the Chicago police department with broad discretionary power may or may not be an anachronistic throwback to Jim Crow, but the Supreme Court justice who wishes to do so believes himself to be the heir of such a throwback—and that that is a good thing.

THE FINAL REASON for Thomas's embrace of harsh policing is that he believes it will contribute to African Americans' success in the capitalist market and the development of virtues that are critical to such success. The relationship between punishment and capitalism is not a topic that receives much attention in mainstream debates about markets and states; indeed, much of the popular discussion of contemporary conservatism and neoliberalism assumes that they unleashed the market and rolled back the state.[58] But as several astute studies have shown, what the modern right and the neoliberal center have sought, and often achieved, is to redirect the state away from its social democratic and welfarist functions and to concentrate its power on policing and punishment.[59] And rather than simply remove the market from all regulation, the modern right and neoliberal center have used those policing and punishment powers to shore up markets in multiple ways: by threatening poor and working-class people with the prospect of punishment should they not conform to the market's dictates; by policing neighborhoods and cities to make them safer for investment; by turning proverbially lazy and criminally inclined dependents, often coded as black, into responsible market actors; and by engineering a sea change in how we think about the self and the state, with punitiveness understood to be the key to well-being while welfare and social democracy are seen as disabling threats.

From his earliest days as a conservative to his most recent judgments as a jurist, Thomas has been at the forefront of this movement for carceral capitalism—despite his forceful pronouncements about the distinction between the white state and the black market, and about the need for African Americans to cease paying attention to the state and concentrate more on the market. As it turns out, by Thomas's own analysis, the black market is intimately related to, and dependent on, the white state.

During the Reagan administration, one of the more popular ideas on the right was the creation of enterprise zones. Most prominently associated with Jack Kemp—Republican congressman from Buffalo, George H. W. Bush's secretary of housing, and Bob Dole's running mate in 1996—enterprise zones were thought to be the answer to urban blight and decay. Through a combination of tax incentives, relaxation of business regulations, and development, companies would be enticed to move to inner cities, where they would offer residents jobs and infrastructure. But in a 1985 symposium of black conservatives, where enterprise zones received near-universal support, Thomas neatly swiped them off the table, arguing instead that policing and punishment had to be the centerpiece of any vision of black economic development.

> The first priority is to control the crime. The sections where the poorest people live aren't really livable. If people can't go to school, or rear their families, or go to church without being mugged, how much progress can you expect in a community? Who would do business in a community that looks like an armed camp, where the only people who inhabit the streets after dark are the criminals?
>
> There were lots of black businesses before enterprise zones, even in segregation. My grandfather was a businessman. But blacks cannot stay in business if they are robbed every two minutes, or if they are mugged, or if customers are mugged in and out of the establishment, or if people are hanging out selling drugs in front of it. If you want to encourage business in these areas, then stopping crime has got to be at the top of the list.[60]

In order to invest in a neighborhood, businesses need to be assured basic levels of public safety and civic order. Beyond just being protected from actual violence, the businessman and the customer must be free of the menace of violence. Criminal elements, even if their activity is non-violent, must also be removed: they create an atmosphere of fear, undermining the possibility of legal business transactions. In *Chicago v. Morales*, Thomas made a point of mentioning that among the many victims of Chicago's gangs were black consumers too "afraid to shop."[61] Heavy policing and the realistic prospect of state punishment thus provide the necessary if not sufficient conditions for the buying and selling that are the foundation of a capitalist economy.

But carceral capitalism requires more than just the state's protection of simple economic trades. What the police are protecting and promoting is also the social infrastructure upon which a capitalist society depends. The specific institutions Thomas called out in that 1985 symposium were schools, families, and churches. These are the institutions that cultivate, ideally, the virtues and habits necessary for middle-class success: responsibility, discipline, deferred gratification, respect for authority, temperance, prudence, and thrift. Thomas has spoken forcefully of the effects of crime on children's schooling and family life. A general tolerance of crime, he says, has "incredibly significant effects on the ability of school principals . . . to enforce standards of decency and conduct." Crime and violence also affect the families struggling to make ends meet so that kids can get their education: "How can the parents or older brothers and sisters of these children lead productive lives if economic and educational opportunity are stymied by rampant community violence and disorder?"[62] Again, these are the types of victims Thomas highlighted in *Chicago v. Morales*: "good, decent people who must struggle to overcome their desperate situation, against all odds, in order to raise their families, earn a living, and remain good citizens."[63]

Beyond protecting schools and churches so that families can lead "productive lives," policing and punishment are meant to make people into market actors, the selves of capitalism. In addition to responsibility, discipline, prudence, and so forth, good market actors are defined by their relationship to property: their respect for it, their desire for it, their refusal to trespass against it. The property owner must be a "prudent ward of his interests."[64] Among the manners and mores, the rules of propriety, that Thomas claims he learned from his grandparents and in the shadow of the police was this: "We knew that we were not to litter or damage the property of another, regardless of how much the property was worth."[65] As Thomas sees it, one of the consequences of the rights revolution, with its limitations on policing and punishing, is that it undercut the respect for private property that capitalism depends upon. "If the government does not punish harmful conduct," Thomas writes, "we send a dangerous message to society"—not just to the unpunished violator of private property but to all members of society, lawful and unlawful alike. "What are we telling . . . the upstanding public housing tenant who respects others' property and well being, when our law fails to express outrage at those who do wrong?"[66]

If the upstanding custodian and caretaker of private property has been the chief victim of the rights revolution, its chief beneficiary, in Thomas's view, has been the violator of that property. After the drug dealer and the rapist, no criminals vex Thomas as much as the vagrant and the beggar. These are the ancient demons of the market society, lacking in land and money—the two forms of property, fixed and mobile, that such a society prizes. The vagrant and the beggar recur throughout Thomas's writings and opinions. After the rights revolution, he writes, "vagrants and others who regularly roamed the streets had rights that could not be circumscribed by the community's sense of decency or decorum." Once "government discretion had to be curbed," cities were prevented from enforcing "broad vagrancy or anti-panhandling laws."[67] While Thomas went to great lengths in *Chicago v. Morales* to separate anti-loitering ordinances from the history of Jim Crow, lest a direct association between the two make Chicago's law appear racially suspect, he happily joined the city's ordinance to the history of vagrancy laws meant to police the mores of property and social class. "The vagrant has been very appropriately described," Thomas wrote, quoting approvingly from an 1886 treatise, "as the chrysalis of every species of criminal. A wanderer through the land, without home ties, and without apparent means of support, what but criminality is to be expected from such a person?"[68]

What Thomas's writings, speeches, and opinions about carceral capitalism ultimately reveal is just how much his ideas about punishment, authority, and the market are framed by a particular demographic and geography: not black people in general, but poor and working-class black people living in the inner city. Carceral capitalism is not a project for wealthy African Americans or other people of color; they struggle with the more rarefied stigmas and anxieties of success that Thomas describes in his critiques of affirmative action. Carceral capitalism is for a lower stratum of African Americans who, Thomas believes, need the harsh hand of the punitive state. For it is that stratum, located in the inner cities, that Thomas believes has been most affected by the rights revolution: "The transformation of the criminal justice system has had and will continue to have its greatest impact in our urban areas. It is there that modern excuses for criminal behavior abound— poverty, substandard education, faltering families, unemployment, a lack of respect for authority because of deep feelings of oppression."[69] The inner city is a swamp not simply of criminal behavior but of bad behavior in general: not minding one's manners, failing in school, not rising up and out into the middle class.

Thomas has always seen a connection between class and criminality. In discussing how punishment and policing can create good market actors, he is explicitly thinking of poor blacks in the inner cities, who, he believes, lack the necessary habits and virtues. The proximity of the black urban poor to crime, whether as victims or perpetrators, has everything to do with their distance from capitalism: it is in poor, black urban areas that Thomas sees the culture of excuses as being rampant. It might even be said that it was there that the rights revolution was meant to have its greatest effect: "How can we hold the poor responsible for their actions, some asked, when our society does little to remedy the social conditions of the ill-educated and unemployed in our urban areas?"[70] As a result, Thomas says, "many in today's society do not expect the less fortunate to accept responsibility for (and overcome) their present circumstances. . . . They are instead given the right to fret and complain, and are encouraged to avoid responsibility and self-help."[71] It stands to reason, then, that it is in those same areas, among those same poor and working-class black people, that the punitive state has the potential to have its greatest effect. If it is the task of policing and punishment "to ensure a greater degree of personal responsibility in our society," where else but in poor urban black communities, where Thomas believes the levels of personal responsibility are low, will policing and punishment have a more potent impact?[72]

If that comes at the price of tolerating a racist police force and a racist prison system, so be it, Thomas suggests. Black people have suffered worse in the past—and, by his lights, gained more because of it. Perhaps the same will be true in the future.

GIVEN THE ASSOCIATIONS between federalism and states' rights—that is, between federalism and the political language of white supremacy, an association Thomas is more than aware of—it's astonishing how openly Thomas embraces not just federalism but a view of federalism associated with the slaveocracy and Jim Crow.[73] Prior to the Civil War, it was common among Southern defenders of slavery to argue that the Constitution was not a national charter of the American people—the "We the People of the United States" that opens the Preamble to the Constitution—but instead a compact of sovereign states. It was the states (or the citizens of states assembled in their state conventions) that adopted the Constitution. And because the Constitution derives its authority from the states voluntarily compacting with each other, any state at any time could deny that Constitution its authority by withdrawing itself from the compact. In the twentieth century, as the civil rights movement began making increasing demands for a strengthened national government to end Jim Crow, that states' rights version of federalism was resurrected by the movement's opponents. By 1964, it became the keystone of the conservative backlash against civil rights.[74]

Thomas does not go that far. He does not assert that the Constitution is a compact of sovereign states or that states have the right to withdraw from the compact. Nor does he use phrases like "states' rights." Yet while Thomas concedes that the Constitution derives its authority from the people, he does insist, quite strenuously, that these people are not "the undifferentiated people of the Nation as a whole" but instead "the people of each individual State."[75] That may seem like a distinction without a difference, but in constitutional and conservative circles it signals an attentiveness, even solicitude, for a tradition of pro-state thinking associated with the Southern position during Jim Crow.

In *U.S. Term Limits, Inc. v. Thornton* (1995), for example, one of the more important federalism cases of the last quarter century, Thomas took repeated exception to the notion of an "undifferentiated people of the Nation as a whole"; some version of the phrase appears six times in his opinion.[76] The point was partially to resist any unified conception of political identity or political citizenship located at the level of the nation-state: "The people of each State have retained their independent political identity," Thomas proclaimed. Echoing the master class's position before and after the Civil War, he insisted that American citizenship is still divided between the state and the national, as in *Dred Scott* and *Slaughter-House* and *Cruikshank*: "There always remains a meaningful distinction between someone who is a citizen of the United States and of Massachusetts."[77] Even more striking than these endorsements of a differentiated citizenship have been Thomas's firm affirmations of the sovereignty of states. In a key speech on the topic of federalism, Thomas invoked state sovereignty seventeen times. "Our system of federalism," he said, "not only diffuses power, but it also creates independent sovereigns. . . . The state of Virginia, my home state, for example, is sovereign in a way that an administrative division of France is not. Virginia has its own government, it has plenary control over certain subjects, it administers areas such as criminal law and education with substantial, if not complete, policy-making freedom, its governmental operations cannot be 'commandeered' or taxed by another sovereign."[78]

Thomas's Black Constitution depends on a "nationalization of constitutional rights"—preventing states, for instance, from infringing on the Second Amendment right to bear arms.[79] Thomas's White Constitution, by contrast, involves a significant devolution of rights, with national citizenship yielding to states. It is an almost complete reversal of the Black Constitution, championing the very state sovereignty that the struggle for emancipation was supposed to overcome.

One of the main reasons for this is discipline and punishment.[80] As much as Thomas invokes federalism as an abstract liberty check on the national government, it is clear from his writings that he wishes to empower the states as sovereigns with the power to punish. This is his counterattack on the criminal justice element of the rights revolution, which had its greatest effect on state and local governments. "The very same ideas that prompted the judicial revolution in due process rights," Thomas complains, "circumscribed the authority of local communities to set standards for decorum and civility on the streets or in the public schools" and "made it far more difficult for the criminal justice system to hold people responsible for the consequences of their harmful acts." The federal courts' scrutiny of the states' criminal justice systems, he says, "denies society the right to punish some admitted offenders, and intrudes on state sovereignty to a degree matched by few exercises of federal judicial authority."[81] To fix society, those due process rights of individuals must be limited or taken away. And any reinvigoration of the power to punish will have to involve a significant rollback of federal power and a reinvigoration of the states. That is what federalism, as Thomas understands it, is designed in part to do.[82] That is the White Constitution in a nutshell.

"Young children cannot learn in schools if they are besieged by drugs and constant threats of violence," Thomas wrote in an essay on the rights revolution. "Nor, for that matter, can they lead normal lives if so many street corners, sandlots and apartment buildings are fixed places of business for drug dealers and other criminals."[83] What is to be done about this? How should government address the problem—and which level of government should do it? In *United States v. Lopez*, which involved the Gun-Free School Zones Act, Thomas and the Court confronted precisely this issue of violence and schoolchildren. The Court's liberals, eager to restrict gun possession, saw the Constitution's Commerce Clause as the ideal instrument for that project. Show the negative effects of guns near schools on the children's learning, demonstrate the long-term economic impact of those poor learning conditions, and you have a straightforward argument for the exercise of federal power. In his essay on the rights revolution, Thomas did not reject or refuse that causality; he accepted it. Yet rather than allowing the federal government to address the problem of gun possession through the Commerce Clause—which would place the issue within the remedial mold of liberal regulation—Thomas insisted that it be addressed through the states. There, it would be handled as the problem Thomas believed it to be: not an obstacle to good education that must be dealt with by the federal government, but as individual acts of immorality that needed to be policed and punished by a carceral state.[84]

The states are the realm of common law, a body of law rooted in feudal Britain and brought over to the colonies, which survived the introduction of the Constitution and the manifold changes that increasing nationalism brought to the country. At the federal level, by contrast, there is only the Constitution and federal statutes.[85] But in the states, common law still rules. That has a deep personal meaning for Thomas. In his first year of law school, he read a passage from Oliver Wendell Holmes: "The common law is not a brooding omniscience in the sky but the articulate voice of some sovereign or quasi-sovereign that can be identified." Upon reading it, Thomas writes, "I thought at once of Daddy, the brooding omnipresence of my childhood and youth. 'He could make me cry just by looking at me,' Pigeon often said. But as I grew older, made my own way in the world, and raised a son, I came to appreciate what I had not understood as a child: I had been raised by the greatest man I have ever known."[86] Thomas's White Constitution empowers the policing and punishing elements of the state. But that is only a means to an end. The utopian vision that Thomas sees beyond the carceral state is the creation of a new generation of black patriarchs—terrifying enough to make their children cry and thereby to teach them how to survive another chapter in America's long history of white supremacy.[87]

Clarence Thomas's America

Clarence Thomas is the most extreme justice on the Supreme Court. He is also the most emblematic. His jurisprudence may be a bitter mix of right-wing revanchism and black nationalism, but it is distinctively American and of the moment. It begins with the belief that racism is permanent, the state is ineffective, and politics is feeble, and ends with a dystopia that looks painfully familiar: men armed to the teeth, people locked up in jails, money ruling all, and racial conflict as far as the eye can see. It reflects the anxious aspiration and curdled disappointment of a society that spent the better part of the twentieth century trying to overcome white supremacy and the Gilded Age only to see their rehabilitation in the twenty-first. It rehearses and repeats that experience of defeat, with no sign of exit or end. It returns to scenes of ancient injury and present wrong, not to repair the first or right the second but to tell us that neither righting nor repair can be done.

From its beginnings, race has been the master explainer for such a state of affairs. Race was meant to signal the impregnability of nature to the demands of democracy, the immunity of social life to political transformation. Race was the work of God, declared Southern race theorist Josiah Nott, and "no human power can change the fiat of the

Almighty." Taking stock of the effort to revolutionize the condition of former slaves after the Civil War, Nott confidently predicted that "all the powers of the Freedmen's Bureau . . . cannot prevail against" the force of race.[1] Though this naturalistic account of race is less ascendant today than it was in Nott's time, its vision of permanence lives on in our accounts of racism. Racism is now thought to be as immutable and intractable as race once was.[2] It is a social current that courses so far beneath our feet as to lie beyond our grasp. It powers the whole in a way that cannot be done away with. It yields a vision of politics that sees our agency, our room for action and maneuver, as radically constrained. It explains and forecasts defeat.

The same goes for the two other elements in Thomas's jurisprudence. As an economic system, capitalism may entail restless dynamism and creative destruction, but its role in our polity is anything but creative or dynamic. The business of capitalism is to take the great questions of society—justice, equality, freedom, distribution—off the table of public deliberation. Capitalism's most ardent proponents say that it functions best when it is untouched by democracy, when it is protected from the conscious and collective interference of citizens acting through their government. And while for a brief stretch of the twentieth century the Constitution was envisioned as a living experiment, a text to be revised and revisited through argument and amendment, its function today is the opposite. Through the Senate and the Electoral College, both of which privilege the interests of a numerical minority from mostly white states over the interests of democratic, multiracial majorities; through the elevation of the Supreme Court to the status of talisman, where the fate of the nation hinges on nine men and women educated at the most elite schools; and through the doctrine of originalism, the Constitution has reverted to what it has been throughout most of American history: a source of overwhelming, anti-democratic constraint.

We live in a world of deep division and polarization. Yet while factions may fight because of a yawning divide between them, a battle may be fiercest precisely when two armies are contending on the same ground. The jurisprudence of Clarence Thomas suggests we're in that type of moment. It's not that Thomas's critics agree with his opinions about the Voting Rights Act or the Equal Protection Clause. It's that the underlying vision—of the permanence and autonomy of race, of the inability of politics to overcome social disrepair, of the ineffectiveness of state action—is so widely shared. Perhaps that explains Thomas's enigmatic silence on the bench. What need is there to speak when the rest of us are saying his words?

If Thomas begins from premises that are shared yet arrives at conclusions from which we recoil, that might argue for closer scrutiny of the steps he takes along the way. One might, for example, accept his claim that the roots of racism are "undiscoverable"—suggesting that racism is transhistorical, with origins deep in our neurons or psychology or some other source—yet refuse to give up the struggle against racism.[3] One might agree that racism is a permanent stain on the soul of America yet choose to wage a moral battle against what is essentially a version of original sin. One might accept his claim that racism is everywhere in time and space, then turn that claim against his defense of the carceral state—though in the name of what sort of antiracist ideal (and whether such ideals can survive professions of racism's ontological reality) remains unclear.

But that need not be our only response. When brought face-to-face with an enemy whose vision we share, we may ask ourselves not where he goes wrong, but where we did. We may wonder whether we're not trapped in the same historical moment as he, making sense of the same defeats of the last century in not dissimilar ways. We may ask whether we, in the shadow of defeat, have simply come to accept and repeat, without realizing it, the story he has been telling us for decades. And then we may come to a realization: that the task at hand is not to retrace and rebut his moves from premise to conclusion, but to go back and start again with different premises.

NOTES

A note on citations: I've used a modified version of standard legal citation methods for court opinions. As is customary, when Thomas is writing the opinion of the Court, I cite the name of the case, its page numbers in the *United States Reports* or the *Supreme Court Reporter*, and the year of the decision. If Thomas's opinion is a dissent or concurrence, I note that. Because Thomas is the author of most of the opinions cited here, I do not cite him as the author. When citing the opinions of other justices, I note the author and whether they are writing for the Court, in dissent, or in concurrence. For cases decided before Thomas's 1991 ascension to the Court, however, I cite the author only if the opinion is a dissent or concurrence.

INTRODUCTION

1. David Cay Johnston, *The Making of Donald Trump* (Brooklyn: Melville House, 2016), 93–94.
2. Though Justice Scalia wrote the opinion in *District of Columbia v. Heller*, the contemporary Court's first major gun rights decision, it was Thomas who first argued, in *Printz*, that the right to bear arms is a personal or individual right as opposed to a reference to state militias. And as Jeffrey Toobin has rightly said of *Citizens United*, the Court's controversial campaign finance decision of 2011, "The opinion was Kennedy's, but the victory was Thomas's." *Printz v. United States*, 521 U.S. 898, 938 (1997) (concurring); Jeffrey Toobin, *The Oath: The Obama White House and the Supreme Court* (New York: Anchor, 2012, 2013), 243–44; Ralph A. Rossum, *Understanding*

Clarence Thomas: The Jurisprudence of Constitutional Restoration (Lawrence: University Press of Kansas, 2014), 109; Steven B. Lichtman, "Black Like Me: The Free Speech Jurisprudence of Clarence Thomas," *Penn State Law Review* 114 (Fall 2009), 431–37. As of December 2018, the exact number of Thomas's opinions was 709, based on searches of multiple databases— Ballotpedia, Wikipedia, Washington University Law, and LexisNexis. Of these 709 opinions, 49 were related to orders such as dissents from or concurrences with grants and denials of certiorari.

3. Jeffrey Toobin, "Partners," *New Yorker* (August 29, 2011), 41; Oliver Roeder and Amelia Thomson-DeVeaux, "How Brett Kavanaugh Would Change the Supreme Court," *FiveThirtyEight* (July 9, 2018), https://fivethirtyeight.com /features/how-brett-kavanaugh-would-change-the-supreme-court/; Andrew Witherspoon and Harry Stevens, "Where Brett Kavanaugh Sits on the Ideological Spectrum," *Axios* (July 10, 2018), https://www.axios.com/brett -kavanaugh-conservative-ideological-political-views-9d009f84-0e0a-4ebf -ac82-084489a108f2.html; Elliott Ash and Daniel L. Chen, "What Kind of Judge Is Brett Kavanaugh? A Quantitative Analysis," *Cardozo Law Review* (2018), 70–100, http://cardozolawreview.com/what-kind-of-judge-is-brett -kavanaugh/. As the *New York Times* reporter Adam Liptak has written, Thomas often will write an opinion, joined by no one, in which he takes a position that "can seem idiosyncratic and therefore inconsequential"—in just eight days in February 2019 alone, Thomas urged the Court to overturn three long-standing precedents protecting citizens from libel suits by public officials, guaranteeing poor citizens the right to counsel, and assuring women of the right to an abortion—only to have the Court slowly come around to it years later. Adam Liptak, "That's a Settled Precedent? Thomas Disagrees," *New York Times* (March 5, 2019), A13.

4. Jane Mayer and Jill Abramson, *Strange Justice: The Selling of Clarence Thomas* (Boston: Houghton Mifflin, 1994), 199–200; Jeffrey Rosen, "Radical Constitutionalism," *New York Times Magazine* (November 26, 2010), MM34, https://www.nytimes.com/2010/11/28/magazine/28FOB-idealab-t .html; Toobin, *The Oath*, 230–50; Toobin, "Partners," 41, 48, 51.

5. *National Institute of Family and Life Advocates v. Becerra*, 138 S. Ct. 2361 (2018); *District of Columbia v. Wesby*, 138 S. Ct. 537 (2018); *Ohio v. American Express*, 138 S. Ct. 2274 (2018); Dahlia Lithwick and Mark Joseph Stern, "The Clarence Thomas Takeover," *Slate* (August 2, 2017), https://slate.com/news-and-politics/2017/08/clarence-thomas-legal-vision -is-becoming-a-trump-era-reality.html; Mark Sherman, "22 former Justice Thomas clerks have jobs thanks to Trump," *AP News* (August 4, 2018), https://www.apnews.com/ebda07542740484c86ea192caaf357a9.

6. The former clerks are: Brinton Lucas (Justice), Heath Tarbert (Treasury), Eric McArthur (Justice), Jeffrey B. Wall (Justice), Neomi Rao (Office of Management and Budget), Sigal Mandelker (Treasury), Eric Grant (Justice), Steven G. Bradbury (Treasury), Rebekah Ricketts (Office of U.S. Attorneys), and Steven McAllister (Office of U.S. Attorneys). Spencer S. Hsu, "Federal judge

in D.C. weighs ordering administration to restart 'dreamers' program," *Washington Post* (March 14, 2018), https://www.washingtonpost.com/local /public-safety/federal-judge-in-dc-weighs-ordering-administration-to-restart -dreamers-program/2018/03/14/883b5178-27a7-11e8-bc72-077aa4dab9ef _story.html; Jane Chong, "Argument Summary: Hawaii v. Trump," *Lawfare-Blog* (May 16, 2017), https://www.lawfareblog.com/argument-summary -hawaii-v-trump; *Masterpiece Cakeshop v. Colorado Civil Rights Commission*, amicus brief, http://www.scotusblog.com/wp-content/uploads/2017/09 /16-111-tsac-USA.pdf.

7. U.S. Court of Appeals: Allison Eid, James Ho, Gregory Katsas, Eric D. Miller, Neomi Rao, Allison Jones Rushing, and David Stras; District Court: Martha Pacold and Carl Nichols; Specialty Courts: Emin Toro and Gregory Maggs. Also see Ian Millhiser, "Clarence Thomas is the Most Important Legal Thinker in America," ThinkProgress.org (July 3, 2018), https://thinkprogress.org /clarence-thomas-most-important-legal-thinker-in-america-c12af3d08c98/.

8. "List of federal judges appointed by Donald Trump," Wikipedia, https://en .wikipedia.org/wiki/List_of_federal_judges_appointed_by_Donald_Trump, accessed on December 31, 2018; "List of law clerks on the Supreme Court of the United States," Wikipedia, https://en.wikipedia.org/wiki/List_of_law _clerks_of_the_Supreme_Court_of_the_United_States, accessed on December 31, 2018.

9. Juan Williams, "A Question of Fairness," *Atlantic Monthly* (February 1987), 73.

10. Bill Kaufmann, "Clarence Thomas," *Reason* (November 1987), 32.

11. Lithwick and Stern, "The Clarence Thomas Takeover."

12. *Hearings before the Senate Committee on the Judiciary*, 102nd Cong., 1st sess., September 10, 11, 12, 13, 17, 19, 20, 1991, and October 11, 12, 13, 1991, Part 1, 366, 369, 370, 380; Part 2, 668, 670, 741, 742, 745, 748, 1116; Part 3, 47, 202, 403, 466, 472.

13. *Senate Confirmation Hearings*, Part 1, 109; Part 3, 403; Thomas, "Black Americans & the Constitution," *The New Federalist Papers*, ed. J. Jackson Barlow et al. (Lanham, MD: University Press of America, 1988), 308–309; Juan Williams, "Black Conservatives, Center Stage," *Washington Post* (December 16, 1980), A21. Also see Kimberlé Crenshaw, "We Still Haven't Learned from Anita Hill's Testimony," *New York Times* (September 27, 2018), https:// www.nytimes.com/2018/09/27/opinion/anita-hill-clarence-thomas-brett -kavanaugh-christine-ford.html.

14. The best accounts of the Thomas-Hill controversy remain Mayer and Abramson, *Strange Justice*, and Timothy M. Phelps and Helen Winternitz, *Capitol Games: The Inside Story of Clarence Thomas, Anita Hill, and a Supreme Court Nomination* (New York: HarperPerennial, 1992). For a more recent look at the charges, with new information from other sources, see Jill Abramson, "Do You Believe Her Now?," *New York* (February 18, 2018), http://nymag.com/daily/intelligencer/2018/02/the-case-for-impeaching -clarence-thomas.html.

15. Lori A. Ringhand and Paul M. Collins Jr., "Neil Gorsuch and the Ginsburg Rules," *Chicago-Kent Law Review* 93 (2018), 486–87, 492, 500–504.

16. Thomas, speech to the Heritage Foundation (June 18, 1987), reprinted as "Why Black Americans Should Look to Conservative Policies," *Human Events* (July 27, 1991), 17, and as "What Conservatives Can Offer Blacks," *St. Louis Post-Dispatch* (July 14, 1991), 3B; Chester A. Higgins, Sr., "'We Are Going to Enforce the Law!' Interview with Clarence Thomas, Chairman, EEOC," *The Crisis* (February 1983), 51. Also see Thomas, "Black America Under the Reagan Administration," *Policy Review* (Fall 1985), 35.

17. Andrew Peyton, *Clarence Thomas: A Biography* (San Francisco: Encounter, 2001), 173; Thomas, "Why Black Americans Should Look to Conservative Policies," 12.

18. As Thomas pointed out in a law review article not long before his confirmation hearings, "Conservatives need to realize that their audience is not one composed of simple lawyers." On and off the bench, he wrote, conservatives should be mindful of the fact that "our struggle, as conservatives and political actors, is not simply another litigation piece or technique. This is a political struggle." In the words of another commentator, "Thomas may not write his separate opinions for his contemporaries—perhaps he writes them for the future." Thomas, "The Higher Law Background of the Privileges or Immunities Clause of the Fourteenth Amendment," *Harvard Journal of Law and Public Policy* 12 (1989), 68; Hannah Weiner, "The Next 'Great Dissenter'? How Clarence Thomas Is Using the Words and Principles of John Marshall Harlan to Craft a New Era of Civil Rights," *Duke Law Journal* 58 (2008), 175.

19. Thomas, "A Right to Think for Myself," *St. Louis Post-Dispatch* (April 2, 1998), B3.

20. Thomas's project here is similar to that of other black conservatives and black Republicans. See Angela D. Dillard, *Guess Who's Coming to Dinner Now? Multicultural Conservatism in America* (New York: New York University Press, 2001), 15; Leah Wright Rigueur, *The Loneliness of the Black Republican* (Princeton, NJ: Princeton University Press, 2015), 124–25.

21. Kevin Merida and Michael A. Fletcher, *Supreme Discomfort: The Divided Soul of Clarence Thomas* (New York: Doubleday, 2007), 29.

22. Indeed, while some black nationalist groups looked explicitly to other nations in the decolonizing world for alternative models of a new constitutional order, Thomas recoils at the slightest suggestion that the Court should consider international law or the statutes of other countries. *Foster v. Florida*, 537 U.S. 990, 990* (2002) (concurring in denial of writ of certiorari); *Johnson v. Bredesen*, 558 U.S. 1067, 1072 (2009) (concurring); Aziz Rana, "Colonialism and Constitutional Memory," *UC Irvine Law Review* 5 (2015), 285–86.

23. Tommie Shelby, *We Who Are Dark: The Philosophical Foundations of Black Solidarity* (Cambridge, MA: Harvard University Press, 2005), 27, 28–29, 32, 47, 53, 266n17; Michael C. Dawson, *Black Visions: The Roots of Contemporary African-American Political Ideologies* (Chicago: University of Chicago Press, 2001), 100–102, 122–23, 129–30, 316.

24. In his classic study, Wilson Moses issues "a challenge to those who have viewed black nationalism as if it were invariably a leftist movement," and goes so far as to claim that during "the Golden Age of Black Nationalism"—from the 1850s through the 1920s—"the ideology was conservative rather than radical." Wilson Jeremiah Moses, *The Golden Age of Black Nationalism, 1850–1925* (New York: Oxford University Press, 1978), 11. My argument about Thomas does not depend upon any such claims about the inherently conservative nature of black nationalism. I am instead interested in the overlap between black conservatism and black nationalism, which is usefully surveyed and discussed in Rigueur, *Loneliness of the Black Republican,* 68, 89, 124; Dawson, *Black Visions,* 87, 89, 92–93, 100–122, 130, 282; Dean E. Robinson, *Black Nationalism in American Politics and Thought* (New York: Cambridge University Press, 2001), 125–27, 133–34; Robert L. Allen, *Black Awakening in Capitalist America: An Analytical History* (Trenton, NJ: Africa World Press, 1990), 18, 68, 153–56, 158–64, 182–92, 216, 245; Shelby, *We Who Are Dark,* 71–78, 103–7; and *Black Conservatism: Essays in Intellectual and Political History,* ed. Peter Eisenstadt (New York: Garland, 1999); xiv, xviii–xix.

25. John Ganz, "The Forgotten Man," *The Baffler* (December 15, 2017), https://thebaffler.com/latest/the-forgotten-man-ganz; Julian Sanchez and David Weigel, "Who Wrote Ron Paul's Newsletters?," *Reason* (January 16, 2008), http://reason.com/archives/2008/01/16/who-wrote-ron-pauls-newsletter /singlepage; Murray Rothbard, "Judge Thomas and Black Nationalism," *Rothbard-Rockwell Report* II (September 1991), 5. I am grateful to John Ganz for bringing the Rothbard article to my attention.

26. *Black Conservatism;* Lewis A. Randolph, "A Historical Analysis and Critique of Contemporary Black Conservatism," *Western Journal of Black Studies* 19 (Fall 1995), 149–63; Angela K. Lewis, "Black Conservatism in America," *Journal of African American Studies* 8 (March 2005), 3–13; Dawson, *Black Visions,* 281–302.

27. Corey Robin, *The Reactionary Mind: Conservatism from Edmund Burke to Donald Trump* (New York: Oxford University Press, 2018), 52–55, 195–200, 224–26, 239–42, 268–69.

28. On the racism of the contemporary Republican Party, see Donald R. Kinder and Allison Dale-Riddle, *The End of Race? Obama, 2008, and Racial Politics in America* (New Haven, CT: Yale University Press, 2011); Theda Skocpol and Vanessa Williamson, *The Tea Party and the Remaking of Republican Conservatism* (New York: Oxford University Press, 2013), 4, 11, 56–57, 68, 71–72, 76, 79, 81, 193–96; Chris S. Parker and Matt Bareto, *Change They Can't Believe In: The Tea Party and Reactionary Politics in America* (Princeton, NJ: Princeton University Press, 2013); Diana C. Mutz, "Status threat, not economic hardship, explains the 2016 presidential vote," *Proceedings of the National Academy of Sciences* 115 (May 8, 2018), E4330–E4339, http://www.pnas.org/content/pnas/115/19/E4330.full.pdf; Brian F. Schaffner, Matthew MacWilliams, and Tatishe Nteta, "Understanding White Polarization

in the 2016 Vote for President: The Sobering Role of Racism and Sexism," *Political Science Quarterly* 133 (Spring 2018), 9–34.

29. Peyton, *Clarence Thomas*, 247.

30. Statement of Niara Sudarkasa (September 17, 1991), *Senate Confirmation Hearings*, Part 1, 76–78; Manning Marable, "Clarence Thomas and the Crisis of Black Political Culture," in *Race-ing Justice, En-gendering Power: Essays on Anita Hill, Clarence Thomas, and the Construction of Social Reality*, ed. Toni Morrison (New York: Pantheon, 1992), 80–82; "Roundtable: Doubting Thomas," *Tikkun* 6 (September/October 1991), 23–24. I am grateful to Larry Glickman for bringing this roundtable, in which Cruse participated, to my attention.

31. Robert Pear, "Despite Praising Farrakhan in 1983, Thomas Denies Anti-Semitism," *New York Times* (July 13, 1991), L7.

32. Sam Zagoria, "What Jesse Jackson Said," *Washington Post* (February 22, 1984), https://www.washingtonpost.com/archive/politics/1984/02/22/what-jesse-jackson-said/6c09b7fe-5cfe-4fbf-b14b-456e377c89ce/; Milton Coleman, "A Reporter's Story," *Washington Post* (April 8, 1984), https://www.washingtonpost.com/archive/opinions/1984/04/08/a-reporters-story/807486fd-b978-484d-8110-e5a544d072aa/; *Blacks and Jews: Alliances and Arguments*, ed. Paul Berman (New York: Delacorte, 1994); Adolph Reed Jr., "What Color Is Antisemitism," in *Class Notes: Posing as Politics and Other Thoughts on the American Scene* (New York: New Press, 2000), 33–35.

33. Phelps and Winternitz, *Capitol Games*, 44–48; Mayer and Abramson, *Strange Justice*, 51, 117–18.

34. Merida and Fletcher, *Supreme Discomfort*, 106–19, 266–67, 283, 294, 371, 375–376; Peyton, *Clarence Thomas*, 126–28; Ken Foskett, *Judging Thomas: The Life and Times of Clarence Thomas* (New York: Harper-Perennial, 2004), 74, 99–101, 103–12; Diane Brady, *Fraternity* (New York: Spiegel & Grau, 2012), 73–75, 126–28, 141–60, 170–71; Jeffrey Rosen, "Moving On," *New Yorker* (April 29, 1996), 66–73.

35. Rossum, *Understanding Clarence Thomas*, 4, 221; Scott Douglas Gerber, *First Principles: The Jurisprudence of Clarence Thomas* (New York: New York University Press, 1999).

36. Cedric Merlin Powell, "Justice Thomas, *Brown*, and Post-Racial Determinism," *Washburn Law Journal* 53 (2014), 451–77; Stephen F. Smith, "Clarence X? The Black Nationalist Behind Justice Thomas's Constitutionalism," *New York University Journal of Law & Liberty* 4 (2009), 583–625; Nicole Stelle Garnett, "But for the Grace of God, There Go I: Justice Thomas and the Little Guy," *New York University Journal of Law & Liberty* 4 (2009), 626–47; Cedric Merlin Powell, "Rhetorical Neutrality: Colorblindness, Frederick Douglass, and Inverted Critical Race Theory," *Cleveland State Law Review* 56 (2008), 832–94; Tomiko Brown-Nagin, "The Transformative Racial Politics of Justice Thomas? The *Grutter v. Bollinger* Opinion," *Journal of Constitutional Law* 7 (February 2005), 787–807; Angela Onwuachi-Willig, "Just Another Brother on the Supreme Court? What Justice Clarence

Thomas Teaches Us About the Influence of Racial Identity," *Iowa Law Review* 90 (March 2005), 933–1009; Angela Onwuachi-Willig, "Using the Master's 'Tool' to Dismantle His House: Why Justice Clarence Thomas Makes the Case for Affirmative Action," *Arizona Law Review* 47 (Spring 2005), 113–65; Guy-Uriel E. Charles, "Colored Speech: Cross Burnings, Epistemics, and the Triumph of the Crits?," *Georgetown Law Journal* 93 (2005), 575–632; Kendall Thomas, "Reading Clarence Thomas," *National Black Law Journal* 18 (2004), 224–38; Mark Tushnet, "Clarence Thomas's Black Nationalism," *Howard Law Journal* 47 (Winter 2004), 323–39.

37. LexisNexis search (December 28, 2018).

38. LexisNexis search (July 11, 2018). Each year, the *Harvard Law Review* publishes statistics comparing the number of opinions written by each justice. Though the *Law Review*'s statistics don't include opinions related to Court orders, they are nonetheless useful for comparative purposes. For the terms beginning in the fall of 2012 and ending in the spring of 2018, see "The Statistics," *Harvard Law Review* 127 (2013), 408; "The Statistics," *Harvard Law Review* 128 (2014), 401; "The Statistics," *Harvard Law Review* 129 (2015), 381; "The Statistics," *Harvard Law Review* 130 (2016), 507; and "The Statistics," *Harvard Law Review* 131 (2017), 403.

39. Ralph Ellison, *Invisible Man* (New York: Vintage, 1947, 1980), 3; Foskett, *Judging Thomas*, 82, 102, 290–91; Thomas, *My Grandfather's Son: A Memoir* (New York: HarperPerennial, 2007), 63, 245, 251; Brady, *Fraternity*, 192; Kauffman, "Clarence Thomas," 32; Merida and Fletcher, *Supreme Discomfort*, 102, 357–58, 368; Mayer and Abramson, *Strange Justice*, 51; Peyton, *Clarence Thomas*, 107–8, 129; Phelps and Winternitz, *Capitol Games*, 42–43.

40. Tonja Jacobi and Matthew Sag, "The New Oral Argument: Justices as Advocates," *Notre Dame Law Review* 94 (2019), 1161–254; Barry Sullivan and Megan Canty, "Interruptions in Search of a Purpose: Oral Argument in the Supreme Court, October Terms 1958–60 and 2010–12," *Utah Law Review* 5 (2015), 1005–82; Timothy R. Johnson, James F. Spriggs II, and Paul J. Wahlbeck, "Oral Advocacy Before the United States Supreme Court: Does It Affect the Justices' Decisions?," *Washington University Law Review* (2007), 457–527.

41. Onwuachi-Willig, "Just Another Brother on the Supreme Court?," 933; Merida and Fletcher, *Supreme Discomfort*, 326; Foskett, *Judging Thomas*, 231, 297.

42. "The Second Annual William French Smith Memorial Lecture: A Conversation with Justice Clarence Thomas," *Pepperdine Law Review* 37 (2009), 11; Jan Crawford Greenburg, *Supreme Conflict: The Inside Story of the Struggle for Control of the United States Supreme Court* (New York: Penguin, 2007), 115, 117, 120, 124–25.

43. Also like Thomas, Marshall was criticized for a second marriage to a woman who was not African American. Onwuachi-Willig, "Just Another Brother on the Supreme Court?," 935–36; Brown-Nagin, "The Transformative Racial Politics of Justice Thomas?," 803; Terry Eastland, "While Justice Sleeps,"

National Review (April 21, 1989); Merida and Fletcher, *Supreme Discomfort*, 261, 265.

44. Merida and Fletcher, *Supreme Discomfort*, 256; Thomas, "Be Not Afraid," Francis Boyer Lecture, American Enterprise Institute Annual Dinner (February 13, 2001), http://www.aei.org/publication/be-not-afraid/.

45. Thomas, "Be Not Afraid"; Foskett, *Judging Thomas*, 268.

46. Thomas's tenure and jurisprudence have been compared to Black's. See Toobin, "Partners," 41; Lichtman, "Black Like Me," 419, 441, 447–48, 452–55. An early version of the comparison, issued more as a challenge to Thomas, can be found in A. Leon Higginbotham Jr., "An Open Letter to Justice Clarence Thomas from a Federal Judicial Colleague," in *Race-ing Justice, En-gendering Power*, 26.

47. Dawson, *Black Visions*, 104, 324; Robinson, *Black Nationalism*, 127; Manning Marable, *Malcolm X: A Life of Reinvention* (New York: Penguin, 2011), 199–201.

1. RACE MAN

1. Kevin Merida and Michael A. Fletcher, *Supreme Discomfort: The Divided Soul of Clarence Thomas* (New York: Doubleday, 2007), 37, 59–69; Andrew Peyton, *Clarence Thomas: A Biography* (San Francisco: Encounter, 2001), 60, 79; Ken Foskett, *Judging Thomas: The Life and Times of Clarence Thomas* (New York: HarperPerennial, 2004), 52, 55, 62–63, 72–73.

2. Kim Masters, "EEOC's Thomas: Ready to Sing a Different Tune?," *Legal Times* (December 24/31, 1984), 2, 5; Thomas, speech at *Headway* Magazine National Leadership Conference (September 1998), reprinted in *Headway* 10 (December 31, 1998), 10, and in "Black Conservatives Have Walked a Long Way," *Richmond Times-Dispatch* (April 18, 1999), F1; Thomas, "No Room at the Inn: The Loneliness of the Black Conservative," in *Black and Right: The Bold New Voice of Black Conservatives in America*, ed. Stan Faryna, Brad Stetson, and Joseph G. Conti (Westport, CT: Praeger, 1997), 4; Merida and Fletcher, *Supreme Discomfort*, 154; Peyton, *Clarence Thomas*, 221; Foskett, *Judging Thomas*, 83. Thomas frequently recurs to the parallels between America's racial autocracy and authoritarianism in other countries: "But [Ronald Reagan's] point, as I take it, is that we must continue to recognize evil and call it for what it is, whether we find it abroad or at home. The zeal needed to fight tyranny abroad is the same quality of soul needed to fight for freedom at home." "Conservatives should be as adamant about freedom here at home as we are about freedom abroad." Thomas, "Civil Rights as a Principle Versus Civil Rights as an Interest," in *Assessing the Reagan Years*, ed. David Boaz (Washington, DC: Cato, 1988), 401–2; Thomas, speech to the Heritage Foundation (July 18, 1987), reprinted as "Why Black Americans Should Look to Conservative Policies," *Human Events* (July 27, 1991), 11, 17.

3. Ron Suskind, "And Clarence Thomas Wept," *Esquire* (July 1998), 70.

4. Thomas, *My Grandfather's Son: A Memoir* (New York: HarperPerennial, 2007), 5.

5. Ibid., 6–7.

6. Ibid., 7–8.

7. Peyton, *Clarence Thomas*, 7; Mark Tushnet, *A Court Divided: The Rehnquist Court and the Future of Constitutional Law* (New York: Norton, 2006, 2005), 97; *The Autobiography of Benjamin Franklin* (Mineola, NY: Dover, 1996), 22–23, 26, 46, 48, 80; *Narrative of the Life of Frederick Douglass, an American Slave, Written by Himself,* ed. William Andrews and William McFeely (New York: Norton, 1997), 28, 32, 34; Booker T. Washington, *Up from Slavery,* ed. William L. Andrews (New York: Norton, 1996), 44–45; *The Autobiography of Malcolm X* (New York: Ballantine, 1964), 73, 77, 80, 219–70.

8. Chester A. Higgins, Sr., "'We Are Going to Enforce the Law!' Interview with Clarence Thomas, Chairman, EEOC," *The Crisis* (February 1983), 51; "The Second Annual William French Smith Memorial Lecture: A Conversation with Justice Clarence Thomas," *Pepperdine Law Review* 37 (2009), 13; Thomas, *My Grandfather's Son,* 29–30; Juan Williams, "A Question of Fairness," *Atlantic Monthly* (February 1, 1987), 74; Jane Mayer and Jill Abramson, *Strange Justice: The Selling of Clarence Thomas* (Boston: Houghton Mifflin, 1994), 45; Merida and Fletcher, *Supreme Discomfort,* 61. For a sensitive and nuanced treatment of these issues, which raises important questions about Thomas's memory of these slights, see Merida and Fletcher, *Supreme Discomfort,* 61–64.

9. Mayer and Abramson, *Strange Justice,* 45; Foskett, *Judging Thomas,* 59–62. On the ambiguities of Thomas's class status, see Toni Morrison, "Introduction: Friday on the Potomac," in *Race-ing Justice, En-gendering Power: Essays on Anita Hill, Clarence Thomas, and the Construction of Social Reality,* ed. Toni Morrison (New York: Pantheon, 1992), xx–xxi; Merida and Fletcher, *Supreme Discomfort,* 55–60; Foskett, *Judging Thomas,* 18–19, 42.

10. Foskett, *Judging Thomas,* 61–62, 111. Also see Merida and Fletcher, *Supreme Discomfort,* 49.

11. Tommie Shelby, *We Who Are Dark: The Philosophical Foundations of Black Solidarity* (Cambridge, MA: Harvard University Press, 2005), 75–76.

12. Thomas, *My Grandfather's Son,* 92; Jeffrey Rosen, "Moving On," *New Yorker* (April 29/May 6, 1996), 68; Peyton, *Clarence Thomas,* 248; Merida and Fletcher, *Supreme Discomfort,* 64, 136, 144–45; Mayer and Abramson, *Strange Justice,* 45–46, 136; Foskett, *Judging Thomas,* 223.

13. Thomas, *My Grandfather's Son,* 92; Foskett, *Judging Thomas,* 134.

14. W.E.B. Du Bois, "On Being Ashamed of Oneself: An Essay on Race Pride," *The Crisis* (September 1933), 199. For a sensitive discussion of this essay and how it relates to Du Bois's theories of black leadership, see Shelby, *We Who Are Dark,* 80–94.

15. Merida and Fletcher, *Supreme Discomfort,* 104; Peyton, *Clarence Thomas,*

116. More generally, see Diane Brady, *Fraternity* (New York: Spiegel & Grau, 2012).

16. Martha Biondi, *The Black Revolution on Campus* (Berkeley: University of California Press, 2012), 2, 4, 29.

17. Brady, *Fraternity*, 24, 59; Peyton, *Clarence Thomas*, 114; Merida and Fletcher, *Supreme Discomfort*, 104, 107.

18. Brady, *Fraternity*, 38, 77–82; Foskett, *Judging Thomas*, 97; Thomas, letter to the editor, *Wall Street Journal* (April 20, 1987), 23.

19. Thomas, *My Grandfather's Son*, 78. Also see "The Second Annual William French Smith Memorial Lecture," 13.

20. Thomas, Savannah State College Commencement Address (June 9, 1985), in Thomas, *Confronting the Future: Selections from the Senate Confirmation Hearings and Prior Speeches* (Washington, DC: Regnery Gateway, 1992), 37; Chris Moody, "Clarence Thomas: Society Is Overly Sensitive About Race," Yahoo! News (February 11, 2014), https://www.yahoo.com/news/clarence -thomas-on-race-194104252.html; Angela Onwuachi-Willig, "Just Another Brother on the Supreme Court? What Justice Clarence Thomas Teaches Us About the Influence of Racial Identity," *Iowa Law Review* 90 (March 2005), 967; Thomas, "The New Intolerance," Law Day Address, Walter F. George School of Law, Mercer University (May 1993), http://www.americanrhetoric .com/speeches/clarencethomasthenewintolerance.htm; Merida and Fletcher, *Supreme Discomfort*, 96–98; Mayer and Abramson, *Strange Justice*, 49; Peyton, *Clarence Thomas*, 85, 89–90; Thomas, *My Grandfather's Son*, 35–36; Foskett, *Judging Thomas*, 70, 74–75, 79–80.

21. Biondi, *The Black Revolution*, 15.

22. Vivian Gornick, *The Situation and the Story: The Art of Personal Narrative* (New York: Farrar, Straus & Giroux, 2002).

23. Foskett, *Judging Thomas*, 82; Biondi, *The Black Revolution*, 2.

24. Biondi, *The Black Revolution*, 25–26.

25. Brady, *Fraternity*, 73; Foskett, *Judging Thomas*, 99.

26. Brady, *Fraternity*, 137; Foskett, *Judging Thomas*, 104.

27. Merida and Fletcher, *Supreme Discomfort*, 109, 165; Brady, *Fraternity*, 126, 137; Foskett, *Judging Thomas*, 109–10; Thomas, *My Grandfather's Son*, 181; Timothy M. Phelps and Helen Winternitz, *Capitol Games: The Inside Story of Clarence Thomas, Anita Hill, and a Supreme Court Nomination* (New York: HarperPerennial, 1992)), 115.

28. *Autobiography of Malcolm X*, 221, 224; Steve Estes, *I Am a Man! Race, Manhood, and the Civil Rights Movement* (Chapel Hill: University of North Carolina Press, 2005), 7–8, 91, 153–77; Biondi, *The Black Revolution*, 26–28.

29. Thomas is a fan of Spike Lee's films, especially the racially explosive *Do the Right Thing* (1989), and has expressed a desire to meet Lee in person. Merida and Fletcher, *Supreme Discomfort*, 108, 283, 371; *United States v. Fordice*, 505 U.S. 717, 745 (1992) (concurring); *Missouri v. Jenkins*, 515 U.S. 70, 114 (1995) (concurring); Bill Kauffman, "Clarence Thomas," *Reason* (Novem-

ber 1987), 32; Williams, "A Question of Fairness," 73; Rosen, "Moving On," 70; Foskett, *Judging Thomas*, 97; Phelps and Winternitz, *Capitol Games*, 14; Peyton, *Clarence Thomas*, 128.

30. Merida and Fletcher, *Supreme Discomfort*, 108, 119, 165; Peyton, *Clarence Thomas*, 127; Foskett, *Judging Thomas*, 102–3; Stefan Fatsis, "No Viet Cong Ever Called Me Nigger: The Story Behind the Famous Quote Muhammad Ali Probably Never Said," *Slate* (June 8, 2016), http://www.slate.com/articles/sports/sports_nut/2016/06/did_muhammad_ali_ever_say_no_viet_cong_ever_called_me_nigger.html.

31. The interview appeared in the October 22, 1996, issue of the magazine *Neopolitique*, which was published by the university's School of Government and is now defunct. http://justicethomas.blogspot.com/2007/09/neopolitique-interview.html; email to the author from Chris Roslan (March 5, 2018).

32. Biondi, *The Black Revolution*, 2; *Hearings Before the Senate Committee on the Judiciary*, 102nd Cong., 1st sess., September 10, 11, 12, 13, 17, 19, 20, 1991, and October 11, 12, 13, 1991, Part 1, 367.

33. Journalists and Thomas offer different accounts of this incident. Merida and Fletcher, *Supreme Discomfort*, 118–119; Thomas, *My Grandfather's Son*, 59; Foskett, *Judging Thomas*, 109; Peyton, *Clarence Thomas*, 129; Brady, *Fraternity*, 169.

34. Kauffman, "Clarence Thomas," 32; Brady, *Fraternity*, 126–27; Thomas, *My Grandfather's Son*, 67; Foskett, *Judging Thomas*, 109; Peyton, *Clarence Thomas*, 127.

35. Depending on their sources, journalistic accounts of Thomas's role in the walkout—whether it was his idea or not—differ. In his memoir, Thomas says, "I was one of the BSU members who supported the idea of simply leaving a place where we no longer felt welcome," but his classmates assign him more of a leading role. Thomas, *My Grandfather's Son*, 57; Merida and Fletcher, *Supreme Discomfort*, 114–15; Foskett, *Judging Thomas*, 105–8; Brady, *Fraternity*, 143–60; Peyton, *Clarence Thomas*, 121–25.

36. Foskett, *Judging Thomas*, 108; Peyton, *Clarence Thomas*, 125.

37. Brady, *Fraternity*, 92, 102, 124; Merida and Fletcher, *Supreme Discomfort*, 111; Mayer and Abramson, *Strange Justice*, 51–52; Thomas, *My Grandfather's Son*, 54–55, 58–61; Peyton, *Clarence Thomas*, 117, 126; Cedric Johnson, *Revolutionaries to Race Leaders: Black Power and the Making of African American Politics* (Minneapolis: University of Minnesota Press, 2007), 54–56.

38. Shelby, *We Who Are Dark*, 31; Dean E. Robinson, *Black Nationalism in American Politics and Thought* (New York: Cambridge University Press, 2001), 6.

39. Shelby, *We Who Are Dark*, 28–29, 32, 47, 53, 266n17; Robinson, *Black Nationalism*, 2, 100; Michael C. Dawson, *Black Visions: The Roots of Contemporary African-American Political Ideologies* (Chicago: University of Chicago Press, 2001), 92, 101.

40. Johnson, *Revolutionaries to Race Leaders*, 75–76; Robinson, *Black*

Nationalism, 63, 97, 99. "Most black leaders have occasionally shown black nationalist elements in their thinking." Wilson Jeremiah Moses, *The Golden Age of Black Nationalism, 1850–1925* (New York: Oxford University Press, 1978, 1988), 6.

41. Higgins, "'We Are Going to Enforce the Law!,'" 50; Brady, *Fraternity*, 192; Kauffman, "Clarence Thomas," 32.

42. Peyton, *Clarence Thomas*, 119; Thomas, *My Grandfather's Son*, 47–48.

43. Brady, *Fraternity*, 193, 205; Mark Savolis (head archivist at Holy Cross), email to author, December 4, 2017; Thomas, *My Grandfather's Son*, 69. For more on Thomas's achievements at Holy Cross, see Foskett, *Judging Thomas*, 110–11, 115.

44. Thomas, *My Grandfather's Son*, 64–65; Merida and Fletcher, *Supreme Discomfort*, 122–23; Peyton, *Clarence Thomas*, 136; Foskett, *Judging Thomas*, 119–20.

45. Juan Williams, "Black Conservatives, Center Stage," *Washington Post* (December 16, 1980), A21; Thomas, *My Grandfather's Son*, 70; Mayer and Abramson, *Strange Justice*, 49; Merida and Fletcher, *Supreme Discomfort*, 96–98; Peyton, *Clarence Thomas*, 85.

46. Thomas, *My Grandfather's Son*, 74.

47. Williams, "A Question of Fairness," 75.

48. Williams, "A Question of Fairness," 75; Peyton, *Clarence Thomas*, 141, 277, 286, 347; Thomas, *My Grandfather's Son*, 137, 216, 231–32; Mayer and Abramson, *Strange Justice*, 144; Phelps and Winternitz, *Capitol Games*, 90.

49. Thomas, *My Grandfather's Son*, 75; Foskett, *Judging Thomas*, 120.

50. Thomas, "The New Intolerance."

51. John McWhorter, "Racism in America Is Over," *Forbes* (December 30, 2008), https://www.forbes.com/2008/12/30/end-of-racism-oped-cx_jm_1230mcwhorter.html; Dinesh D'Souza, *The End of Racism: Principles for a Multiracial Society* (New York: Free Press, 1995); James J. Heckman, "Detecting Discrimination," *Journal of Economic Perspectives* 12 (Spring 1998), 101–16; Desmond S. King and Rogers M. Smith, "'Without Regard to Race': Critical Ideational Development in Modern American Politics," *Journal of Politics* 76 (July 2014), 958–71; Leah Wright Rigueur, *The Loneliness of the Black Republican* (Princeton, NJ: Princeton University Press, 2015), 309–10. I'm grateful to Phil Klinkner for pointing me to some of these sources.

52. William Raspberry, "Are the Problems of Blacks Too Big for Government to Solve?," *Washington Post* (July 17, 1983), C3; Thomas, Savannah State Address, 37; Thomas, "Black America Under the Reagan Administration," *Policy Review* (Fall 1985), 34, 41; Kauffman, "Clarence Thomas," 33; Williams, "A Question of Fairness," 72.

53. Williams, "A Question of Fairness," 72; Thomas, *My Grandfather's Son*, 163.

54. Merida and Fletcher, *Supreme Discomfort*, 141; Peyton, *Clarence Thomas*, 155.

55. Kauffman, "Clarence Thomas," 33; Thomas, "Why Black Americans Should

Look to Conservative Policies," 12. Also see Thomas, speech to Pacific Research Institute, San Francisco (August 10, 1987), in *Senate Confirmation Hearings*, Part 1, 158; Thomas, "No Room at the Inn," 5, 8–9, 12; Thomas, "Black America Under the Reagan Administration," 35–36; Thomas, letter to the editor, *New Republic* (March 7, 1988), 2, 41; Thomas, "Republicans Can Win Black Votes," *New Pittsburgh Courier* (March 7, 1987), 4; Merida and Fletcher, *Supreme Discomfort*, 162; Mayer and Abramson, *Strange Justice*, 78; Thomas, *My Grandfather's Son*, 146–47, 179; Peyton, *Clarence Thomas*, 202, 273ff, 293–94; Foskett, *Judging Thomas*, 197–98.

56. Mayer and Abramson, *Strange Justice*, 186; also see Mayer and Abramson, *Strange Justice*, 144, and Peyton, *Clarence Thomas*, 286.

57. Williams, "A Question of Fairness," 80. Also see Thomas, *My Grandfather's Son*, 108; Mayer and Abramson, *Strange Justice*, 78–79.

58. Thomas, *My Grandfather's Son*, 236. Also see Foskett, *Judging Thomas*, 260–61.

59. Masters, "EEOC's Thomas," 2.

60. Cited in Robinson, *Black Nationalism*, 31. That distinction between transparency and deception (and self-deception) also runs throughout Stokely Carmichael and Charles Hamilton's *Black Power*, which came out one year before Thomas headed north. What differentiates their account from Thomas's is that they map a distinction between overt and covert racism onto their distinction between individual and institutional racism. Individual racism is overt, Carmichael and Hamilton argue, and thus elicits criticism and condemnation. Institutional racism is "less overt, far more subtle, less identifiable in terms of *specific* individuals committing the acts." It has the support of "respected forces in the society" and "'respectable' individuals." It is just as destructive as individual racism—more destructive, in fact—but because it cannot be sited in individuals, because it is hidden by a veneer of respectability and legitimacy, it "receives far less public condemnation" than individual racism. These markers of the distinction between individual and institutional racism—opacity, respectability, and pervasiveness—find their way into Thomas's conceptualization of race sincerity. Though Thomas briefly flirted with the idea of institutional racism, as we'll see in chapter 5, that idea ultimately dropped out of his mature thought and jurisprudence. What remained is the distinction between overtness and covertness, but reconfigured as moral attributes of the self: a person is racially honest or dishonest, candid or duplicitous. What for Carmichael and Hamilton were the outer characteristics of institutional racism became, in Thomas's hands, the distinguishing marks between two types of individual racist. Kwame Ture (formerly known as Stokely Carmichael) and Charles Hamilton, *Black Power: The Politics of Liberation* (New York: Vintage, 1967, 1992), 4–5.

61. Thomas, *My Grandfather's Son*, 75–76.

62. Malcolm X, "God's Judgment of White America," in *The End of White World Supremacy: Four Speeches by Malcolm X*, ed. Imam Benjamin Karim (New York: Arcade, 1971), 137.

63. Foskett, *Judging Thomas*, 121, 131.
64. Thomas, *My Grandfather's Son*, 63, 245, 251; Kauffman, "Clarence Thomas," 32; Merida and Fletcher, *Supreme Discomfort*, 102, 357–58, 368; Mayer and Abramson, *Strange Justice*, 51; Peyton, *Clarence Thomas*, 107–8, 129; Foskett, *Judging Thomas*, 82, 102, 290–91; Phelps and Winternitz, *Capitol Games*, 42–43; Brady, *Fraternity*, 192.
65. Thomas, "Black America Under the Reagan Administration," 41; *Adarand Constructors, Inc. v. Peña*, 515 U.S. 200, 241 (1995) (concurring); *Grutter v. Bollinger*, 539 U.S. 306, 356 (2003) (concurring in part and dissenting in part).
66. Thomas, "Remembering an Island of Hope in an Era of Despair," *Lincoln Review* (Spring 1986), 56; Thomas, *My Grandfather's Son*, x; Thomas, "Freedom: A Responsibility, Not a Right," *Ohio Northern University Law Review* 21, no. 1 (1994), 4; *Senate Confirmation Hearings*, Part 4, 9; Brady, *Fraternity*, 4–5; Kauffman, "Clarence Thomas," 31; Suskind, "And Clarence Thomas Wept," 146.
67. Thomas, speech to Pacific Research Institute, 155–56.
68. Thomas, "Victims and Heroes in the 'Benevolent State,'" *Harvard Law and Public Policy Review* 19 (Spring 1996), 672, 679, 682. Also see Rosen, "Moving On," 66–67; Phelps and Winternitz, *Capitol Games*, 112.
69. Thomas, "Freedom: A Responsibility, Not a Right," 3; Thomas, speech to Pacific Research Institute, 158. Thomas's thinking here resonates with some of the arguments of Martin Delaney, the nineteenth-century thinker and activist who founded the black nationalist tradition in the United States. Shelby, *We Who Are Dark*, 35–37.
70. Thomas, "Victims and Heroes," 679. Thomas also says, "No one tries if they know at the end of the day they won't get full credit for the victory." Suskind, "And Clarence Thomas Wept," 146.
71. Thomas, Savannah State Address, 38; Thomas, "Black America Under the Reagan Administration," 41.
72. Masters, "EEOC's Thomas," 5; Merida and Fletcher, *Supreme Discomfort*, 67; Williams, "A Question of Fairness," 74.

2. STIGMAS

1. Thomas did dissent from one part of the majority's decision that upheld government requirements that donations be reported and disclosed. In Thomas's view, the Court's conservatives should have struck down these requirements as well. *Citizens United v. FEC*, 558 U.S. 310, 480 (2010) (concurring in part and dissenting in part).
2. *Citizens United v. FEC*, 558 U.S. 310, 446 (2010) (Stevens, dissenting).
3. *McDonald v. City of Chicago*, 561 U.S. 742, 856 (2010) (concurring).
4. *McDonald v. City of Chicago*, 561 U.S. 742, 856n22 (2010) (concurring).
5. Adam Liptak, "Justice Defends Ruling on Finance," *New York Times* (February 3, 2010), A17.

6. In a 2018 immigration case that originated with the Obama administration, Thomas opened his dissent with a lengthy disquisition on the history of immigration law. He made a special point of noting that early opposition to the federal government deporting immigrants reflected less the Jeffersonians' openness to immigrants than the Southern slaveholders' fear that federal control over immigration policy could lead to the federal government prohibiting a state government from preventing free black people from entering the state. *Sessions v. Dimaya*, 138 S. Ct. 1204, 1246n4 (2018) (dissenting).

7. David G. Savage, "Supreme Court Leaves in Place California's 10-day Wait for Gun Buyers, Rejects 2nd Amendment Challenge," *Los Angeles Times* (February 20, 2018), http://www.latimes.com/politics/la-na-pol-court-guns-20180220-story.html.

8. *Silvester v. Becerra*, 138 S. Ct. 945, 945 (2018) (dissenting from denial of certiorari). Thomas reiterates his complaint that the Court does not take Second Amendment rights (or other rights favored by conservatives) as seriously as it does rights favored by liberals in *Friedman v. City of Highland Park*, 136 S. Ct. 447, 449–50 (2015) (dissenting from denial of certiorari); *Arrigoni Enterprises v. Town of Durham*, 136 S. Ct. 1409, 1411 (2016) (dissenting from denial of certiorari); *Peruta v. California*, 137 S. Ct. 1995, 1999 (2017) (dissenting from denial of certiorari).

9. *Georgia v. McCollum*, 505 U.S. 42, 61 (1992) (concurring). One year later, Thomas made the same point in a speech: "We would be kidding ourselves if we didn't admit that racial stereotypes still linger in 1993." Thomas, "The New Intolerance," Law Day Address, Walter F. George School of Law, Mercer University (May 1993), http://www.americanrhetoric.com/speeches/clarencethomasthenewintolerance.htm.

10. *Zelman v. Simmons-Harris*, 536 U.S. 639, 683 (2002) (concurring).

11. *Parents Involved in Community Schools v. Seattle School District No. 1*, 551 U.S. 701, 767–68 (2007) (concurring).

12. *Adarand Constructors, Inc. v. Peña*, 515 U.S. 270 (1995) (Souter, dissenting).

13. *Georgia v. McCollum*, 505 U.S. 42, 48–49, 57, 59 (1992) (Blackmun).

14. *Georgia v. McCollum*, 505 U.S. 42, 59 (1992) (Blackmun).

15. *Georgia v. McCollum*, 505 U.S. 42, 59–60 (1992) (Rehnquist, concurring); *Georgia v. McCollum*, 505 U.S. 42, 62–69 (1992) (O'Connor, dissenting); *Georgia v. McCollum*, 505 U.S. 42, 69–70 (1992) (Scalia, dissenting).

16. *Georgia v. McCollum*, 505 U.S. 42, 60 (1992) (concurring).

17. *Georgia v. McCollum*, 505 U.S. 42, 61 (1992) (concurring).

18. *Georgia v. McCollum*, 505 U.S. 42, 48–49, 58–59 (1992) (Blackmun).

19. *Georgia v. McCollum*, 505 U.S. 42, 60, 61 (1992) (concurring). In a separate case involving a different set of issues concerning race and juries, Thomas wrote, "Jurors do not leave their knowledge of the world behind when they enter a courtroom." *Dawson v. Delaware*, 503 U.S. 159, 171 (1992) (dissenting). Thomas also showed a concern about the effects of the outside world on juries, albeit not in the context of racial prejudice, in *Dietz v. Bouldin*, 136 S. Ct. 1885, 1897 (2016) (dissenting).

20. Thomas is not the only conservative justice who takes a dim view of the possibilities of eliminating race prejudice in jury trials. Justice Scalia made similar claims in private memos ("the unconscious operation of irrational sympathies and antipathies, including racial, upon jury decisions and [hence] prosecutorial decisions is real . . . and ineradicable") and Court opinions ("all groups tend to have particular sympathies and hostilities—most notably, sympathies towards their own group members"). There is a crucial difference between the two justices, however. Scalia believed that racism is merely a form of group identification, a tribalism that expresses itself in partiality toward insiders and dislike of outsiders. Because tribalism is ubiquitous—Jews bond with Jews, Catholics with Catholics, and so on—there's nothing peculiar or particular about white racism. It's just another form of collective self-love, with no peculiar stigmatic effect on any one group. Thomas, by contrast, believes that white racism is not garden-variety group narcissism. *Powers v. Ohio*, 499 U.S. 400, 424 (2001) (Scalia, dissenting); Biskupic, *American Original*, 154, 157. See *Davis v. Minnesota*, 511 U.S. 1115, 1117–18 (1994) (dissenting from denial of certiorari), which Scalia joined, for a potential counter to this claim about the difference between Thomas and Scalia.

21. *Zelman v. Simmons-Harris*, 536 U.S. 639 (2002) (Rehnquist).

22. United States Census Bureau (2000). Social Explorer Tables (SE). Retrieved from https://www.socialexplorer.com/tables/C2000/R11826577. I am grateful to Joshua Garoon and Daniel Burton for providing me with this data.

23. *Zelman v. Simmons-Harris*, 536 U.S. 639, 681 (2002) (concurring).

24. Harvard legal scholar Mark Tushnet has claimed that Thomas is the only Supreme Court justice to quote both Du Bois and Douglass in his opinions. In a blog post, I repeated this claim, but a commenter pointed out that Justice William O. Douglas cites both Douglass and Du Bois in a 1968 case. Mark Tushnet, *A Court Divided: The Rehnquist Court and the Future of Constitutional Law* (New York: Norton, 2005, 2006), 97; Mark Tushnet, "Clarence Thomas's Black Nationalism," *Howard Law Journal* (Winter 2004), 323; Corey Robin, "Eleven Things You Did Not Know About Clarence Thomas," *Crooked Timber* (April 18, 2014), http://crookedtimber.org/2014/04/18/eleven-things-you-did-not-know-about-clarence-thomas/; *Jones v. Alfred H. Mayer Co.*, 392 U.S. 409, 444, 446 (1968) (Douglas, concurring).

25. *Zelman v. Simmons-Harris*, 536 U.S. 639, 676, 681, 682, 684 (2002) (concurring).

26. *Virginia v. Black*, 538 U.S. 343, 348–50 (2003) (O'Connor); *Virginia v. Black*, 538 U.S. 343, 393–394 (2003) (dissenting).

27. *Virginia v. Black*, 538 U.S. 343, 365–66 (2003) (O'Connor).

28. *Virginia v. Black*, 538 U.S. 343, 388–89 (2003) (dissenting).

29. *Virginia v. Black*, 538 U.S. 343, 352, 356 (2003) (O'Connor).

30. *Virginia v. Black*, 538 U.S. 343, 388, 391 (2003) (dissenting). Also see Calvin J. TerBeek, "Write Separately: Justice Clarence Thomas's 'Race Opinions' on the Supreme Court," *Texas Journal on Civil Liberties and Civil Rights* 11 (Spring 2006), 201; Stephen F. Smith, "Clarence X? The Black Nationalist

Behind Justice Thomas's Constitutionalism," *New York University Journal of Law & Liberty* 4 (2009), 595–96.

31. Several years earlier, the Court had held that a municipality may not prevent the Ku Klux Klan from erecting a cross in a public square. Such a prohibition, the Court ruled, would interfere with the Klan's exercise of religion and thus violate the Establishment Clause. Thomas concurred with the Court's judgment, but, anticipating the race-conscious move he would make in *Virginia v. Black*, he also wrote that "the erection of such a cross" by the Klan "is a political act, not a Christian one." The goal of the Klan is "to establish a racist white government in the United States," he noted; the Klan cross is "a symbol of white supremacy and a tool for intimidation and harassment." As with his later opinion in the cross-burning case, Thomas used race to suggest that the issue at stake in *Capitol Square Review* "may not have truly involved the Establishment Clause" at all. *Capitol Square Review and Advisory Board v. Pinette*, 515 U.S. 753, 770–71 (1995) (concurring). Conversely, Thomas can be extraordinarily indifferent to the question of racist speech in the workplace, bending over backward to classify it as protected First Amendment speech. That may have as much to do with his opposition to the state's interference in the market and the workplace, a topic explored in chapter 5. *Avis Rent a Car System v. Oscar Aguilar*, 529 U.S. 1138 (2000) (dissenting from denial of certiorari).

32. *Johnson v. California*, 543 U.S. 499 (2005) (O'Connor).

33. *Johnson v. California*, 543 U.S. 499, 526 (2005) (dissenting). Ironically, in a Texas affirmative action case discussed in chapter 3, Thomas accused defenders of affirmative action of making the same move: "Finally, while the University admits that racial discrimination in admissions is not ideal, it asserts that it is a temporary necessity because of the enduring race consciousness of our society. . . . Yet again, the University echoes the hollow justifications advanced by the segregationists." *Fisher v. University of Texas*, 570 U.S. 297, 325 (2013) (concurring).

34. *Johnson v. California*, 543 U.S. 499, 524, 532, 535 (2005) (dissenting); *Plessy v. Ferguson*, 163 U.S. 537, 550 (1896).

35. *Johnson v. California*, 543 U.S. 499, 527, 545 (2005) (dissenting).

36. *Parents Involved in Community Schools v. Seattle School District No. 1*, 551 U.S. 701, 768, 769, 769n17 (2007) (concurring). Also see *Beard v. Banks*, 548 U.S. 521, 536 (2006) (concurring); *Thompson v. McNeil*, 556 U.S. 1114, 1118 (2009) (concurring in denial of certiorari).

37. *Campbell v. Louisiana*, 523 U.S. 392, 403 (1998) (concurring in part and dissenting in part); Linda Greenhouse, "Justices Rule About Race of Grand Jury," *New York Times* (April 22, 1998), A22.

38. *Campbell v. Louisiana*, 523 U.S. 392, 395, 396, 398, 400 (1998) (Kennedy).

39. *Campbell v. Louisiana*, 523 U.S. 392, 403, 405–6, 406n2, 408 (1998) (concurring in part and dissenting in part).

40. Juan Williams, "Black Conservatives, Center Stage," *Washington Post* (December 16, 1980), A21.

41. Cf. Thomas, "Rule of Law: The New Intolerance," *Wall Street Journal* (May 12, 1993), A15; Kendall Thomas, "Reading Clarence Thomas," *National Black Law Journal* 18 (2004), 234–35.

42. *Hearings Before the Senate Committee on the Judiciary*, 102nd Cong., 1st sess., September 10, 11, 12, 13, 17, 19, 20, 1991, and October 11, 12, 13, 1991, Part 4, 202, 203, 205.

43. *Missouri v. Jenkins*, 515 U.S. 70, 114 (1995) (concurring).

44. For an excellent discussion of the role of racial stigma in Thomas's thinking, see Tomiko Brown-Nagin, "The Transformational Politics of Justice Thomas? The *Grutter v. Bollinger* Opinion," *Journal of Constitutional Law* 7 (February 2005), 787–807.

45. *Adarand Constructors, Inc. v. Peña*, 515 U.S. 200, 241 (1995) (concurring); *Fisher v. University of Texas*, 570 U.S. 297, 333 (2013) (concurring).

46. Thomas, "Affirmative Action Goals and Timetables: Too Tough? Not Tough Enough!," *Yale Law & Policy Review* 5 (Spring–Summer 1987), 403.

47. Barbara J. Fields, "Whiteness, Racism, and Identity," *International Labor and Working Class History* 60 (October 2001), 48–56; Karen E. Fields and Barbara J. Fields, *Racecraft: The Soul of Inequality in American Life* (New York: Verso, 2012), 115–21.

48. "The Second Annual William French Smith Memorial Lecture: A Conversation with Justice Clarence Thomas," *Pepperdine Law Review* 37 (2009), 22–23.

49. *Missouri v. Jenkins*, 515 U.S. 70, 122, 138 (1995) (concurring).

50. Kwame Ture (formerly known as Stokely Carmichael) and Charles V. Hamilton, *Black Power: The Politics of Liberation* (New York: Vintage, 1967, 1992), 54; Cedric Johnson, *Revolutionaries to Race Leaders: Black Power and the Making of African American Politics* (Minneapolis: University of Minnesota Press, 2007), 112. Also see Dean E. Robinson, *Black Nationalism in American Politics and Thought* (New York: Cambridge University Press, 2001), 99.

51. Thomas, "Affirmative Action Goals and Timetables," 403.

52. *Obergefell v. Hodges*, 135 S. Ct. 2584, 2631, 2639 (2015) (dissenting). In the summer of 1981, after separating from his first wife, Thomas moved in with an old friend. Every morning, he listened to George Benson's "The Greatest Love of All," and according to the friend's girlfriend, sang the song at the top of his lungs. Thomas tells a slightly different story but admits he was especially moved by these lyrics: "No matter what they take from me / They can't take away my dignity." Jane Mayer and Jill Abramson, *Strange Justice: The Selling of Clarence Thomas* (Boston: Houghton Mifflin, 1994), 81; Thomas, *My Grandfather's Son: A Memoir* (New York: HarperPerennial, 2007), 136–37.

53. Thomas, "Victims and Heroes in the 'Benevolent State,'" *Harvard Law and Public Policy Review* 19 (Spring 1996), 683.

54. Orlando Patterson, *Freedom: Volume I: Freedom in the Making of Western Culture* (New York: Basic, 1991), 277–84.

55. *Grutter v. Bollinger*, 539 U.S. 306, 353 (2003) (concurring in part and dissenting in part).

3. SEPARATE BUT EQUAL

1. Ken Foskett, *Judging Thomas: The Life and Times of Clarence Thomas* (New York: HarperPerennial, 2004), 288–89; Thomas, *My Grandfather's Son: A Memoir* (New York: HarperPerennial, 2007), 137, 216, 232; Andrew Peyton, *Clarence Thomas: A Biography* (San Francisco: Encounter, 2001), 141, 277, 286, 347; Jane Mayer and Jill Abramson, *Strange Justice: The Selling of Clarence Thomas* (Boston: Houghton Mifflin, 1994), 144; Timothy M. Phelps and Helen Winternitz, *Capitol Games: The Inside Story of Clarence Thomas, Anita Hill, and a Supreme Court Nomination* (New York: Harper-Perennial, 1992), 90.

2. Joan Biskupic, *American Original: The Life and Constitution of Supreme Court Justice Antonin Scalia* (New York: Farrar, Straus & Giroux, 2009), 160. For other examples of the conservative critique of affirmative action, see *Regents of the University of California v. Bakke*, 483 U.S. 265, 299 (1978); *Fullilove v. Klutznick*, 448 U.S. 448, 522–26 (1980) (Stewart, dissenting); *Richmond v. J. A. Croson*, 488 U. S. 469, 493–94 (1989); *Richmond v. J. A. Croson*, 488 U.S. 520–21 (1989) (Scalia, concurring); *Adarand Constructors, Inc. v. Peña*, 515 U.S. 200, 227, 229–30 (1995) (O'Connor); *Adarand Constructors, Inc. v. Peña*, 515 U.S. 200, 239 (1995) (Scalia, concurring); *Grutter v. Bollinger*, 359 U.S. 306, 389–93 (2003) (Kennedy, dissenting); *Fisher v. University of Texas*, 136 S. Ct. 2198, 2215 (2016) (Alito, dissenting); Thomas M. Keck, *The Most Activist Supreme Court in History: The Road to Modern Judicial Conservatism* (Chicago: University of Chicago Press, 2004), 139–40.

3. Scott D. Gerber, "Clarence Thomas, *Fisher v. University of Texas*, and the Future of Affirmative Action in Higher Education," *University of Richmond Law Review* 50 (2016), 1169–92; Nathan W. Dean, "The Primacy of the Individual in the Political Philosophy and Civil Rights Jurisprudence of Justice Clarence Thomas," *George Mason University Civil Rights Law Journal* 14 (2004), 36–37, 57; Scott Douglas Gerber, *First Principles: The Jurisprudence of Clarence Thomas* (New York: New York University Press, 1999), 50.

4. Clint Bolick, *The Affirmative Action Fraud: Can We Restore the American Civil Rights Vision?* (Washington, DC: Cato Institute, 1996); Terry Eastland, *Ending Affirmative Action: The Case for Colorblind Justice* (New York: Basic, 1997); Desmond S. King and Rogers M. Smith, " 'Without Regard to Race': Critical Ideational Development in Modern American Politics," *Journal of Politics* 76 (July 2014), 958–71; Keck, *Most Activist Supreme Court*, 143–48, 181, 186–89; Mark Tushnet, *In the Balance: Law and Politics on the Roberts Court* (New York: Norton, 2013), 134–41.

5. Randall Kennedy is one of the few scholars to have noticed that Thomas's "opposition to affirmative action has to do not so much with alleged unfairness to whites—the central theme of many white conservatives—but instead with his perception that it is bad for blacks." Kennedy does claim,

however, that Thomas believes the race-conscious measures of Jim Crow, which were designed to subjugate African Americans, are equivalent to the race-conscious measures designed to undo the effects of Jim Crow. I don't think the evidence sustains that claim, at least as Kennedy construes it. Randall Kennedy, *Sellout: The Politics of Racial Betrayal* (New York: Pantheon, 2008), 97, 125–26. One of the few instances where Thomas makes such a claim occurs not in an affirmative action case but in a voting rights case, where Thomas cites a 1979 equal protection decision having to do with jury selection: "This exacting scrutiny [of race-based criteria] makes sense because '[d]iscrimination on the basis of race' is 'odious in all aspects.'" *Bethune-Hill v. Virginia State Board of Elections*, 137 S. Ct. 788, 805 (2017) (concurring in part and dissenting in part).

6. Thomas, "Current Litigation Trends and Goals at the EEOC," *Labor Law Journal* (April 1983), 213. On Thomas's various positions on affirmative action during the Reagan years, see chapter 4, note 17.

7. Phelps and Winternitz, *Capitol Games*, 97–98. In the one instance I've found from the 1980s where Thomas made the equivalence argument, he did so by reference not to Jim Crow or white supremacy in the United States but by analogy to South African apartheid: "I bristle at the thought, for example, that it is morally proper to protest against minority racial preferences in South Africa while arguing for such preferences here." Thomas, "The Equal Employment Opportunity Commission: Reflections on a New Philosophy," *Stetson Law Review* 15 (1985), 35.

8. Ronald Suresh Roberts, *Clarence Thomas and the Tough Love Crowd: Counterfeit Heroes and Unhappy Truths* (New York: New York University Press, 1995), 121.

9. Thomas, "Victims and Heroes in the 'Benevolent State,'" *Harvard Law and Public Policy Review* 19 (Spring 1996), 680–81.

10. *Fisher v. University of Texas*, 570 U.S. 297, 331 (2013) (concurring).

11. *Adarand Constructors, Inc. v. Peña*, 515 U.S. 200, 241 (1995) (concurring); *Missouri v. Jenkins*, 515 U. S. 70, 120–21 (1995) (concurring); *Grutter v. Bollinger*, 539 U.S. 306, 377 (2003) (concurring in part and dissenting in part); *Parents Involved in Community Schools v. Seattle School District No. 1*, 551 U.S. 701, 759 (2007) (concurring); *Fisher v. University of Texas*, 570 U.S. 297, 331 (2013) (concurring). In his second year on the Court, Thomas did author an equal protection opinion in which he claimed that a government set-aside plan giving preferences to women and African Americans disadvantaged whites. What's notable about the opinion, however, is that in addition to coming early in Thomas's tenure, the opinion also garnered the support of defenders of affirmative action like Justices Stevens and Souter. Much of the case revolved around narrower and more technical questions, and Thomas did not pursue its claims later. *Northeastern Florida Chapter of the Associated General Contractors of America v. Jacksonville*, 508 U.S. 656 (1993).

12. Biskupic, *American Original*, 161, 175.

13. *Adarand Constructors, Inc. v. Peña*, 515 U.S. 200, 240–41 (1995) (concurring).

14. Edmund Morgan, *American Slavery, American Freedom: The Ordeal of Colonial America* (New York: Norton, 1975); Karen E. Fields and Barbara J. Fields, *Racecraft: The Soul of Inequality in American Life* (New York: Verso, 2012), 111–48.

15. *Adarand Constructors, Inc. v. Peña*, 515 U.S. 200, 243 (1995) (Stevens, dissenting).

16. *Fisher v. University of Texas*, 570 U.S. 297, 328–30 (2013) (concurring).

17. *Fisher v. University of Texas*, 570 U.S. 297, 328–30 (2013) (concurring); *Parents Involved in Community Schools v. Seattle School District No. 1*, 551 U.S. 701, 778n27 (2007) (concurring).

18. Kwame Ture (formerly known as Stokely Carmichael) and Charles Hamilton, *Black Power: The Politics of Liberation* (New York: Vintage, 1967, 1992), 61.

19. *Grutter v. Bollinger*, 539 U.S. 306, 367–68 (2003) (concurring in part and dissenting in part).

20. *Grutter v. Bollinger*, 539 U.S. 306, 373 (2003) (concurring in part and dissenting in part). Also see *Fisher v. University of Texas*, 515 U.S. 297, 334 (2013) (concurring).

21. *Adarand Constructors, Inc. v. Peña*, 516 U.S. 200, 270 (1995) (Souter, dissenting).

22. "The Second Annual William French Smith Memorial Lecture: A Conversation with Justice Clarence Thomas," *Pepperdine Law Review* 37 (2009), 22–23; *Adarand Constructors, Inc. v. Peña*, 515 U.S. 200, 241 (1995) (concurring); *Fisher v. University of Texas*, 515 U.S. 297, 333–34 (2013) (concurring).

23. *Fullilove v. Klutznick*, 448 U.S. 448, 545 (1980) (Stevens, dissenting); *Richmond v. J. A. Croson*, 488 U.S. 469, 516–17 (1989) (Stevens, concurring).

24. *Adarand Constructors, Inc. v. Peña*, 515 U.S. 200, 247–48 (1995) (Stevens, dissenting).

25. *Adarand Constructors, Inc. v. Peña*, 515 U.S. 200, 228–29 (1995) (O'Connor, concurring); *Grutter v. Bollinger*, 539 U.S. 306, 328 (2003) (O'Connor). In his dissent in *Fisher II*, Justice Alito seems, at first glance, to rely on this argument from stigma, but it's more narrowly tailored to the specifics of the University of Texas's affirmative action plan, and to the university's response to *Fisher I*, than it is to affirmative action as such. *Fisher v. University of Texas*, 136 S. Ct. 2198, 2215 (2016) (Alito, dissenting).

26. *Grutter v. Bollinger*, 539 U.S. 306, 343 (2003).

27. *Grutter v. Bollinger*, 539 U.S. 306, 386 (2003) (Rehnquist, dissenting).

28. *Grutter v. Bollinger*, 539 U.S. 306, 350 (2003) (concurring in part and dissenting in part).

29. *Grutter v. Bollinger*, 539 U.S. 306, 360 (2003) (concurring in part and dissenting in part).

30. *Grutter v. Bollinger*, 539 U.S. 306, 369 (2003) (concurring in part and dissenting in part).

31. *Grutter v. Bollinger*, 539 U.S. 306, 361, 367, 368, 370 (2003) (concurring in part and dissenting in part).

32. *Grutter v. Bollinger*, 539 U.S. 306, 367–68 (2003) (concurring in part and dissenting in part).

33. Harvard law scholar Tomiko Brown-Nagin argues that Thomas's position here parallels that of "the most radical voice in the litigation" over the law school's affirmative action program, a group of student activists known as BAMN. Thomas's position, Brown-Nagin adds, also contains "elements of the critique that scholars on the political left"—including Derrick Bell, Charles Lawrence, and Patricia Williams—"have made against traditional notions of merit for years." Thomas, incidentally, gave Derrick Bell's *And We Are Not Saved* a surprisingly sympathetic review in the pages of the *Wall Street Journal*. Tomiko Brown-Nagin, "The Transformational Politics of Justice Thomas? The *Grutter v. Bollinger* Opinion," *Journal of Constitutional Law* 7 (February 2005), 796–98, 799–804; Thomas, "The Black Experience: Rage and Reality," *Wall Street Journal* (October 12, 1987), 18. The invisible dialogue between Thomas and Critical Race Theory is discussed in Scott Douglas Gerber, *First Principles: The Jurisprudence of Clarence Thomas* (New York: New York University Press, 1999), 69–112.

34. *Grutter v. Bollinger*, 539 U.S. 306, 350 (2003) (concurring in part and dissenting in part).

35. *Grutter v. Bollinger*, 539 U.S. 306, 350 (2003) (concurring in part and dissenting in part).

36. *Grutter v. Bollinger*, 539 U.S. 306, 361 (2003) (concurring in part and dissenting in part).

37. *Grutter v. Bollinger*, 539 U.S. 306, 356 (2003) (concurring in part and dissenting in part).

38. *Grutter v. Bollinger*, 539 U.S. 306, 368 (2003) (concurring in part and dissenting in part). Along the same lines, Thomas writes: "Michigan has no compelling interest in having a law school at all, much less an *elite* one." "Having decided to use the LSAT, the Law School must accept the constitutional burdens that come with this decision. The Law School may freely continue to employ the LSAT and other allegedly merit-based standards in whatever fashion it likes. What the Equal Protection Clause forbids . . . is the use of these standards hand-in-hand with racial discrimination." *Grutter v. Bollinger*, 539 U.S. 306, 358, 370 (2003) (concurring in part and dissenting in part).

39. *Grutter v. Bollinger*, 539 U.S. 306, 370–71 (2003) (concurring in part and dissenting in part).

40. *Regents of the University of California v. Bakke*, 483 U.S. 265, 311–23 (1978).

41. *Grutter v. Bollinger*, 539 U.S. 306, 356 (2003) (concurring in part and dissenting in part).

42. *Fisher v. University of Texas*, 570 U.S. 297, 323 (2013) (concurring).

43. *Grutter v. Bollinger*, 539 U.S. 306, 355, 372 (2003) (concurring in part and dissenting in part).

44. *Grutter v. Bollinger*, 539 U.S. 306, 354, 355, 357, 361, 362, 364, 370, 372 (2003) (concurring in part and dissenting in part); *Parents Involved in Com-*

munity Schools v. Seattle School District No. 1, 551 U.S. 701, 750n3 (2007) (concurring).

45. *Grutter v. Bollinger*, 539 U.S. 306, 372n11–373 (2003) (concurring in part and dissenting in part). Also see *Parents Involved in Community Schools v. Seattle School District No. 1*, 551 U.S. 701, 750n3 (2007) (concurring).

46. *Adarand Constructors, Inc. v. Peña, Inc.*, 515 U.S. 200, 241 (1995) (concurring).

47. In the *Bakke* decision, Justice Powell made a similar reference to the Gilded Age jurisprudence of the Court: "It is far too late to argue that the guarantee of equal protection to all persons permits the recognition of special wards entitled to a degree of protection greater than that accorded others." That reference to special wards echoes a line from *Lochner v. New York*: "They [workers] are in no sense wards of the state." *Regents of the University of California v. Bakke*, 483 U.S. 265, 295 (1978); *Lochner v. New York*, 198 U.S. 45, 57 (1905). Justice Kennedy cited, without elaborating, that portion of Powell's *Bakke* opinion in *Fisher v. University of Texas*, 570 U.S. 297, 307 (2013) (Kennedy).

48. *Adarand Constructors, Inc. v. Peña*, 515 U.S. 200, 241 (1995) (concurring).

49. *Adarand Constructors, Inc. v. Peña*, 515 U.S. 200, 240 (1995) (concurring).

50. *Grutter v. Bollinger*, 539 U.S. 306, 354 (2003) (concurring in part and dissenting in part); *Fisher v. University of Texas*, 515 U.S. 297, 332 (2013) (concurring).

51. Juan Williams, "A Question of Fairness," *Atlantic Monthly* (February 1, 1987), 75; Bill Kauffman, "Clarence Thomas," *Reason* (November 1, 1987), 31; Foskett, *Judging Thomas*, 134; Thomas, *My Grandfather's Son*, 56, 92; Thomas, "Black America Under the Reagan Administration," *Policy Review* (Fall 1985), 31.

52. Foskett, *Judging Thomas*, 5; Michael C. Dawson, *Black Visions: The Roots of Contemporary African-American Political Ideologies* (Chicago: University of Chicago Press, 2001), 281–82, 300–302, 312–13.

53. *Grutter v. Bollinger*, 539 U.S. 306, 349 (2003) (concurring in part and dissenting in part).

54. Richard L. Hasen, *The Justice of Contradictions: Antonin Scalia and the Politics of Disruption* (New Haven, CT: Yale University Press, 2018), 80.

55. Ron Suskind, "And Clarence Thomas Wept," *Esquire* (July 1998), 73.

56. *Grutter v. Bollinger*, 539 U.S. 306, 364–65, 371–72 (2003) (concurring in part and dissenting in part); *Fisher v. University of Texas*, 515 U.S. 297, 331–34 (2013) (concurring).

57. Mark A. Graber, "Clarence Thomas," *Biographical Encyclopedia of the Supreme Court: The Lives and Legal Philosophies of the Justices*, ed. Melvin I. Urofsky (Washington, DC: CQ Press, 2006), 542–53.

58. Kevin Merida and Michael A. Fletcher, *Supreme Discomfort: The Divided Soul of Clarence Thomas* (New York: Doubleday, 2007), 67.

59. In *Brown*, the Court invoked the "modern authority" of "psychological knowledge" as part of its decision, citing the doll experiments of social psychologists

Kenneth and Mamie Clark, in which black children given the choice of a black or a white doll tended to describe the white one as the "nice" doll they preferred to play with. Their choice of the white dolls was interpreted to mean that they had internalized white society's message of their inferiority, leading the Court to argue that separating schoolchildren on the basis of race "generates a feeling of inferiority [in the black students] as to their status in the community that may affect their hearts and minds in a way unlikely ever to be undone." Even if the state distributed material resources equally to segregated schools, the *Brown* Court reasoned, the mere fact of separation would undermine the self-esteem, the confidence and motivation, of black students, making it difficult for them to learn and develop at the same rate or to the same extent as white students. According to Thomas, that turn to psychology, which he claims is rife throughout the legal profession, is illegitimate. It relies upon the dubious status of internal "feelings" rather than objective externalities of justice and the law. "Psychological injury" and "psychological feelings of inferiority," he wrote in one opinion, are "irrelevant." *Brown v. Board of Education of Topeka, Kansas*, 347 U.S. 483, 494 (1954); Thomas, "An Afro-American Perspective: Toward a 'Plain Reading' of the Constitution," *Howard Law Journal* 30 (1987), 698–99; "Comments of Justice Clarence Thomas," *Thurgood Marshall Law Review* 23 (Fall 1997), 8; Thomas, "Civil Rights as a Principle Versus Civil Rights as an Interest," in *Assessing the Reagan Years*, ed. David Boaz (Washington, DC: Cato, 1988), 392–93; *Missouri v. Jenkins*, 515 U.S. 70, 121 (1995) (concurring). For a fuller discussion of the role of psychology in the Court's civil rights jurisprudence as well as in broader political and cultural debates about race, see Daryl Michael Scott, *Contempt and Pity: Social Policy and the Image of the Damaged Black Psyche, 1880–1996* (Chapel Hill: University of North Carolina Press, 1997).

60. Thomas, "Remembering an Island of Hope in an Era of Despair," *Lincoln Review* (Spring 1986), 58; Thomas, "Minorities, Youth, and Education," *Journal of Labor Research* 3 (Fall 1982), 444; Thomas, "Civil Rights as a Principle," 393.

61. *Hearings Before the Senate Committee on the Judiciary*, 102nd Cong., 1st sess., September 10, 11, 12, 13, 17, 19, 20, 1991, and October 11, 12, 13, 1991, Part 1, 488.

62. *Missouri v. Jenkins*, 515 U.S. 70, 120, 122 (1995) (concurring). Also see Thomas's dismissal of concerns about "racial imbalance," and how "racial imbalance is not segregation." *Parents Involved in Community Schools v. Seattle School District No. 1*, 551 U.S. 701, 749 (2007) (concurring).

63. Thomas, "The Black Experience," 18. Also see *Senate Confirmation Hearings*, Part 1, 250; Thomas, "Thomas Sowell and the Heritage of Lincoln," *Lincoln Review* (Spring 1988), 7, 9, 11. Thomas does write elsewhere that a colorblind Constitution is "a necessary condition for a colorblind society," but he does not claim that it will bring about such a society. Indeed, he claims

that such a society "is certainly beyond the power of legislation alone." Thomas, "An Afro-American Perspective," 700.

64. Peyton, *Clarence Thomas*, 196–97; Thomas, "Black colleges not alone," *Afro-American* (April 23, 1983), 4; Martha Biondi, *The Black Revolution on Campus* (Berkeley: University of California Press, 2012), 33–35; Merida and Fletcher, *Supreme Discomfort*, 152–53; Phelps and Winternitz, *Capitol Games*, 89, 144–45.

65. Thomas, "Minorities, Youth, and Education," 437. Also see Chester A. Higgins, Sr., "'We Are Going to Enforce the Law!' Interview with Clarence Thomas, Chairman, EEOC," *The Crisis* (February 1983), 52.

66. Jeffrey Rosen, "Moving On," *New Yorker* (April 29, 1996), 66. Also see Andy Guess, "Clarence Thomas, Champion of Black Colleges," *Inside Higher Ed* (September 10, 2008), https://www.insidehighered.com/news/2008/09/10/thomas.

67. Graber, "Clarence Thomas," 542–53.

68. Peyton, *Clarence Thomas*, 277.

69. *Fisher v. University of Texas*, 570 U.S. 229, 332–33 (2013) (concurring).

70. *Grutter v. Bollinger*, 539 U.S. 306, 372 (2003) (concurring in part and dissenting in part).

71. *Grutter v. Bollinger*, 539 U.S. 306, 364 (2003) (concurring in part and dissenting in part); *Fisher v. University of Texas*, 570 U.S. 229, 332–33 (2013) (concurring).

72. *Grutter v. Bollinger*, 539 U.S. 306, 364–65 (2003) (concurring in part and dissenting in part).

73. *United States v. Fordice*, 505 U.S. 717, 748 (1992) (concurring).

74. *Parents Involved in Community Schools v. Seattle School District No. 1*, 551 U.S. 701, 763–66 (2007) (concurring); *Grutter v. Bollinger*, 539 U.S. 306, 364–65 (2003) (concurring in part and dissenting in part).

75. *United States v. Fordice*, 505 U.S. 717, 745, 748, 749 (1992) (concurring).

4. WHITE MAN, BLACK MARKET

1. Thomas, *My Grandfather's Son: A Memoir* (New York: HarperCollins, 2007), 73, 86–89; Ken Foskett, *Judging Thomas: The Life and Times of Clarence Thomas* (New York: HarperPerennial, 2004), 128–35; Kevin Merida and Michael A. Fletcher, *Supreme Discomfort: The Divided Soul of Clarence Thomas* (New York: Doubleday, 2007), 132–36; Andrew Peyton, *Clarence Thomas: A Biography* (San Francisco: Encounter, 2001), 147–50.

2. Speech at *Headway* Magazine National Leadership Conference (September 1998), reprinted in *Headway* 10 (December 31, 1998), 10, and in "Black Conservatives Have Walked Long Way," *Richmond Times-Dispatch* (April 18, 1999), F1; Merida and Fletcher, *Supreme Discomfort*, 112–13, 353; Thomas, *My Grandfather's Son*, 76–77; Foskett, *Judging Thomas*, 128, 256; Peyton, *Clarence Thomas*, 150, 502.

3. In his *Reason* interview, Thomas claims that the Sowell volume that inspired him was *The Economics and Politics of Race*. But that book did not come out until 1983. In his memoir, Thomas correctly reports the title as *Race and Economics*. Bill Kauffman, "Clarence Thomas," *Reason* (November 1, 1987), 30; Thomas, *My Grandfather's Son*, 107; Foskett, *Judging Thomas*, 142; Peyton, *Clarence Thomas*, 162–62; Merida and Fletcher, *Supreme Discomfort*, 141–43.

4. Thomas, *My Grandfather's Son*, 107; Merida and Fletcher, *Supreme Discomfort*, 143; Kay Cole James, interview with Clarence Thomas (1996), http://justicethomas.blogspot.com/2007/09/neopolitique-interview.html; Thomas Sowell, *A Personal Odyssey* (New York: Free Press, 2000), 270; "Sexual Equality Under the Fourteenth and Equal Rights Amendments: Panel Discussion," *Washington University Law Review* 1 (1979), 205–6. I am grateful to Irin Carmon for bringing the Sowell memoir and this law review article to my attention, which helped confirm the presence of Bader Ginsburg at this debate.

5. Peyton, *Clarence Thomas*, 153, 164; Merida and Fletcher, *Supreme Discomfort*, 141; Foskett, *Judging Thomas*, 146.

6. Thomas, *My Grandfather's Son*, 133, 137; Juan Williams, "Black Conservatives, Center Stage," *Washington Post* (December 16, 1980), A21; Leah Wright Rigueur, *The Loneliness of the Black Republican: Pragmatic Politics and the Pursuit of Power* (Princeton, NJ: Princeton University Press, 2014), 294–300.

7. Jane Mayer and Jill Abramson, *Strange Justice: The Selling of Clarence Thomas* (Boston: Houghton Mifflin, 1994), 70; Thomas, *My Grandfather's Son*, 106–7.

8. Thomas Sowell, *Race and Economics* (New York: David McKay, 1975), xvi, 48, 51–52, 53, 127, 128, 140, 142.

9. Ibid., 13–14.

10. Ibid., 29–30.

11. After he joined the Court, Thomas retained his interest in the relationship between slavery and capitalism, patiently explaining to journalist Jeffrey Rosen the differences between the Marxist analysis of Eugene Genovese's *Roll, Jordan, Roll* and the econometric analysis of Robert Fogel and Stanley Engerman's *Time on the Cross*. Jeffrey Rosen, "Moving On," *New Yorker* (April 29, 1996), 73.

12. Kay Cole James, interview with Clarence Thomas (1996), http://justicethomas.blogspot.com/2007/09/neopolitique-interview.html.

13. Thomas, *My Grandfather's Son*, 59–65.

14. Thomas, *My Grandfather's Son*, 61–62; Diane Brady, *Fraternity* (New York: Spiegel & Grau, 2012), 170, 180–81; Foskett, *Judging Thomas*, 280.

15. Thomas, *My Grandfather's Son*, 72–73.

16. Peyton, *Clarence Thomas*, 138; Kim Masters, "EEOC's Thomas: Ready to Sing a Different Tune?," *Legal Times* (December 24/31, 1984), 2.

17. A good example of Thomas's ambivalence in the early 1980s can be found in

his "Current Litigation Trends and Goals at the EEOC," *Labor Law Journal* (April 1983), 208–14. Also see Thomas, "Black America Under the Reagan Administration," *Policy Review* (Fall 1985), 41; Chester A. Higgins, Sr., "'We Are Going to Enforce the Law!' Interview with Clarence Thomas, Chairman, EEOC," *The Crisis* (February 1983), 52. As late as 1987, Thomas was suggesting he was open to the idea of criminal prosecution and punishment, including jail, for violators of antidiscrimination law. Thomas, "Affirmative Action Goals and Timetables: Too Tough? Not Tough Enough!" *Yale Law & Policy Review* 5 (Spring–Summer 1987), 408. The most comprehensive (and highly critical) discussion of Thomas's changing positions on affirmative action during his time at the EEOC is the memorandum prepared by the Lawyers Committee for Civil Rights Under Law and presented to the Senate during Thomas's confirmation hearings. See Memorandum (n.d.), 51–76, *Hearings Before the Senate Committee on the Judiciary*, 102nd Cong., 1st sess., September 10, 11, 12, 13, 17, 19, 20, 1991, and October 11, 12, 13, 1991, Part 2, 203–28. Also see "Judge Clarence Thomas: 'An Overall Disdain for the Rule of Law,'" People for the American Way, July 30, 1991, 11–14, in *Senate Confirmation Hearings*, Part 2, 829–32; Timothy M. Phelps and Helen Winternitz, *Capitol Games: The Inside Story of Clarence Thomas, Anita Hill, and a Supreme Court Nomination* (New York: HarperPerennial, 1992), 96–97, 103–9; Foskett, *Judging Thomas*, 167; Merida and Fletcher, *Supreme Discomfort*, 160, 162; Peyton, *Clarence Thomas*, 223, 240–44.

18. For an excellent account of the contradictions of the 1970s, see the essays gathered in *Rightward Bound: Making America Conservative in the 1970s*, ed. Bruce J. Schulman and Julian Zelizer (Cambridge, MA: Harvard University Press, 2008).

19. Daniel Rodgers offers a vivid rendition of this disaffection, as it was registered in the intellectual sphere, in his *Age of Fracture* (Cambridge, MA: Harvard University Press, 2012).

20. Martha Biondi, *The Black Revolution on Campus* (Berkeley: University of California Press, 2012), 21–22.

21. Thomas J. Sugrue, *Sweet Land of Liberty: The Forgotten Struggle for Civil Rights in the North* (New York: Random House, 2008), 494–97.

22. Tommie Shelby, *We Who Are Dark: The Philosophical Foundations of Black Solidarity* (Cambridge, MA: Harvard University Press, 2005), 26, 30, 103–4; Wilson Jeremiah Moses, *The Golden Age of Black Nationalism, 1850–1925* (New York: Oxford University Press, 1978, 1988), 7, 9, 45; Dean E. Robinson, *Black Nationalism in American Politics and Thought* (New York: Cambridge University Press, 2001), 4–5; Robert L. Allen, *Black Awakening in Capitalist America* (Trenton, NJ: Africa World Press, 1990 [1969]), 19, 23; Michael C. Dawson, *Black Visions: The Roots of Contemporary African-American Political Ideologies* (Chicago: University of Chicago Press, 2001), 133, 316, 322.

23. Sugrue, *Sweet Land of Liberty*, 494–95.

24. Cedric Johnson, *Revolutionaries to Race Leaders: Black Power and the Making of African American Politics* (Minneapolis: University of Minnesota Press, 2007), 95; James Williams, "Wanted: A Basis for Unity in Black Education," *The Crisis* 80 (August–September 1973), 247; Sugrue, *Sweet Land of Liberty*, 445–48.

25. Johnson, *Revolutionaries to Race Leaders*, xxiii, 35–36, 62, 79–80, 104–5; Sugrue, *Sweet Land of Liberty*, 497–505.

26. Charles Hamilton, "Afterword, 1992," in Kwame Ture (formerly known as Stokely Carmichael) and Charles Hamilton, *Black Power: The Politics of Liberation* (New York: Vintage, 1967, 1992), 208–11.

27. Johnson, *Revolutionaries to Race Leaders*, 57–68; Allen, *Black Awakening in Capitalist America*, 17–19, 21–22, 48; Sugrue, *Sweet Land of Liberty*, 433–34, 440–41; Robinson, *Black Nationalism in American Politics and Thought*, 73, 77, 79, 94.

28. *The Business of Black Power: Community Development, Capitalism, and Corporate Responsibility in Postwar America*, ed. Laura Warren Hill and Julia Rabig (Rochester, NY: University of Rochester Press, 2012), 4, 16, 25–26, 30–31, 41, 45–46; Allen, *Black Awakening in Capitalist America*, 153–56, 158–64, 182–92, 216–45; Sugrue, *Sweet Land of Liberty*, 427–43.

29. *The Autobiography of Malcolm X* (New York: Ballantine, 1964), 281; Juan Williams, "A Question of Fairness," *Atlantic Monthly* (February 1, 1987), 73.

30. Johnson, *Revolutionaries to Race Leaders*, 125.

31. For an eye-opening set of accounts, particularly at the local level, see the essays collected in *Black Power at Work: Community Control, Affirmative Action, and the Construction Industry*, ed. David Goldberg and Trevor Griffey (Ithaca, NY: Cornell University Press, 2010).

32. Sugrue, *Sweet Land of Liberty*, 442; Rigueur, *The Loneliness of the Black Republican*, 136–37, 149–64.

33. Sugrue, *Sweet Land of Liberty*, 443; Allen, *Black Awakening in Capitalist America*, 227–31.

34. Rigueur, *The Loneliness of the Black Republican*, 296.

35. Amiri Baraka, "Malcolm as Ideology," *The LeRoi Jones/Amiri Baraka Reader*, ed. William J. Harris (New York: Basic, 1999), 509.

36. Thomas, *My Grandfather's Son*, 46.

37. Joshua Bloom and Waldo E. Martin Jr., *Black Against Empire: The History and Politics of the Black Panther Party* (Oakland: University of California Press, 2013, 2016), 159.

38. Thomas, "Savannah State College Commencement Address" (June 9, 1985), in Thomas, *Confronting the Future: Selections from the Senate Confirmation Hearings and Prior Speeches* (Washington, DC: Regnery Gateway, 1992), 34.

39. William Raspberry, "Are the Problems of Blacks Too Big for Government to Solve?," *Washington Post* (July 17, 1983), C3.

40. Nancy MacLean, *Freedom Is Not Enough: The Opening of the American Workplace* (Cambridge, MA: Harvard University Press, 2006), 236–37.

41. Juan Williams, "Black Conservatives, Center Stage," *Washington Post* (December 16, 1980), A21. Also see Thomas, "No Room at the Inn: The Loneliness of the Black Conservative," in *Black and Right: The Bold New Voice of Black Conservatives in America*, ed. Stan Faryna, Brad Stetson, and Joseph G. Contti (Westport, CT: Praeger, 1997), 7.

42. Peyton, *Clarence Thomas*, 173–74.

43. *Headway* 10 (December 31, 1998), 10; "Black Conservatives Have Walked a Long Way," *Richmond Times-Dispatch* (April 18, 1999), F1; Thomas, speech to the annual convention of the National Bar Association (Memphis, 1998), reprinted as "Justice Thomas Answers His Critics," *New York Post* (July 31, 1998), 25. Dillard describes a similar phenomenon among other black conservatives wrestling with and laying claim to the tradition of black nationalism. See Angela D. Dillard, *Guess Who's Coming to Dinner Now? Multicultural Conservatism in America* (New York: New York University Press, 2001), 31–32.

44. Thomas, "With Liberty . . . for All," 43. After working in the Reagan and Bush administrations, libertarians Chip Mellor and Clint Bolick (who had been close to Thomas when they worked together at the EEOC, and who played a critical role in pushing for Thomas's nomination to the Court) deftly challenged state licensing laws in court in part by working with plaintiffs of color such as African American hair braiders in San Diego. Jeffrey Rosen, "The Unregulated Offensive," *New York Times Magazine* (April 17, 2005), 47. On the relationship between race and licensing laws from a libertarian perspective, see David E. Bernstein, *Only One Place of Redress: African Americans, Labor Regulations, and the Courts from Reconstruction to the New Deal* (Durham, NC: Duke University Press, 2001), 28–45.

45. Thomas, letter to the editor, *Washington Times* (September 2, 1987), A9; Peyton, *Clarence Thomas*, 299–300; Thomas, "Black America Under the Reagan Administration," 36; Thomas, "Thomas Sowell and the Heritage of Lincoln," *Lincoln Review* (Spring 1988), 13–15; Thomas, "Thank You, Walter Williams," *Human Events* (October 6, 2003), 3.

46. Phelps and Winternitz, *Capitol Games*, 87–88; Raspberry, "Are the Problems of Blacks Too Big for Government to Solve?," C3. Also see Sowell, *Race and Economics*, 166–68.

47. Thomas, "Victims and Heroes in the 'Benevolent State,'" *Harvard Law and Public Policy Review* 19 (Spring 1996), 682; "Justice Thomas Answers His Critics," 25.

48. Sowell makes a similar claim. Sowell, *Race and Economics*, 3, 30–33, 60, 126.

49. Raspberry, "Are the Problems of Blacks Too Big for Government to Solve?," C3.

50. Ibid.

51. Lyndon Johnson, Commencement Address at Howard University (June 4, 1965), http://www.presidency.ucsb.edu/ws/?pid=27021.

52. Raspberry, "Are the Problems of Blacks Too Big for Government to Solve?," C3.

53. As Thomas put it, "You're using a statute at the employment level to try to deal with that, okay? . . . We're trying to remedy all of that with this one little enfeebled statute! It simply isn't going to happen." Raspberry, "Are the Problems of Blacks Too Big for Government to Solve?," C3.

54. Thomas, letter to the editor, *Christian Science Monitor* (March 10, 1987), 17; Thomas, letter to the editor, *New York Times* (February 1, 1987), F22.

55. Thomas, "Black America Under the Reagan Administration," 33; Williams, "A Question of Fairness," 79.

56. Kauffman, "Clarence Thomas," 32.

57. Williams, "A Question of Fairness," 72. Also see Thomas, "Thomas Sowell and the Heritage of Lincoln," 13–14.

58. Peyton, *Clarence Thomas*, 300.

59. Thomas, speech to Pacific Research Institute, *Senate Confirmation Hearings*, Part 1, 154; Merida and Fletcher, *Supreme Discomfort*, 58, 61–62.

60. Thomas, "Victims and Heroes," 681.

61. On one occasion, Thomas did offer a mild endorsement of wage labor, but it applied only to younger people: "I never would have had my first job if I had to make the minimum wage, but the benefits of the job were more than just the salary: getting up, going to work, working hard, doing a good job, not destroying my boss's equipment, just being responsible." On another occasion, in which he celebrated the "dignity" of labor, he didn't discuss the wage but instead focused on the value of physical labor and hard work. And when he did finally mention the wage, it was merely to say that the individual had a "natural right to earn from one's labor" and that anything that detracted from that notion was a form of slavery. Thomas, "Black America Under the Reagan Administration," 37; Thomas, speech to Pacific Research Institute, in *Senate Confirmation Hearings*, Part 1, 164, 165, 166.

62. Thomas, *My Grandfather's Son*, 46–47; Peyton, *Clarence Thomas*, 66–67. Thomas's antipathy to wage labor is notable, given how often he invokes the authority of Frederick Douglass, for whom, at least in his earlier writing, the wage was a critical emblem of freedom. *Grutter v. Bollinger*, 539 U.S. 306, 349 (2003) (concurring in part and dissenting in part); *Narrative of the Life of Frederick Douglass, an American Slave, Written by Himself*, ed. William Andrews and William McFeeley (New York: Norton, 1997), 74. In his later years, Douglass became more ambivalent about wage labor. Cf. his "Address to the People of the United States" (1883), in *Frederick Douglass: Selected Speeches and Writings*, ed. Philip S. Foner (Chicago: Lawrence Hill Books, 1950, 1999), 676–79.

63. Thomas, "Freedom: A Responsibility, Not a Right: Kormendy Lecture," *Ohio Northern University Law Review* 21, no. 1 (1994), 10.

64. Thomas, speech to Pacific Research Institute, 154–56; Peyton, *Clarence Thomas*, 34, 65–66; Thomas, *My Grandfather's Son*, 46–47.

65. Raspberry, "Are the Problems of Blacks Too Big for Government to Solve?," C3.

66. Interestingly, in an article where Thomas attempts to set out that "success (as well as failure) is the result of one's own talents, morals, decisions, and actions," he winds up arguing the very opposite: that much of the failure and weakness of individuals in contemporary society is due to a pervasive legal culture and set of institutions that encourage that failure and sustain that weakness, and that Thomas owes his success to "my family and my community" that did so much "to reinforce this message of self-determination and self-worth." Thomas, "Victims and Heroes," 671, 682–83.

67. Thomas, speech to Pacific Research Institute, 155; Thomas, "Freedom: A Responsibility," 10.

68. Johnson, *Revolutionaries to Race Leaders*, 65. The patriarchal elements of black nationalism, with its heavy investment in the status of black men, are usefully explored in E. Frances White, "Africa on My Mind: Gender, Counter Discourse and African-American Nationalism," *Journal of Women's History* 2 (Spring 1990), 73–97; Shelby, *We Who Are Dark*, 8–9, 122–23, 226–27; Allen, *Black Awakening in Capitalist America*, 168–71; Robinson, *Black Nationalism*, 68–69, 113–14.

69. Thomas, "Freedom: A Responsibility," 4.

70. Merida and Fletcher, *Supreme Discomfort*, 55–60; Foskett, *Judging Thomas*, 18–19, 42. The pride Thomas takes in his grandfather's stature and achievements also sits uneasily with his claims that Anderson was at the bottom of Savannah's black community, the object of ridicule and scorn from lighter-skinned, wealthier African Americans.

71. Toni Morrison, "Introduction: Friday on the Potomac," in *Race-ing Justice, En-gendering Power: Essays on Anita Hill, Clarence Thomas, and the Construction of Social Reality*, ed. Toni Morrison (New York: Pantheon, 1992), xx–xxi.

72. Pacific Research Institute mission statement, https://www.pacificresearch.org /mission-statement/.

73. Ibid., 156–58.

74. Ibid., 158.

75. Ibid., 157.

76. Ibid., 154.

5. AGAINST POLITICS

1. Angela D. Dillard, *Guess Who's Coming to Dinner Now? Multicultural Conservatism in America* (New York: New York University Press, 2001), 41.

2. Juan Williams, "A Question of Fairness," *Atlantic Monthly* (February 1, 1987), 79.

3. *Morse v. Republican Party of Virginia* 517 U.S. 186, 253 (1996) (dissenting); *Lopez v. Monterey County*, 525 U.S. 266, 291–92 (1999) (dissenting); *Arizona v. Inter Tribal Council of Arizona*, 570 U.S. 1, 22 (2013)

(dissenting); *Husted v. A. Philip Randolph Institute*, 138 S. Ct. 1833, 1848 (2018) (concurring). Thomas repeats that move of deferring to the states in other voting rights cases that are not about ballot access: *Cook v. Gralike*, 531 U.S. 510, 530 (2001) (concurring); *Northwest Austin v. Holder*, 557 U.S. 193, 212, 226–29 (2009) (concurring in part and dissenting in part); *Perry v. Perez*, 565 U.S. 388, 399 (2012) (concurring); *Shelby County v. Holder*, 570 U.S. 529, 557 (2013 (concurring); *Evenwel v. Abbott*, 136 S. Ct. 1120, 1133 (2016) (concurring). Whether the case is about ballot access or voting power, Thomas is willing to use the Court—or to defer to lower courts—in order to overrule the actions of state legislatures when he believes race has been a factor in their decisions. He is more likely to see race as a factor, however, when those legislatures are acting to enhance the voting rights or power of African Americans. When they are not acting on behalf of that interest, Thomas tends to view their actions as being in accordance with "traditional, race-neutral" principles. Whatever the jurisprudential integrity of these decisions, they are in keeping with Thomas's skepticism about the project of enhancing the voting power of African Americans. *Bush v. Vera*, 517 U.S. 952, 1001 (1996) (concurring); *Hunt v. Cromartie*, 526 U.S. 541, 547 (1999); *Easley v. Cromartie*, 532 U.S. 234, 265–67 (2001) (dissenting).

4. *Holder v. Hall*, 512 U.S. 874, 891–92, 896–97, 900, 902, 909, 912, 924, 939 (1994) (concurring).

5. *Holder v. Hall*, 512 U.S. 874, 876–82, 885.

6. *Johnson v. De Grandy*, 512 U.S. 997, 1031–32 (1994) (dissenting); *Reno v. Bossier Parish School Board*, 520 U.S. 471, 490 (1997) (concurring); *Georgia v. Ashcroft*, 539 U.S. 461, 492 (2003) (concurring); *Bartlett v. Strickland*, 556 U.S. 1, 26 (2009) (concurring); *Cooper v. Harris*, 137 S. Ct. 1455, 1485–86 (2017) (concurring); *Abbott v. Perez*, 138 S. Ct. 2305, 2335 (2018) (concurring).

7. *Holder v. Hall*, 512 U.S. 874, 907 (1994) (concurring).

8. *Holder v. Hall*, 512 U.S. 874, 903 (1994) (concurring). Though the term "racial groups" applies in theory to whites, Asian Americans, Latinx, and other groups, it's clear from his opinion that Thomas is thinking of African Americans. And while some have argued that Thomas is making a descriptive, perhaps even normative, claim that African Americans don't have a collective interest as a group—that is, each black person has only an individual interest, which may or may not have anything to do with race—that is not the thrust of Thomas's argument in *Holder*. Scott Douglas Gerber, *First Principles: The Jurisprudence of Clarence Thomas* (New York: New York University Press, 1999), 86–97; Scott D. Gerber, "Clarence Thomas, *Fisher v. University of Texas*, and the Future of Affirmative Action in Higher Education," *University of Richmond Law Review* 50 (2016), 1183; Nathan W. Dean, "The Primacy of the Individual in the Political Philosophy and Civil Rights Jurisprudence of Justice Clarence Thomas," *George Mason University Civil Rights Law Journal* 14 (2004), 48; Ralph Rossum, *Understanding*

Clarence Thomas: The Jurisprudence of Constitutional Restoration (Lawrence: University Press of Kansas, 2014), 190.

9. *Holder v. Hall*, 512 U.S. 874, 906 (1994) (concurring). It's telling how absent opposition to racial essentialism is from Thomas's opinion, given that it played a critical role in his discourse at an earlier phase of his conservatism. See Thomas, "Pluralism Lives: Blacks *Don't* All Think Alike," *Los Angeles Times* (November 15, 1985), C9. On the other hand, during his brief tenure on the Court of Appeals, Thomas did author one opinion where he accepted without challenge the claim that radio stations owned by African Americans were more likely to offer programming and news that was of interest to African Americans than were stations not owned by African Americans. There were no such disparities, Thomas went on to argue, in the case of gender: stations owned by women were not more likely to support women-related programming than were other stations. Though Thomas, as an appellate judge, was following the Court's findings with respect to race, the distinctions drawn between race and gender do suggest a greater sympathy to notions of there being programming of distinct interest to African Americans that African American ownership would facilitate—which makes Thomas's distrust of arguments on the Court about the translation of African American views into organized political interests all the more stark. *Lamprecht v. FCC*, 958 F.2d 382 (1992).

10. *Holder v. Hall*, 512 U.S. 874, 906 (1994) (concurring). This element of Thomas's opinion in *Holder* builds on his long-standing insistence that though African Americans have collective interests and a shared fate, they should resist the impulse to pursue those interests or contest that fate through electoral means. In the 1980s, wrote Williams, Thomas rejected "civil rights as a matter of corporate struggle and group equity." Yet he was equally critical of a fellow black conservative who, he claimed, "minimizes the unique problems of blacks usually portrayed as a *group* experience." The target of Thomas's critique, in other words, was not the idea that African Americans are a group but the idea of politically mobilizing African Americans as a group—"Blacks [voting] as Blacks," as he put it, blacks voting as a collectively organized, self-identified, coherent bloc. Williams, "A Question of Fairness," 79; Thomas, "With Liberty . . . For All," *Lincoln Review* (Winter–Spring 1982), 42.

11. *Holder v. Hall*, 512 U.S. 874, 898–901, 918–19 (1994) (concurring).

12. *Holder v. Hall*, 512 U.S. 874, 899, 900 (1994) (concurring).

13. For a fuller discussion of these issues, see Paul Frymer, *Uneasy Alliances: Race and Party Competition in America* (Princeton, NJ: Princeton University Press, 1999).

14. Thomas, "Why Black Americans Should Look to Conservative Policies," 17; Thomas, "Republicans Can Win Black Votes," *New Pittsburgh Courier* (March 7, 1987), 4; Leah Wright Rigueur, *The Loneliness of the Black Republican* (Princeton, NJ: Princeton University Press, 2015), 261.

15. *Holder v. Hall*, 512 U. S. 874, 899, 900, 919 (1994) (concurring). Thomas came to a similar conclusion about the disutility of the "influence" model, albeit for different reasons, in *Reno v. Bossier Parish School Board*, 520 U.S. 471, 491 (1997) (concurring).

16. *Holder v. Hall*, 512 U.S. 874, 901 (1994) (Thomas, concurring).

17. *Holder v. Hall*, 512 U.S. 874, 905, 906, 928, 936 (1994) (concurring). Emphasis added. In a more recent voting rights case, Thomas was even more explicit in his construction: "Long ago, the DOJ [Department of Justice] and special-interest groups like the ACLU hijacked the [Voting Rights] Act, and they have been using it ever since to achieve their vision of maximized black electoral strength, often at the expense of the voters they purport to help." *Alabama Legislative Black Caucus v. Alabama*, 135 S. Ct. 1257, 1288 (2015) (dissenting). In *Easley*, Thomas continued to portray African Americans as objects, emphasizing that the North Carolina legislature drew its racially gerrymandered district lines "based on the stereotype that blacks are reliable Democratic voters." *Easley v. Cromartie*, 532 U.S. 234, 266–67 (2001) (dissenting).

18. Albert O. Hirschman, *The Rhetoric of Reaction: Perversity, Futility, Jeopardy* (Cambridge, MA: Harvard University Press, 1991), 43–44, 46.

19. Thomas, "EEOC Chairman Confronts Difficult Challenges," *Skanner* 8 (April 20, 1983), 5; speech to the American Society of Personnel Administrators (1983), cited in Timothy M. Phelps and Helen Winternitz, *Capitol Games: The Inside Story of Clarence Thomas, Anita Hill, and a Supreme Court Nomination* (New York: HarperPerennial, 1992), 97–98.

20. "Judge Clarence Thomas: A Record Lacking in Support of Women's Legal Rights," National Women's Law Center (August 20, 1991), 29–31, 57–59, 70–74, and "Endangered Liberties: What Judge Clarence Thomas' Record Portends for Women," Women's Legal Defense Fund (July 30, 1991), 26–29, in *Hearings Before the Senate Committee on the Judiciary*, 102nd Cong., 1st sess., September 10, 11, 12, 13, 17, 19, 20, 1991, and October 11, 12, 13, 1991, Part 2, 316–18, 344–46, 357–61, 409–12.

21. Thomas, "Pay Equity and Comparable Worth," *Labor Law Journal* 34 (January 1, 1983), 4, 7–8.

22. Thomas, letter to the editor, *Washington Post* (July 3, 1985), A16; also see letter to the editor, *Washington Post* (July 1, 1984), C6.

23. Thomas, "Thomas Sowell and the Heritage of Lincoln," *Lincoln Review* 8 (Winter 1988), 15–16.

24. Phelps and Winternitz, *Capitol Games*, 103, 109; Peyton, *Clarence Thomas*, 259, 262, 276.

25. *Senate Confirmation Hearings*, Part 2, 100, 107; "On the Nomination of Clarence Thomas as an Associate Justice of the United States Supreme Court," Lawyers Committee for Civil Rights Under Law (1991), 40–46, in *Senate Confirmation Hearings*, Part 2, 192–98; "Judge Clarence Thomas: A Record Lacking in Support of Women's Legal Rights," 70–71, in *Senate Confirmation Hearings*, Part 2, 357–58.

26. *Texas Department of Housing and Community Affairs v. Inclusive Communities Project*, 135 S. Ct. 2507, 2525 (2015) (Kennedy); *Texas Department of Housing and Community Affairs v. Inclusive Communities Project*, 135 S. Ct. 2507, 2532 (2015) (Alito, dissenting); *Griggs v. Duke Power Co.*, 401 U. S. 424, 431 (1971).

27. *Texas Department of Housing and Community Affairs v. Inclusive Communities Project*, 135 S. Ct. 2507, 2526 (2015) (dissenting).

28. "Disparate-impact doctrine defies reality itself. In their quest to eradicate what they view as institutionalized discrimination, disparate-impact proponents doggedly assume that a given racial disparity at an institution is a product of that institution rather than a reflection of the disparities that exist outside of it." Among advocates of disparate impact, there is an "unstated—and unsubstantiated—assumption," writes Thomas, "that, in the absence of discrimination, an institution's racial makeup would mirror that of society." But that assumption fails to reckon with the fact that "the absence of racial disparities in multiethnic societies has been the exception, not the rule." *Texas Department of Housing and Community Affairs v. Inclusive Communities Project*, 135 S. Ct. 2507, 2529–30 (2015) (dissenting).

29. Interestingly, in non-race-related cases where Thomas voices his opposition to disparate impact—one in the context of age, another in the context of religion, and two in the context of poverty—he includes no larger sociological analysis of inequalities involving age, religion, or poverty, as he does in the context of race. In these cases, his analysis is much more straightforwardly legal and formal. *Lewis v. Casey*, 518 U.S. 343, 373–77 (1996) (concurring); *M.L.B. v. S.L.J.*, 519 US. 102, 133–39 (1996) (dissenting); *Meacham v. Knolls Atomic Power Lab*, 554 U.S. 84, 104 (2008) (concurring in part and dissenting in part); *EEOC v. Abercrombie & Fitch*, 135 S. Ct. 2028, 2037 (2015) (concurring in part and dissenting in part).

30. Hirschman, *Rhetoric of Reaction*, 7, 11, 57–58.

31. *Kelo v. City of New London*, 545 U.S. 469, 472–75 (2005) (Stevens); Ilya Somin, "The Story behind Kelo v. City of New London," *Washington Post* (May 29, 2015), https://www.washingtonpost.com/news/volokh-conspiracy/wp/2015/05/29/the-story-behind-the-kelo-case-how-an-obscure-takings-case-came-to-shock-the-conscience-of-the-nation.

32. Even though race plays a role, albeit limited, in the classic conservative treatment of eminent domain and the Takings Clause, it seems to play almost no role at all in the conservative Court's Takings jurisprudence. See Richard A. Epstein, *Takings: Private Property and the Power of Eminent Domain* (Cambridge, MA: Harvard University Press, 1985), 210–15, 324–25.

33. *Kelo v. City of New London*, 545 U.S. 469, 483–87 (2005) (Stevens); *Kelo v. City of New London*, 545 U.S. 469, 501 (2005) (O'Connor, dissenting).

34. *Kelo v. City of New London*, 545 U.S. 469, 505 (2005) (O'Connor, dissenting).

35. While Thomas's opinion in *Kelo* is his sole Takings opinion to address the question of race, his other Takings and regulatory Takings opinions are much

shorter and address narrower, more technical questions. See *Eastern Enterprises v. Apfel*, 524 U.S. 498, 538–39 (1998) (concurring); *Tahoe-Sierra Preservation Council v. Tahoe Regional Planning Agency*, 535 U.S. 302, 355–56 (2002) (dissenting); *Horne v. Department of Agriculture*, 135 S. Ct. 2419, 2433 (2015) (concurring); *Arrigoni Enterprises v. Town of Durham*, 136 S. Ct. 1409 (2016) (dissenting from denial of certiorari); *Murr v. Wisconsin*, 137 S. Ct. 1957–58 (2017) (dissenting).

36. Video clip from "A Conversation with James Baldwin," interview by Dr. Kenneth Clark, recorded May 24, 1963, http://openvault.wgbh.org/catalog/V_C 03ED1927DCF46B5A8C82275DF4239F9.

37. *Kelo v. City of New London*, 545 U.S. 469, 522 (2005) (dissenting).

38. *Kelo v. City of New London*, 545 U.S. 469, 521 (2005) (dissenting).

39. *United States v. Carolene Products*, 304 U.S. 144, 152n4 (1938).

40. In a 2016 abortion case, Thomas noted that through Footnote 4, the mid-century liberal Court "created a new taxonomy of preferred rights," which "simultaneously transformed judicially created rights like the right to abortion into preferred constitutional rights, while disfavoring many of the rights actually enumerated in the Constitution." *Whole Woman's Health v. Hellerstedt*, 136 S. Ct. 2292, 2328–29 (2016) (dissenting).

41. *Kelo v. City of New London*, 545 U.S. 469, 521 (2005) (dissenting).

42. *Kelo v. City of New London*, 545 U.S. 469, 522 (2005) (dissenting). It's telling that whereas Thomas is at best indifferent to questions of race in the context of criminal and defendant rights—as we'll see in chapter 9, in fact, he seems to welcome the infliction of harsh criminal penalties on black and brown people—he is extremely sensitive to issues of race in the context of civil forfeiture cases, where the penalties involve the deprivation of property. *Leonard v. Texas*, 137 S. Ct. 847, 848 (2017) (concurring in denial of certiorari).

43. Thomas offers an especially stringent interpretation of the so-called state action doctrine in *Brentwood Academy v. Tennessee Secondary School Athletic Association*, 531 U.S. 288, 305 (2001).

44. *Heart of Atlanta Motel v. United States*, 379 U.S. 241, 261 (1965).

45. *Heart of Atlanta Motel v. United States*, 379 U.S. 241, 279 (1965) (Douglas, concurring).

46. Richard Wright, *Native Son* (New York: New American Library, 1964), 23–24.

47. *Senate Confirmation Hearings*, Part 1, 373–74.

48. *Gibbons v. Ogden*, 22 U.S. 1 (1824).

49. Jack Balkin, *Living Originalism* (Cambridge, MA: Belknap Press of Harvard University Press, 2011), 149–50; Akhil Reed Amar, *America's Constitution: A Biography* (New York: Random House, 2005), 107–8. More generally, see Emma Rothschild, *Economic Sentiments: Adam Smith, Condorcet, and the Enlightenment* (Cambridge, MA: Harvard University Press, 2001); Sankar Muthu, "Conquest, Commerce, and Cosmopolitanism in Enlightenment Political Thought," in *Empire and Modern Political Thought*, ed. Sankar Muthu (New York, Cambridge: Cambridge University Press, 2012), 199–231;

Albert Hirschman, *The Passions and the Interests: Political Arguments for Capitalism Before Its Triumph* (Princeton, NJ: Princeton University Press, 1977). For a sharp challenge to this account of the Framers' view of commerce, see Randy E. Barnett, "Jack Balkin's Interaction Theory of 'Commerce,'" *University of Illinois Law Review* (2012), 623–67; Randy E. Barnett, "The Original Meaning of the Commerce Clause," *University of Chicago Law Review* 68 (Winter 2001), 101–47.

50. *Narrative of the Life of Frederick Douglass, an American Slave, Written by Himself,* ed. William L. Andrews and William S. McFeely (New York: Norton, 1997), 34; also see 28, 30, 32.

51. The language of "spillover effects" is Balkin's. See Balkin, *Living Originalism,* 181.

52. *United States v. Lopez,* 514 U.S. 549, 558–61 (1995) (Rehnquist). In a follow-up case in 2000, Rehnquist's language was even stronger: "our cases have upheld Commerce Clause regulation of intrastate activity *only* where that activity is economic in nature." *United States v. Morrison,* 529 U.S. 598, 613 (2000) (Rehnquist). Also see Andrew Koppelman, *The Tough Luck Constitution and the Assault on Health Care* (New York: Oxford University Press, 2013), 49–60. I am grateful to Keith Whittington and Andy Koppelman for helping me with this account of Rehnquist's decision in *Lopez,* which is ambiguous, at times confusing.

53. *United States v. Lopez,* 514 U.S. 549, 585 (1995) (concurring).

54. According to UCLA law professor Eugene Volokh, "There is conventional wisdom about what's possible, like 'Whatever you think about the Commerce Clause, no one is going back to the pre-1937 approach.' . . . Thomas has shown that sometimes the conventional wisdom is wrong." Jeffrey Toobin, "Partners," *New Yorker* (August 29, 2011), 51. Also see *Adoptive Couple v. Baby Girl,* 570 U.S. 637, 659 (2013) (concurring); Mark A. Graber, "Clarence Thomas," *Biographical Encyclopedia of the Supreme Court: The Lives and Legal Philosophies of the Justices,* ed. Melvin I. Urofsky (Washington, DC: CQ Press, 2006), 542–53; Mark A. Graber, "Clarence Thomas and the Perils of Amateur History," in *Rehnquist Justice: Understanding the Court Dynamic,* ed. Earl M. Maltz (Lawrence: University Press of Kansas, 2003), 86.

55. *Gonzalez v. Raich,* 545 U.S. 1, 58–59 (2005) (dissenting). Also see *Taylor v. United States,* 136 S. Ct. 2074, 2083 (2016) (dissenting).

56. *Gibbons v. Ogden,* 22 U.S. 1, 190 (1824).

57. In his *Lopez* concurrence, Thomas also argued against the second part of the test Rehnquist adopted in *Lopez,* that the activity in question must "substantially" affect interstate commerce. That stipulation, said Thomas, is not strict enough and does not comport with the understanding of the Commerce Clause at the time of its adoption. The Framers were well aware that many activities affect interstate commerce, Thomas said. Yet they did not empower Congress, under the Commerce Clause, to regulate those activities or activities that "substantially" affect interstate commerce. *United States v. Lopez,*

514 U.S. 549, 585 (1995) (concurring); also see *United States v. Morrison*, 529 U.S. 598, 627 (2000) (concurring); *Printz v. United States*, 521 US. 898, 937 (1997) (concurring); *National Federation of Independent Business v. Sebelius*, 567 U.S. 519, 708 (2012) (dissenting); *Taylor v. United States*, 136 S. Ct. 2074, 2086–89 (2016) (dissenting). Thomas made the point again in *Raich*, where he concluded that the Commerce Clause does not empower Congress to regulate "activities that substantially affect interstate commerce." *Gonzalez v. Raich*, 545 U.S. 1, 67 (2005) (dissenting).

58. *Gonzalez v. Raich*, 545 U.S. 1, 70 (2005) (dissenting).
59. *United States v. Morrison*, 529 U.S. 598, 627 (2000) (concurring).
60. *Gonzalez v. Raich*, 545 U.S. 1, 69n7 (2005) (dissenting).
61. Thomas, "Black America Under the Reagan Administration," *Policy Review* (Fall 1985), 35.
62. *Gonzalez v. Raich*, 545 U.S. 1, 70 (2005) (dissenting).

6. MEN OF MONEY

1. Thomas, speech to Pacific Research Institute, San Francisco (August 10, 1987), in *Hearings Before the Senate Committee on the Judiciary*, 102nd Cong., 1st sess., September 10, 11, 12, 13, 17, 19, 20, 1991, and October 11, 12, 13, 1991, Part 1, 156, 160.
2. The irony of Thomas's position here is that while it appeals to a certain recognizable stereotype of midcentury liberalism, some of the pioneering decisions on the Court that helped to undermine these distinctions between speech and money, economic rights and human rights, were written and/or joined by liberals on the Court: William Brennan is considered to be the primary author and force behind *Buckley v. Valeo*, which held that the government cannot impose restrictions on campaign expenditures. The *Virginia Pharmacy* decision, which played such a critical role in the development of the commercial speech doctrine discussed below, was authored by Harry Blackmun and joined by Brennan and Thurgood Marshall; conservative William Rehnquist was the lone dissenter (though Rehnquist would later abandon his opposition to the protection of commercial speech, joining Thomas's opinion in *Rubin v. Coors Brewing Co.*). Indeed, according to Columbia law scholar Jeremy Kessler, that move to blur the distinction between economic activity and First Amendment activity was first made by two of the Court's great midcentury liberals: William Douglas and Hugo Black. Jeremy K. Kessler, "The Early Years of First Amendment Lochnerism," *Columbia Law Review* 116 (2016), 1915–2004.
3. Thomas, speech to Pacific Research Institute, 167; also see 154, 159, 164.
4. Thomas, letter to the editor, *Washington Times* (September 2, 1987), A9. While Thomas seeks to elevate money and economics in his philosophy, the narrative he tells of his life oddly denigrates the moral status of money. In between his time at the Office of the Attorney General in Missouri and his move to Washington, Thomas had a stint at Monsanto, the chemical con-

glomerate. He lasted two years. Upon quitting, Thomas later explained, "I made a decision . . . not to ever work for money. I would never take a job for money, never switch jobs for money. So often we think, 'I can make 15 or 20 percent more if I move here.' But that would mean either that I wasn't working for something that was meaningful for me, or if I was working for something meaningful, that it was for sale." In his memoir, Thomas is even more unsparing about his decision to leave the corporate world: "I saw that my personal definition of success was as mistaken as the decision I'd made to go to work there. I had manufactured artificial goals as a means of motivating myself, using my longing for money, cars, and other material possessions to create a false sense of purpose. They had worked on me like spoonfuls of sugar—a jolt of energy that soon faded, leaving behind the pangs of a deeper hunger." Ken Foskett, *Judging Thomas: The Life and Times of Clarence Thomas* (New York: HarperPerennial, 2004), 149; Andrew Peyton, *Clarence Thomas: A Biography* (San Francisco: Encounter, 2001), 175; Thomas, *My Grandfather's Son: A Memoir* (New York: HarperPerennial, 2007), 116–17.

5. Jedediah Purdy, "Neoliberal Constitutionalism: Lochnerism for a New Economy," *Law and Contemporary Problems* 77 (2014), 195–213; Robert Post and Amanda Shanor, "Adam Smith's First Amendment," *Harvard Law Review Forum* 128 (2015), 165–82; Amanda Shanor, "The New Lochner," *Wisconsin Law Review* (2016), 133–208.

6. *Janus v. AFSCME, Council 31*, 138 S. Ct. 2448, 2501 (2018) (Kagan, dissenting).

7. John C. Coates IV, "Corporate Speech & the First Amendment: History, Data, and Implications," *Constitutional Commentary* 30 (2015), 250–51, 253. Also see Haley Sweetland Edwards, "The Corporate 'Free Speech' Racket," *Washington Monthly* (January/February 2014), 28–34; Tim Wu, "The Right to Evade Regulation: How Corporations Hijacked the First Amendment," *New Republic* (June 3, 2013), https://newrepublic.com/article/113294/how-corporations-hijacked-first-amendment-evade-regulation.

8. Thomas, speech to Pacific Research Institute, 161.

9. The confluence described here between Thomas's Commerce Clause and First Amendment jurisprudence may address a concern raised by Columbia law professor Jedediah Purdy in his critique of "neoliberal constitutionalism." Responding to the Court's 2012 Obamacare decision, Purdy argues that the specter haunting the majority's decision in *National Federation of Independent Business v. Sebelius* is "the autonomy of the consumer" and "the rights of the individual." As Purdy notes, however, "because the Commerce Clause concerns the powers of Congress, not the rights of individuals, a ruling that invalidates the individual mandate under the Commerce Clause simply means that only state governments, not the federal government, can pass such a law. . . . Under the modern doctrine, there is no such thing as an important, constitutionally protected personal liberty that a state can violate but the federal government cannot, or vice versa." While I think Purdy overstates the theoretical

and political distinctions between the federalism concerns of contemporary Commerce Clause cases going back to *Lopez*, and the rights claims that he sees at the heart, albeit implicitly, of *Sebelius*, the fusion of Thomas's positions on the Commerce Clause and the First Amendment might help us see how that distinction might be bridged by a conservative jurisprudence in practice. Purdy, "Neoliberal Constitutionalism," 195–213.

10. Cited in Dana Gioia, "Business and Poetry," *Hudson Review* (Spring 1983), 147.

11. *Nixon v. Shrink Missouri Government PAC*, 528 U.S. 377, 412, 415, 417 (2000) (dissenting).

12. "The size of the contribution provides a very rough index of the intensity of the contributor's support for the candidate." *Nixon v. Shrink Missouri Government PAC*, 528 U.S. 377, 414 (2000) (dissenting).

13. *Colorado Republican Federal Campaign Committee v. FEC*, 518 U.S. 604, 636 (1996) (concurring in part and dissenting in part); *Nixon v. Shrink Missouri Government PAC*, 528 U.S. 377, 411–12 (2000) (dissenting); *FEC v. Colorado Republican Federal Campaign Committee*, 533 U.S. 431, 466 (2001) (dissenting); *McConnell v. FEC*, 540 U.S. 93, 265 (2003) (concurring and dissenting).

14. Thomas, speech to Pacific Research Institute, 158; Kay Cole James, interview with Clarence Thomas (1996), http://justicethomas.blogspot.com/2007/09 /neopolitique-interview.html; Peyton, *Clarence Thomas*, 290–91, 300; Steven B. Lichtman, "Black Like Me: The Free Speech Jurisprudence of Clarence Thomas," *Penn State Law Review* 114 (Fall 2009), 420, 445; Thomas, "Victims and Heroes in the 'Benevolent State,'" *Harvard Law and Public Policy Review* 19 (Spring 1996), 673; Thomas, "Civil Rights as a Principle Versus Civil Rights as an Interest," in *Assessing the Reagan Years*, ed. David Boaz (Washington, DC: Cato, 1988), 399.

15. Friedrich Hayek, *The Road to Serfdom: Texts and Documents: The Definitive Edition*, ed. Bruce Caldwell (Chicago: University of Chicago Press, 2007), 125.

16. Hayek, *The Road to Serfdom*, 125, 216–17.

17. Ibid., 126.

18. I am grateful to Alex Gourevitch for helping me to clarify this point.

19. Thomas offers an inadvertent illustration in his dissenting opinion in *M.L.B. v. S.L.J.* (1996). In this case, a mother had lost custodial rights over her children to the children's biological father. Unable to pay the necessary court fees to mount an appeal, the mother filed suit claiming that she had been denied equal protection of the law: while wealthier people might be able to afford the state's filing fees, an impoverished person like herself could not. The Court ruled in her favor. At the end of his dissent, Thomas acknowledged that "for many—if not most—parents, the termination of their right to raise their children would be an exaction more dear than any other." That "many—if not most" hints at a personal experience of Thomas's that will prove, as we'll see in the next chapter, to be important to his worldview about

authority. But it also indicates Thomas's belief that there are no universal modes of valuation (not all parents value their children above all else) and that what we do value most is either "more dear" than anything else or lies beyond monetary value. *M.L.B. v. S.L.J.*, 519 U.S. 102, 144 (1996) (dissenting).

20. Hayek, *The Road to Serfdom*, 126. At an earlier moment in Thomas's career, the Hayekian strains of his thinking, the sense of the intimate connection between our morals and our money, could be heard quite clearly: "Because we Americans are a commercial people, we express our freedom most typically in the diverse means by which we take to gain wealth. And this wealth can in turn serve as a means to higher ends." Thomas, "Thomas Sowell and the Heritage of Lincoln," *Lincoln Review* (Spring 1988), 16–17.

21. *Nixon v. Shrink Missouri Government PAC*, 528 U.S. 377, 418 (2000) (dissenting).

22. *Buckley v. Valeo*, 424 U.S. 1, 17, 18, 21, 23, 48, 52–53, 58 (1976).

23. Jeffrey Toobin, *The Oath: The Obama White House and the Supreme Court* (New York: Anchor Books, 2012), 149. The conflict over what counts as speech versus what counts as economic activity is a long one in the United States, with no clear delineation between liberal and conservative positions. As Boston College political scientist Ken Kersch has argued, it was liberals and the labor movement in the first part of the twentieth century who turned economic-related activities that had previously not been considered speech—picketing and union organizing, for instance—into forms of speech. Later, as Kersch shows (and Kessler discusses separately), it was conservatives allied with business who sought to turn management activity in the firm, which liberals and the labor movement had hoped to regulate and constrain, into forms of speech. Ken I. Kersch, "How Conduct Became Speech and Speech Became Conduct: A Political Development Case Study in Labor Law and the Freedom of Speech," *University of Pennsylvania Journal of Constitutional Law* 2 (March 2006), 255–97; Kessler, "Early Years of First Amendment Lochnerism," 1915–2004.

24. Robert C. Post, *Citizens Divided: Campaign Finance Reform and the Constitution* (Cambridge, MA: Harvard University Press, 2014), 46, 200.

25. *Buckley v. Valeo*, 424 U.S. 1, 20–21, 48 (1976).

26. Thomas has made these arguments in a series of concurrences and dissents. *Colorado Republican Federal Campaign Committee v. FEC*, 518 U.S. 604, 635–40 (1996) (concurring in part and dissenting in part); *Nixon v. Shrink Missouri Government PAC*, 528 U.S. 377, 412–20 (2000) (dissenting); *FEC v. Colorado Republican Federal Campaign Committee*, 553 U.S. 431, 465–66 (2001) (dissenting); *FEC v. Beaumont*, 539 U.S. 146, 164–65 (2003) (dissenting); *Randall v. Sorrell*, 548 U.S. 230, 265–267 (2006) (concurring); *McCutcheon v. FEC*, 572 U.S. 185, 228 (2014) (concurring).

27. Lichtman, "Black Like Me," 432.

28. Exodus 4:14–16.

29. *Nixon v. Shrink Missouri Government PAC*, 528 U.S. 377, 412–20 (2000)

(dissenting); *Colorado Republican Federal Campaign Committee v. FEC*, 518 U.S. 604, 636, 638 (1996) (concurring in part and dissenting in part).

30. *Colorado Republican Federal Campaign Committee v. FEC*, 518 U.S. 604, 638–639 (1996) (concurring in part and dissenting in part). Also see *Nixon v. Shrink Missouri Government PAC*, 528 U.S. 377, 414 (2000) (dissenting); *Randall v. Sorrell*, 548 U.S. 230, 266 (2006) (concurring).

31. *Colorado Republican Federal Campaign Committee v. FEC*, 518 U.S. 604, 638 (1996) (concurring in part and dissenting in part); *Nixon v. Shrink Missouri Government PAC*, 528 U.S. 377, 413–18 (2000) (dissenting).

32. *Colorado Republican Federal Campaign Committee v. FEC*, 518 U.S. 604, 636, 640 (1996) (concurring in part and dissenting in part).

33. *Nixon v. Shrink Missouri Government PAC*, 528 U.S. 377, 414, 415 (2000) (dissenting).

34. *Colorado Republican Federal Campaign Committee v. FEC*, 518 U.S. 604, 636n5 (1996) (concurring in part and dissenting in part).

35. Friedrich Hayek, *The Constitution of Liberty*, ed. Ronald Hamowy (Chicago: University of Chicago Press, 2011), 192.

36. "The majority today, by contrast, separates 'corruption' from its *quid pro quo* roots and gives it a new, far-reaching (and speech-suppressing) definition, something like '[t]he perversion of anything from an original state of purity.' . . . And the Court proceeds to define that state of purity, casting aspersions on 'politicians too compliant with the wishes of large contributors.' . . . Presumably, the majority does not mean that politicians should be free of attachments to constituent groups." *Nixon v. Shrink Missouri Government PAC*, 528 U.S. 377, 423–24 (2000) (dissenting).

37. *McConnell v. FEC*, 540 U.S. 93, 274 (2003) (concurring in part and dissenting in part).

38. *Nixon v. Shrink Missouri Government PAC*, 528 U.S. 377, 420 (2000) (dissenting).

39. Thomas Sowell, *Race and Economics* (New York: David McKay, 1975), 128.

40. Lichtman, "Black Like Me," 426.

41. For useful histories and theoretical analyses of commercial speech doctrine, see Alex Kozinski and Stuart Banner, "Who's Afraid of Commercial Speech?," *Virginia Law Review* 76 (May 1990), 627–53; Robert Post, "The Constitutional Status of Commercial Speech," *UCLA Law Review* 48 (October 2000), 1–57; Shanor, "The New Lochner." An important challenge to the historical analysis and assumptions of this literature is offered by Kessler in "The Early Years of First Amendment Lochnerism," 1915–2004.

42. Post and Shanor, "Adam Smith's First Amendment," 165–82; Post, *Citizens Divided*, 45. *Masterpiece Cakeshop v. Colorado Civil Rights Commission*, the wedding-cake case of 2018, suggests how potent such free-speech claims can be. The case concerned a baker in Colorado who refused to make a wedding cake for a same-sex couple. The baker claimed doing so would violate his freedom of religion and freedom of speech. Where the Court's other conservative justices focused on the question of religion, Thomas, joined by Justice

Gorsuch, focused on the question of speech. "Creating and designing custom wedding cakes," said Thomas, is not just a form of economic activity. It is "expressive" conduct—like burning a flag or wearing a black armband—that communicates a message. The baker "considers himself an artist." He "takes exceptional care with each cake that he creates—sketching the design out on paper, choosing the color scheme, creating the frosting and decorations, baking and sculpting the cake, decorating it, and delivering it to the wedding." Though "the cake is eventually eaten, that is not its primary purpose." Its primary purpose is "to communicate the basic message that a wedding is occurring, a marriage has begun, and the couple should be celebrated." Even if the baker is paid for his work, the work is still expressive and communicative: authors, after all, are paid to write books. By forcing the baker to make a wedding cake for a same-sex marriage, the state is requiring him to communicate a statement that he does not believe in or approve of: "that same-sex weddings are 'weddings' and . . . that they should be celebrated." The state, in other words, is forcing the baker to speak. By reconfiguring the baker's economic activity as speech, and the state's regulation of that activity as a restriction on speech, Thomas showed how vast swaths of the economy could be redescribed as speechlike activity and thereby be protected from government regulation, particularly regulation that prohibits discrimination. Recognizing the speechlike elements of commercial activity makes it possible, Thomas concluded, to prevent the Court's other gay rights rulings (and possibly civil rights rulings, though Thomas doesn't mention them) "from being used to 'stamp out every vestige of dissent' and 'vilify Americans who are unwilling to assent to the new orthodoxy.'" *Masterpiece Cakeshop, Ltd. v. Colorado Civil Rights Commission*, 138 S. Ct. 1719, 1742–44, 1748 (2018) (concurring).

43. Justice Scalia, for example, makes a point of declaring in one of his commercial speech opinions that "the core offense of suppressing particular political ideas is not at issue" in the case. *44 Liquormart v. Rhode Island*, 517 U.S. 484, 517 (1996) (Scalia, concurring).

44. Hayek, *Constitution of Liberty*, 97.

45. Ibid., 196.

46. *44 Liquormart v. Rhode Island*, 517 U.S. 484, 520, 522 (1996) (concurring); *Lorillard Tobacco Company v. Reilly*, 533 U.S. 525, 590 (2011) (concurring). Also see *Glickman v. Wileman Brothers & Elliott*, 521 U.S. 457, 504 (1997) (dissenting); *Greater New Orleans Broadcasting Association v. United States*, 527 U.S. 173, 197 (1999) (concurring); *United States v. United Foods*, 533 U.S. 405, 418–19 (2001) (concurring); *Lorillard Tobacco Company v. Reilly*, 533 U.S. 525, 575 (2001) (concurring); *Johanns v. Livestock Marketing Association*, 544 U.S. 550, 567 (2005) (concurring); *Milavetz, Gallop & Milavetz, P.A. v. United States*, 559 U.S. 229, 255 (2010) (concurring); *Matal v. Tam*, 137 S. Ct. 1744, 1769 (2017) (concurring); *National Institute of Family and Life Advocates v. Becerra*, 138 S. Ct. 2361, 2371–72 (2018).

47. Hannah Arendt, "Lying and Politics," in *Crises of the Republic* (New York:

Harcourt Brace, 1972), 3–47; Arendt, "Truth and Politics," in *Between Past and Future* (New York: Viking, 1961, 1968), 227–64.

48. *Lorillard Tobacco Company v. Reilly*, 533 U.S. 525, 578–79 (2011) (concurring).

49. "The first task" of any political movement "is to find the support one believes is there, to reach out somehow to unknown but sympathetic people. In order to do that, the little group of activists must appear to be more than it yet is. . . . Political movements are begun by throwing together a façade, behind which activists rush about trying to raise a building. . . . If they have chosen their moment wisely, the first little group will find people to help it along." Michael Walzer, *Political Action* (New York: NYRB Classics, 2019), 9.

50. *Glickman v. Wileman Brothers & Elliott*, 521 U.S. 457, 505, 505n3 (1997) (dissenting); *Nixon v. Shrink Missouri Government PAC*, 528 U.S. 377, 419–20 (2000) (dissenting). The elitist thrust of this vision can also be seen by comparing Thomas's defense of commercial speech to his indifference about the free-speech rights of employees. When the economic actor is a proprietor or a professional, Thomas is solicitous of his economic speech; when the actor is a worker or an employee, particularly a government employee, Thomas is not so solicitous. *Borgner v. Florida Board of Dentistry*, 537 U.S. 1080 (2002) (dissenting from denial of certiorari); *Lane v. Franks*, 573 U.S. 228, 247 (2014) (concurring); *Heffernan v. Paterson*, 136 S. Ct. 1412, 1420 (2016) (dissenting). The one exception to this rule is racist or hate speech; there, Thomas is solicitous of the free-speech rights of employees, including employees of private firms. *Avis Rent-A-Car v. Aguilar*, 529 U.S. 1138 (2000) (dissenting from denial of certiorari).

7. GRANDFATHERS AND SONS

1. Clarence Thomas, "The Equal Employment Opportunity Commission: Reflections on a New Philosophy," *Stetson Law Review* 15 (1985), 29; Andrew Peyton, *Clarence Thomas: A Biography* (San Francisco: Encounter, 2001), 210–97; Kevin Merida and Michael A. Fletcher, *Supreme Discomfort: The Divided Soul of Clarence Thomas* (New York: Doubleday, 2007), 157–64; Timothy M. Phelps and Helen Winternitz, *Capitol Games: The Inside Story of Clarence Thomas, Anita Hill, and a Supreme Court Nomination* (New York: HarperPerennial, 1992), 93–121; Jane Mayer and Jill Abramson, *Strange Justice: The Selling of Clarence Thomas* (Boston: Houghton Mifflin, 1994), 124–30, 140–44; Ken Foskett, *Judging Thomas: The Life and Times of Clarence Thomas* (New York: HarperPerennial, 2004), 160–81. For a more general history of the EEOC and the struggle for employment equity during the Reagan years, see Nancy MacLean, *Freedom Is Not Enough: The Opening of the American Workplace* (Cambridge, MA: Harvard University Press, 2006), 225–332.

2. Mayer and Abramson, *Strange Justice*, 18, 150–52; Peyton, *Clarence Thomas*,

179, 315–19; Merida and Fletcher, *Supreme Discomfort*, 167–70. Foskett claims Thomas never wanted a seat on the bench until the election of George H. W. Bush and that officials in the Bush administration had to persuade him to take it. Foskett, *Judging Thomas*, 202, 206.

3. Richard H. King, "Rights and Slavery, Race and Racism: Leo Strauss, the Straussians, and the American Dilemma," *Modern Intellectual History* 5 (2008), 55–82; *Toward a More Perfect Union: Writings of Herbert J. Storing*, ed. Joseph M. Bessette (Washington, DC: AEI Press, 1995), 131–220, 236–58.

4. Peyton, *Clarence Thomas*, 286–91, 298–99, 305–9; Thomas, *My Grandfather's Son: A Memoir* (New York: HarperPerennial, 2007), 188; Mayer and Abramson, *Strange Justice*, 141–142; Foskett, *Judging Thomas*, 187–91; Ken Masugi, "Natural Right and Oversight: The Use and Abuse of 'Natural Law' in the Clarence Thomas Hearings," *Political Communication* 9 (1992), 232–35.

5. David Waldstreicher, *Slavery's Constitution: From Revolution to Ratification* (New York: Hill & Wang, 2009), 3, 16; James Oakes, *Freedom National: The Destruction of Slavery in the United States, 1861–1865* (New York: W. W. Norton, 2013), xi–xv, 6–8, 26–42.

6. Scott Douglas Gerber, *First Principles: The Jurisprudence of Clarence Thomas* (New York: New York University Press, 1999), 36–47; Thomas, *My Grandfather's Son*, 188, 231; Phelps and Winternitz, *Capitol Games*, 109–21; Foskett, *Judging Thomas*, 187–92; Mayer and Abramson, *Strange Justice*, 141–42; Peyton, *Clarence Thomas*, 111, 285–309.

7. Masugi, "Natural Right and Oversight," 231, 236–40. Led by Biden, Democrats grilled Thomas on statements he had made throughout the late 1980s indicating that he thought natural law might empower the Supreme Court to strike down economic regulations or uphold restrictions on abortion. Someone compiled a dossier of "Thomas Quotations on Natural Law," complete with a misidentification of Alexander Hamilton as Andrew Hamilton, that Biden read aloud from and introduced into the Senate record. Ever his own worst enemy, Biden got himself into trouble when, in reading out one of these Thomas statements—"I find attractive the arguments of scholars such as Stephen Macedo who defend an activist Supreme Court, which would strike down laws restricting property rights" on the grounds of natural law—he omitted the critical two sentences that followed: "But the libertarian arguments overlooks [sic] the place of the Supreme Court in a scheme of separation of power. One does not strengthen self-government and the rule of law by having the non-democratic branch of government make policy." Utah Republican Orrin Hatch pounced on Biden for the selective quotation, which suggested that Thomas thought the Court should overturn economic legislation in the name of natural law when in fact Thomas had been building to the opposite claim. (Thomas offered a similar critique of libertarianism in his review of Clint Bolick's *Changing Course*.) *Hearings Before the Senate Committee on the Judiciary*, 102nd Cong., 1st sess., September 10, 11,

12, 13, 17, 19, 20, 1991, and October 11, 12, 13, 1991, Part 1, 111–26, 146–49, 168, 170–71, 179–80, 191–93, 218–21, 236–43, 271–77, 426–34, 471–74; Thomas, "A Second Emancipation," *Policy Review* (Summer 1988), 84–85.

8. Gerber, *First Principles*, 36–47, 101–02, 191–93; Ralph A. Rossum, *Understanding Clarence Thomas: The Jurisprudence of Constitutional Restoration* (Lawrence: University Press of Kansas, 2014), 6, 19–21, 184; Mark Tushnet, *A Court Divided: The Rehnquist Court and the Future of Constitutional Law* (New York: W. W. Norton, 2005, 2006), 89, 93–96; Adam J. Hunt, "The Liberal Justice Thomas: An Analysis of Justice Thomas's Articulation and Application of Classical Liberalism," *NYU Journal of Law & Liberty* (2009), 569–71, 575–82; Hannah Weiner, "The Next 'Great Dissenter'? How Clarence Thomas Is Using the Words and Principles of John Marshall Harlan to Craft a New Era of Civil Rights," *Duke Law Journal* 58 (2008), 151–54; Nathan W. Dean, "The Primacy of the Individual in the Political Philosophy and Civil Rights Jurisprudence of Justice Clarence Thomas," *George Mason University Civil Rights Law Journal* 14 (2004), 21–39; John S. Baker, "Natural Law and Justice Thomas," *Regent University Law Review* 12 (2000), 478–80, 497–512; Kirk A. Kennedy, "Reaffirming the Natural Law Jurisprudence of Justice Clarence Thomas," *Regent University Law Review* 9 (1997), 33–87.

9. *Stenberg v. Carhart*, 530 U.S. 914, 980–83 (2000) (dissenting); *Gonzales v. Carhart*, 550 U.S. 124, 168–69 (2007) (concurring); *Whole Women's Health v. Hellerstedt*, 136 S. Ct. 2292, 2321 (2016) (dissenting); *Timbs v. Indiana*, 203 L.Ed. 2d 11, 22 (2019) (concurring).

10. *Stenberg v. Carhart*, 530 U.S. 914, 1002, 1006, 1007, 1009–14 (2000) (dissenting); *Doe v. Bolton*, 410 U.S. 179, 221 (1973) (White, dissenting); *Roe v. Wade*, 410 U.S. 113, 172–77 (1973) (Rehnquist, dissenting).

11. Thomas, "The Higher Law Background of the Privileges or Immunities Clause of the Fourteenth Amendment," *Harvard Journal of Law and Public Policy* 12 (1989), 63–70; Thomas, "An Afro-American Perspective: Toward a 'Plain Reading' of the Constitution—the Declaration of Independence in Constitutional Interpretation," *Howard Law Journal* (1987), 691–703; Thomas, "Black Americans & the Constitution," in *The New Federalist Papers*, ed. J. Jackson Barlow, Dennis J. Mahoney, and John G. West Jr. (Lanham, MD: University Press of America, 1988), 307–9; Thomas, speech to the Heritage Foundation (June 8, 1987), reprinted as "Why Black Americans Should Look to Conservative Policies," *Human Events* (July 27, 1991), 11–12, 17; "Affirmative Action: Cure or Contradiction?," *Center Magazine* (November/December 1987), 20–21; Thomas, "Rewards Belong to Those Who Labor," *Washington Times* (January 18, 1988), F4. A similar set of claims emerges in some of Thomas's writings—but in almost none of his opinions—after his ascension to the Court. Thomas, "No Room at the Inn: The Loneliness of the Black Conservative," in *Black and Right: The Bold New Voice of Black Conservatives in America*, ed. Stan Faryna, Brad Stetson, and Joseph G.

Conti (Westport, CT: Praeger, 1997), 12–13; Thomas, "Why Federalism Matters," *Drake Law Review* 48 (2000), 231–32. Conversely, what is so telling about many of Thomas's post-ascension writings, particularly those that address the question of Lincoln and slavery, is how absent the rhetoric of natural law is in some of them. See, for example, Thomas, "Introduction: Lincoln, *Dred Scott*, and the Preservation of Liberty," in *Lincoln & Liberty*, ed. Lucas E. Morel (Lexington: University Press of Kentucky, 2015), 1–13.

12. William J. Brennan, "Speech to the Text and Teaching Symposium," in *Originalism: A Quarter-Century of Debate*, ed. Steven Calabresi (Washington, DC: Regnery, 2007), 55–70; Thurgood Marshall, "Reflections on the Bicentennial of the United States Constitution," *Harvard Law Review* 101 (November 1987), 1–5.

13. Interestingly, twice during his Senate confirmation hearings, Thomas affirmed a vision of the Constitution as a living document, claiming that the meaning of liberty in the Fourteenth Amendment is "one that evolves over time," that what the framers of that amendment meant at the time of its ratification need not determine "what the term in its totality would mean for the future." Constitutional concepts, he went on to say, are "not frozen in time. Our notions of what liberty means evolves with the country, it moves with our history and our tradition." These concepts are "broad provisions, that . . . [use] our history and tradition evolve." But these were stray comments, not repeated elsewhere in the hearings or in his writings or jurisprudence. *Senate Confirmation Hearings*, Part 1, 274, 277.

14. Thomas, "Judging," *Kansas Law Review* 45 (November 1996), 1–8; Thomas, "Be Not Afraid," Francis Boyer Lecture, American Enterprise Institute, Washington, DC (February 13, 2001), http://www.aei.org/publication/be-not-afraid/; Rossum, *Understanding Clarence Thomas*, 12–31; Gregory E. Maggs, "Which Original Meaning of the Constitution Matters to Justice?," *NYU Journal of Law & Liberty* 4 (2009), 494–516; William H. Pryor Jr., "Justice Thomas, Criminal Justice, and Originalism's Legitimacy," *Yale Law Journal Forum* 127 (2017), 173–81.

15. Mark A. Graber, "Clarence Thomas," *Biographical Encyclopedia of the Supreme Court: The Lives and Legal Philosophies of the Justices*, ed. Melvin I. Urofsky (Washington, DC: CQ Press, 2006), 542–53; Mark A. Graber, "Clarence Thomas and the Perils of Amateur History," in *Rehnquist Justice: Understanding the Court Dynamic*, ed. Earl M. Maltz (Lawrence: University Press of Kansas, 2003), 70–71, 74, 76–77, 79–80, 87–90; Peter J. Smith, "Originalism and Level of Generality," *Georgia Law Review* 51 (2017), 61–65; "Justice Thomas's Inconsistent Originalism," *Harvard Law Review* 121 (March 2008), 1431–38; Doug Kendall and Jim Ryan, "Originalist Sins: The Faux Originalism of Justice Clarence Thomas," *Slate* (August 1, 2007), http://www.slate.com/articles/news_and_politics/jurisprudence/2007/08/originalist_sins.html; Scott Lemieux, "The Limits of Originalism," *American Prospect* (April 18, 2016), http://prospect.org/article/limits-originalism.

16. Rossum, *Understanding Clarence Thomas*, 45–50, 86–94.

17. For an excellent treatment of the role of myth and mythmaking in Thomas's thinking about law and the Constitution, as well as his highly gendered conception of these categories, see Jeffrey R. Dudas, "All the Rage: Clarence Thomas, Paternal Authority, and Conservative Desire," *Law, Culture and the Humanities* 12 (February 2016), 70–105. On the "expressive function" of law, see Cass R. Sunstein, "On the Expressive Function of Law," *University of Pennsylvania Law Review* 144 (1996), 2021–53.

18. *McDonald v. City of Chicago*, 561 U.S. 742, 807 (2010) (concurring); *Evenwel v. Abbott*, 136 S. Ct. 1120, 1140 (2016) (concurring).

19. Thomas, "Why Federalism Matters," 234–37; *U.S. Term Limits v. Thornton*, 514 U.S. 779, 846, 848, 859–860 (1995) (dissenting); Tushnet, *A Court Divided*, 89; Graber, "Clarence Thomas and the Perils of Amateur History," 84; Graber, "Clarence Thomas," 542–53.

20. Peyton, *Clarence Thomas*, 55–56; Foskett, *Judging Thomas*, 50–51; Merida and Fletcher, *Supreme Discomfort*, 45–48; Mayer and Abramson, *Strange Justice*, 33; Dudas, "All the Rage," 9–12; Thomas, *My Grandfather's Son*, 1–2.

21. "The Second Annual William French Smith Memorial Lecture: A Conversation with Justice Clarence Thomas," *Pepperdine Law Review* 37 (2009), 12.

22. Thomas, *My Grandfather's Son*, 1–2.

23. Thomas, Savannah State College Commencement Address (June 9, 1985), in Clarence Thomas, *Confronting the Future: Selections from the Senate Confirmation Hearings and Prior Speeches* (Washington, DC: Regnery Gateway, 1992), 34–35; Thomas, "Black America Under the Reagan Administration," *Policy Review* (Fall 1985), 40.

24. Thomas, *My Grandfather's Son*, 12, 27; Dudas, "All the Rage," 16; Thomas, "The New Intolerance," Law Day Address, Walter F. George School of Law, Mercer University (May 1993), http://www.americanrhetoric.com /speeches/clarencethomasthenewintolerance.htm. Also this: "And let me tell you, even if we felt as kids that the unending work was unfair, there were no negotiations about the work or the rules. . . . By decree of my grandfather, my teachers and my grandmother were always right. And by decree, though not always right, he was never wrong. . . . Regardless of how we were treated by others, we were expected to rise above our circumstances rather than becoming consumed by them or by the natural reactions that stirred within us all." Thomas, "The New Intolerance."

25. William Raspberry, "Are the Problems of Blacks Too Big for Government to Solve?," *Washington Post* (July 17, 1983), C3.

26. I am indebted to Dudas for this point about Thomas's mother. See Dudas, "All the Rage," 14–15. Also see Merida and Fletcher, *Supreme Discomfort*, 87; Peyton, *Clarence Thomas*, 64.

27. Nell Irvin Painter, "Hill, Thomas, and the Use of Racial Stereotype," and Christine Stansell, "White Feminists and Black Realities: The Politics of Authenticity," in *Race-ing Justice, En-gendering Power: Essays on Anita Hill, Clarence Thomas, and the Construction of Social Reality*, ed. Toni Morri-

son (New York: Pantheon, 1992), 201–2, 260–63; "Roundtable: Doubting Thomas," *Tikkun* 6 (September–October 1991), 27.

28. Peyton, *Clarence Thomas*, 256. Also see Raspberry, "Are the Problems of Blacks Too Big for Government to Solve?," C3.

29. Peyton, *Clarence Thomas*, 255–56.

30. Barbara Ehrenreich, *Fear of Falling: The Inner Life of the Middle Class* (New York: Pantheon, 1989), 66–74, 82–91, 167–195; Peter Steinfels, *The Neoconservatives: The Men Who Are Changing America's Politics* (New York: Simon & Schuster, 1979), 53–56, 63–67, 263–269; James Forman Jr., *Locking Up Our Own: Crime and Punishment in Black America* (New York: Farrar, Straus & Giroux, 2017), 127; Matthew D. Lassiter, "Inventing Family Values," in *Rightward Bound: Making America Conservative in the 1970s*, ed. Bruce J. Schulman and Julian E. Zelizer (Cambridge, MA: Harvard University Press, 2008), 13–28; Melinda Cooper, *Family Values: Between Neoliberalism and the New Social Conservatism* (Brooklyn, NY: Zone Books, 2017), 33–117.

31. Donald Atwell Zoll, "Capital Punishment," *National Review* (December 3, 1971), reprinted in *The Rise of Conservatism in America, 1945–2000: A Brief History with Documents*, ed. Ronald Story and Bruce Laurie (Boston: Bedford/St. Martin's, 2008), 84.

32. Midge Decter, "A Letter to the Young (and to Their Parents)," *Atlantic Monthly* (February 1975), reprinted in *Liberal Parents, Radical Children* (New York: Coward, McCann & Geoghegan, 1975), 36–37.

33. Christopher Lasch, *The Culture of Narcissism: American Life in an Age of Diminished Expectations* (New York: W. W. Norton, 1979), 181–82.

34. This was Ralph Dahrendorf's critical description of *The Crisis of Democracy*, the influential report co-authored by Samuel Huntington under the aegis of the Trilateral Commission, which had deep connections to the Carter administration. Steinfels, *The Neoconservatives*, 262, 269.

35. Ehrenreich, *Fear of Falling*, 193.

36. Thomas, "'Rights Revolution' Excesses Weaken Fight Against Crime," *Human Events* 50 (June 10, 1994), 12.

37. Thomas, "'Rights Revolution,'" 13.

38. Thomas, *My Grandfather's Son*, 94–95; Thomas, "'Rights Revolution,'" 12; Jeffrey Rosen, "Moving On," *New Yorker* (April 29, 1996), 67; Thomas, "No Room at the Inn," 13.

39. *Chicago v. Morales*, 527 U.S. 41, 114–15 (1999) (dissenting). Also see *Tharpe v. Sellers*, 138 S. Ct. 545, 553 (2018) (dissenting).

40. Forman, *Locking Up Our Own*, 10, 27, 32, 35, 42, 44–45, 133–36, 141–45.

41. Thomas, "Remembering an Island of Hope in an Era of Despair," *Lincoln Review* (Spring 1986), 58; Thomas, "Black America Under the Reagan Administration," 40; Thomas, Savannah State Address, 34–35.

42. Thomas, "Victims and Heroes in the 'Benevolent State,'" 2–3; Franklin Delano Roosevelt, State of the Union address to Congress (January 11, 1944), http://www.fdrlibrary.marist.edu/archives/address_text.html.

43. Peyton, *Clarence Thomas*, 73; Thomas, "'Rights Revolution,'" 13; Thomas, speech to Pacific Research Institute, in *Senate Confirmation Hearings*, Part 1, 158.

44. Phelps and Winternitz, *Capitol Games*, 214–15; Mayer and Abramson, *Strange Justice*, 219–20; Foskett, *Judging Thomas*, 229, 237.

45. Recent statements of the charges against Thomas, including material related to his tenure on the Court, can be found in Jill Abramson, "Do You Believe Her Now?," *New York* (February 19, 2018), http://nymag.com/intelligencer/2018/02/the-case-for-impeaching-clarence-thomas.html; and Marcia Coyle, "Young Scholar, Now Lawyer, Says Clarence Thomas Groped Her in 1999," *National Law Journal* (October 27, 2016), https://www.law.com/nationallawjournal/almID/1202770918142/Young-Scholar-Now-Lawyer-Says-Clarence-Thomas-Groped-Her-in-1999/.

46. *Senate Confirmation Hearings*, Part 4, 157, 158, 205.

47. Phelps and Winternitz, *Capitol Games*, 332; Peyton, *Clarence Thomas*, 2–3, 343, 380–81; Kendall Thomas, "Strange Fruit," in *Race-ing Justice, Engendering Power*, 367–68.

48. "Comments of Justice Clarence Thomas," *Thurgood Marshall Law Review* 23 (1997), 5; Thomas, *My Grandfather's Son*, 245, 251, 257, 269, 271.

49. Dudas, "All the Rage," 12–26.

50. Phelps and Winternitz, *Capitol Games*, 133.

51. Thomas, "Remembering an Island of Hope," 58.

8. THE BLACK CONSTITUTION

1. *Dred Scott v. Sandford*, 60 U.S. 393, 404–5 (1857).

2. Akhil Reed Amar, *America's Constitution: A Biography* (New York: Random House, 2005), 360, 385; Jack M. Balkin, "The Reconstruction Power," *NYU Law Review* 85 (2010), 1801–61; Eric Foner, "Blacks and the US Constitution 1789–1989," *New Left Review* 183 (September–October 1990), 68–70; Rogers M. Smith, *Civic Ideals: Conflicting Visions of Citizenship in U.S. History* (New Haven, CT: Yale University Press, 1997), 298–317.

3. Foner, "Blacks and the US Constitution," 70.

4. Andrew Peyton, *Clarence Thomas: A Biography* (San Francisco: Encounter, 2001), 247. Also see Thomas, "An Afro-American Perspective: Toward a 'Plain Reading' of the Constitution," *Howard Law Journal* 30 (1987), 993–94; Thomas, "The Higher Law Background of the Privileges or Immunities Clause of the Fourteenth Amendment," *Harvard Journal of Law and Public Policy* 12 (1989), 66.

5. *Evenwel v. Abbott*, 136 S. Ct. 1120, 1140 (2016) (concurring); *McDonald v. City of Chicago*, 561 U.S. 742, 807 (2010) (concurring).

6. Steven Hahn, *A Nation Under Our Feet: Black Political Struggles in the Rural South from Slavery to the Great Migration* (Cambridge, MA: Harvard University Press, 2003), 167, 173–74, 178, 183–84, 186, 203, 206–7, 217, 219–20, 224–25, 265–66, 272–74; Eric Foner, *Reconstruction 1863–1877:*

America's Unfinished Revolution (New York: Harper and Row, 1988), 144–48, 158–63.

7. Smith, *Civic Ideals*, 311.

8. Amar, *America's Constitution*, 351, 361–62; Jack M. Balkin, *Living Originalism* (Cambridge, MA: Belknap Press of Harvard University Press, 2011), 186, 190; Smith, *Civic Ideals*, 327–30.

9. *Slaughter-House Cases*, 83 U.S. 36, 74–80 (1872); *United States v. Cruikshank*, 92 U.S. 542, 549–50 (1875).

10. Cited in Philip Hamburger, "Privileges or Immunities," *Northwestern University Law Review* 105 (2011), 69.

11. Frederick Douglass, "Reconstruction," *Atlantic Monthly* 18 (December 1866), 761–62; Douglas Blackmon, *Slavery by Another Name: The Re-Enslavement of Black Americans from the Civil War to World War II* (New York: Doubleday, 2008).

12. Thomas, "Higher Law Background," 66, 68; Thomas, "Afro-American Perspective," 995.

13. It's true that Justice Hugo Black also urged the Court to rely upon the Privileges or Immunities Clause, but that was not in support of ending racial discrimination but rather on behalf of incorporating the Bill of Rights into the Fourteenth Amendment. Michael Kent Curtis, *No State Shall Abridge: The Fourteenth Amendment and the Bill of Rights* (Durham, NC: Duke University Press, 1986), 2, 4–5, 201–2, 220. Also see John Harrison, "Reconstructing the Privileges or Immunities Clause," *Yale Law Journal* 101 (1992), 1385; *Hague v. Committee for Industrial Organization* 307 U.S. 496, 511 (1939).

14. As Justice Stevens archly noted in a footnote, which quoted directly from one of Thomas's opinions without referencing him by name: "It is no secret that the desire to 'displace' major 'portions of our equal protection and substantive due process jurisprudence' animates some of the passion that attends this interpretive issue." *McDonald v. Chicago*, 561 U.S. 792, 860n3 (2010) (Stevens, dissenting). For a sharp critique of Thomas's Privileges or Immunities jurisprudence, see Hamburger, "Privileges or Immunities," 145n305.

15. In addition to the two Privileges or Immunities cases discussed at length in this chapter, see also *Timbs v. Indiana*, 203 L.E. 2d 11, 16 (2019) (concurring); *Murr v. Wisconsin*, 137 S. Ct. 1933, 1957 (2017) (dissenting); *Brown v. Entertainment Merchants Association*, 564 U.S. 786, 836 (2011) (dissenting).

16. *Saenz v. Roe*, 526 U.S. 489, 492–98, 502–5, 507–10 (1999) (Stevens).

17. *Saenz v. Roe*, 526 U.S. 489, 521, 524, 526, 527–28 (1999) (dissenting).

18. *Saenz v. Roe*, 526 U.S. 489, 524, 527 (1999) (dissenting).

19. *Printz v. United States*, 521 U.S. 898, 938 (1997) (concurring). Also see *Friedman v. Highland Park*, 136 S. Ct. 447, 449 (2015) (dissenting from denial of certiorari).

20. *McDonald v. City of Chicago*, 561 U.S. 742, 750 (2010) (Alito).

21. *McDonald v. City of Chicago*, 561 U.S. 792, 862 (2010) (Stevens, dissenting).

22. Mark Tushnet, *In the Balance: Law and Politics on the Roberts Court* (New York: W. W. Norton, 2013), 178–79; Jefferson Decker, *The Other Rights*

Revolution: Conservative Lawyers and the Remaking of American Government (New York: Oxford University Press, 2016), 187, 197, 208.

23. *McDonald v. City of Chicago*, 561 U.S. 742, 806, 811 (2010) (concurring). Thomas has advanced a procedural interpretation—and rejected a substantive interpretation—of the Due Process Clause on several occasions. *Lawrence v. Texas*, 539 U.S. 558, 605–6 (2003) (dissenting); *NASA v. Nelson*, 562 U.S. 134, 169 (2011) (concurring); *Perry v. New Hampshire*, 565 U.S. 228, 249 (2012) (concurring); *Johnson v. United States*, 135 S. Ct. 2551, 2564, 2569–73 (2015) (concurring); *Sessions v. Dimaya*, 138 S. Ct. 1204, 1244 (2018) (dissenting); *Timbs v. Indiana*, 203 L.E. 2d 11, 21–22 (2019) (concurring).

24. *McDonald v. City of Chicago*, 561 U.S. 742, 858 (2010) (concurring).

25. *McDonald v. City of Chicago*, 561 U.S. 742, 878n23, 906–11 (2010) (Stevens, dissenting).

26. *McDonald v. City of Chicago*, 561 U.S., 742, 920 (2010) (Breyer, dissenting).

27. *McDonald v. City of Chicago*, 561 U.S. 742, 837–38 (2010) (concurring); *Troxel v. Granville*, 530 U.S. 57 80n1 (2000) (concurring).

28. *McDonald v. City of Chicago*, 561 U.S. 742, 805 (2010) (concurring). In one case where Thomas approvingly cites *Heller*'s defense of the right to bear arms as "inherited from our English ancestors" and dedicated to "defense of hearth and home," he does so on behalf of an "elderly" African American woman "who lives alone" (and who was also a well-known longtime civil rights activist in San Francisco). *Jackson v. City and County of San Francisco*, 135 S. Ct. 2799, 2800–2802 (2015) (dissenting from denial of certiorari); Nashelly Chavez, "Community remembers tenaciousness, caring spirit of Bayview activist," *San Francisco Examiner* (January 26, 2016), http://www.sfexaminer.com/community-remembers-tenaciousness-caring-spirit-bayview-activist/.

29. In the earlier *Heller* case, both sides invoked the question of black arms and racial violence only to pursue claims about whether the Second Amendment referred to black militias or black individuals. *McDonald v. City of Chicago*, 561 U.S. 742, 771–78 (2010) (Alito); *McDonald v. City of Chicago*, 561 U.S. 742, 899 (2010) (Stevens, dissenting); *McDonald v. City of Chicago*, 561 U.S. 742, 935 (2010) (Breyer, dissenting); *District of Columbia v. Heller*, 554 U.S. 570, 609–16 (2008) (Scalia); *District of Columbia v. Heller*, 554 U.S. 570, 670–75 (2008) (Stevens, dissenting).

30. *McDonald v. City of Chicago*, 561 U.S. 742, 843 (2010) (concurring).

31. In a 2019 case about whether the Eighth Amendment's proscription of "excessive fines" applies to the states, Thomas relied extensively on the pioneering work of another left-wing scholar of African American history, the Columbia historian Eric Foner. In *Timbs v. Indiana*, the Court ruled unanimously that that Eighth Amendment proscription did apply to the states. But while the Court grounded its ruling in the incorporation doctrine, Thomas took the Privileges or Immunities route. He drew deeply from the archive of African American history, using Foner's magisterial study *Reconstruction* to retell

the story of the Black Codes and the white supremacist backlash against the emancipation of black slaves. Though Justice Ginsburg also referenced that history in her opinion for the Court, Thomas's discussion was longer and more substantive, and only he relied upon Foner's work. *Timbs v. Indiana*, 203 L.E. 2d 11, 27–28 (2019) (concurring).

32. *McDonald v. City of Chicago*, 561 U.S. 742, 844 (2010) (concurring).

33. *McDonald v. City of Chicago*, 561 U.S. 742, 846, 847, 856 (2010) (concurring).

34. Foner, *Reconstruction*, 437; Nicholas Lemann, *Redemption: The Last Battle of the Civil War* (New York: Farrar, Straus & Giroux, 2006), 3–29; Smith, *Civic Ideals*, 334.

35. *United States v. Cruikshank*, 92 U.S. 542, 552–53 (1875); Foner, *Reconstruction*, 530–31; Smith, *Civic Ideals*, 334; *National Rifle Association v. Chicago*, 567 F. 3d 856 (2009).

36. *McDonald v. Chicago*, 561 U.S. 742, 856 (2010) (concurring).

37. *McDonald v. Chicago*, 561 U.S. 742, 845, 858 (2010) (concurring).

38. James Forman Jr., *Locking Up Our Own: Crime and Punishment in Black America* (New York: Farrar, Straus & Giroux, 2017), 69.

39. Forman, *Locking Up Our Own*, 65–70, 254–55; Timothy B. Tyson, *Radio Free Dixie: Robert F. Williams and the Roots of Black Power* (Chapel Hill: University of North Carolina Press, 1999).

40. Steve Estes, *I Am a Man! Race, Manhood, and the Civil Rights Movement* (Chapel Hill: University of North Carolina Press, 2005), 157–58; Joshua Bloom and Waldo E. Martin Jr., *Black Against Empire: The History and Politics of the Black Panther Party* (Oakland: University of California Press, 2013, 2016), 107, 144–45.

41. J. G. A. Pocock, *The Machiavellian Moment: Florentine Political Thought and the Atlantic Republican Tradition* (Princeton, NJ: Princeton University Press, 1975), 88–90, 124–25, 199–204, 209–10, 244–45, 293–95, 281–383; Akhil Reed Amar, *The Bill of Rights: Creation and Reconstruction* (New Haven, CT: Yale University Press, 1998), 46–59, 257–58.

42. Sanford Levinson, "The Embarrassing Second Amendment," *Yale Law Journal* 99 (1989), 637–59; Robert J. Cottrol and Raymond T. Diamond, "The Second Amendment: Toward an Afro-Americanist Reconsideration," *Georgetown Law Journal* 80 (1991), 309–61; Randy E. Barnett and Don B. Kates, "Under Fire: The New Consensus on the Second Amendment," *Emory Law Journal* 45 (Fall 1996), 1139–1259; Amar, *The Bill of Rights*, 258–68.

43. Jeffrey Toobin, *The Oath: The Obama White House and the Supreme Court* (New York: Anchor, 2012, 2013), 21.

44. *McDonald v. Chicago*, 561 U.S. 742, 857 (2010) (concurring).

45. *Plessy v. Ferguson*, 163 U.S. 537, 559 (1896) (Harlan, dissenting); Thomas, "Higher Law Background," 66, 68; Thomas, "An Afro-American Perspective," 992; Thomas, "The Virtue of Defeat: *Plessy v. Ferguson* in Retrospect," *Journal of Supreme Court History* 22 (December 1997), 22–23; Marcia Coyle, *The Roberts Court: The Struggle for the Constitution* (New York: Simon & Schuster, 2013, 2014), 166.

46. Thomas, "The Virtue of Defeat," 21.

47. *Plessy v. Ferguson*, 163 U.S. 537, 559 (1896) (Harlan, dissenting).

48. Thomas, "Judging," *University of Kansas Law Review* 45 (1996), 4; Thomas, "An Afro-American Perspective," 992; Thomas, "The Virtue of Defeat," 23; Ralph A. Rossum, *Understanding Clarence Thomas: The Jurisprudence of Constitutional Restoration* (Lawrence: University Press of Kansas, 2014), 6, 20, 180–81, 186–87, 196–97, 212–13, 266n40; Scott Douglas Gerber, *First Principles: The Jurisprudence of Clarence Thomas* (New York: New York University Press, 1999), 89, 101–3, 109–12; Hannah Weiner, "The Next 'Great Dissenter'? How Clarence Thomas Is Using the Words and Principles of John Marshall Harlan to Craft a New Era of Civil Rights," *Duke Law Journal* 58 (2008), 151–67.

49. *Holder v. Hall*, 512 U.S. 874, 906 (1994) (concurring); *Parents Involved in Community Schools v. Seattle School District No. 1*, 551 U.S. 701, 748, 772n19, 780–81 (2007) (concurring); *Fisher v. University of Texas*, 570 U.S. 297, 325, 327 (2013) (concurring); *Alabama Legislative Black Caucus v. Alabama*, 135 S. Ct. 1257, 1284, 1288 (2015) (dissenting); *Bethune-Hill v. Virginia State Board of Elections*, 137 S. Ct. 788, 807 (2017) (concurring in part and dissenting in part). Also see "The Second Annual William French Smith Memorial Lecture: A Conversation with Justice Clarence Thomas," *Pepperdine Law Review* 37 (2009), 14.

50. Thomas, "Higher Law Background," 66.

51. Thomas, "The Black Experience: Rage and Reality," *Wall Street Journal* (October 12, 1987), 18; Thomas, "Thomas Sowell and the Heritage of Lincoln," *Lincoln Review* (Spring 1988), 7, 9, 11; *Hearings Before the Senate Committee on the Judiciary*, 102nd Cong., 1st sess., September 10, 11, 12, 13, 17, 19, 20, 1991, and October 11, 12, 13, 1991, Part 1, 250.

52. A useful, if ultimately incomplete, discussion of Thomas's view of the rules of the game can be found in "Lasting Stigma: Affirmative Action and Clarence Thomas's Prisoners' Rights Jurisprudence," *Harvard Law Review* 112 (April 1999), 1336.

9. THE WHITE CONSTITUTION

1. Thomas, speech to Federalist Society and Manhattan Institute (May 16, 1994), reprinted as "'Rights Revolution' Excesses Weaken Fight Against Crime," *Human Events* 50 (June 10, 1994), 12; Thomas, "Freedom: A Responsibility, Not a Right," *Ohio Northern University Law Review* 21, no. 1 (1994), 3; Thomas, "Black America Under the Reagan Administration," *Policy Review* (Fall 1985), 41; Thomas, "Remembering an Island of Hope in an Era of Despair," *Lincoln Review* (Spring 1986), 55; Thomas, "Victims and Heroes in the 'Benevolent State,'" *Harvard Law and Public Policy Review* 19 (Spring 1996), 3.

2. Thomas, "'Rights Revolution,'" 12; Thomas, "Remembering an Island of Hope in an Era of Despair," 55; Thomas, speech to the Heritage Foundation

(June 18, 1987), reprinted as "Why Black Americans Should Look to Conservative Policies," *Human Events* (July 27, 1991), 11.

3. Thomas, "Freedom: A Responsibility, Not a Right," 2.
4. Thomas, "'Rights Revolution,'" 12.
5. Ibid., 13.
6. Thomas, "Rewards Belong to Those Who Labor," *Washington Times* (January 18, 1988), F6; Thomas, "Freedom: A Responsibility, Not a Right," 8.
7. Thomas, "Freedom: A Responsibility, Not a Right," 4; Thomas, Savannah State College Commencement Address (June 9, 1985), in Thomas, *Confronting the Future: Selections from the Senate Confirmation Hearings and Prior Speeches* (Washington, DC: Regnery Gateway, 1992), 33, 35, 39.
8. Thomas, "'Rights Revolution,'" 13.
9. *Brumfield v. Cain*, 1355 S. Ct. 2269, 2283, 2285, 2286–87 (2015) (dissenting); *Brumfield v. Cain*, 1355 S. Ct. 2269, 2298 (2015) (Alito, dissenting).
10. *Brown v. Entertainment Merchants Association*, 564 U.S. 786, 823, 828, 836 (2011) (dissenting); *Safford v. Redding*, 557 U.S. 364, 399–400 (2009) (concurring in part and dissenting in part).
11. *Brown v. Entertainment Merchants Association*, 564 U.S. 786, 829, 830 (2011) (dissenting).
12. *Morse v. Frederick*, 551 U.S. 393, 413, 414, 416, 419, 424 (2007) (concurring); *Safford v. Redding*, 557 U.S. 364, 379 (2006) (concurring in part and dissenting in part).
13. *Morse v. Frederick*, 551 U.S. 393, 411, 412, 414 (2007) (concurring); *Safford v. Redding*, 557 U.S. 364, 385 (2006) (concurring in part and dissenting in part)
14. *Rainey v. Chever*, 527 U.S. 1044, 1046 (1999) (dissenting from denial of certiorari).
15. *Turner v. Rogers*, 564 U.S. 431, 458–60 (2011) (dissenting).
16. *Brown v. Entertainment Merchants Association*, 564 U.S. 786, 835, 836 (2011) (dissenting).
17. *Turner v. Rogers*, 564 U.S. 431, 474 (2011) (dissenting).
18. Mark Joseph Stern, "Clarence Thomas, Liberal," *Slate* (June 18, 2013), http://www.slate.com/articles/news_and_politics/jurisprudence/2013/06/clarence_thomas_s_liberal_rulings_how_the_supreme_court_justice_s_originalism.html; Jeremy Byellin, "Clarence Thomas: Deeply Conservative, Yet Uniquely So," *Legal Solutions Blog* (August 7, 2013), http://blog.legalsolutions.thomsonreuters.com/top-legal-news/clarence-thomas-deeply-conservative-yet-uniquely-so/; William H. Pryor Jr., "Justice Thomas, Criminal Justice, and Originalism's Legitimacy," *Yale Law Journal Forum* 127 (2017), 173–81; Marah S. McLeod, "A Humble Justice," *Yale Law Journal Forum* 127 (2017), 199–201; Ralph Rossum, *Understanding Clarence Thomas: The Jurisprudence of Constitutional Restoration* (Lawrence: University Press of Kansas, 2014), 145, 155, 161–63, 178–79.
19. *Alleyne v. United States*, 570 U.S. 99, 109 (2013).
20. *Apprendi v. New Jersey*, 499 U.S. 466, 499–501 (2000) (concurring); *Harris*

v. *United States*, 536 U.S. 545, 575–77 (2002) (dissenting); *Kansas v. Hendricks*, 521 U.S. 346, 359 (1997). In *Hendricks*, a case involving whether it should be the legislature or the psychiatric profession that determines what constitutes a defendant's mental competence, Thomas made a special point of arguing that Kansas's decision was not part of a criminal proceeding but was instead a civil proceeding; it therefore had nothing to do with the imposition of a punishment. Even so, the emphasis on the determinations of the legislature, as opposed to the psychiatric profession, stands out. *Kansas v. Hendricks*, 521 U.S. 346, 361–64 (1997).

21. *Apprendi v. New Jersey*, 499 U.S. 466, 512 (2000) (concurring); *Harris v. United States*, 536 U.S. 545, 575–77 (2002) (dissenting); *Booker v. United States*, 543 U.S. 220, 313 (2005) (dissenting); *Shepard v. United States*, 544 U.S. 13, 26–27 (2005) (concurring); *Rangel-Reyes v. United States*, 547 U.S. 1200, 1202 (2006) (dissenting); *James v. United States*, 550 U.S. 192, 231 (2007) (dissenting); *United States v. O'Brien*, 560 U.S. 218, 240 (2010) (concurring); *Descamps v. United States*, 570 U.S. 254, 280–81 (2013) (concurring); *Mathis v. United States*, 136 S. Ct. 2243, 2258 (2016) (concurring). To this list of cases that protect the rights of individuals against the punitive state, one might add *United States v. Hubbell*, 530 U.S. 27, 49–56 (2000) (concurring); *Indianapolis v. Edmond*, 531 U.S. 32, 56 (2000) (dissenting); *Michaels v. McGrath*, 531 U.S. 1118 (2001) (dissenting from denial of certiorari); *Davis v. Washington*, 547 U.S. 813, 834 (2006) (concurring in part and dissenting in part). See Rossum, *Understanding Clarence Thomas*, 147, 152–53.

22. *Ewing v. California*, 538 U.S. 11, 32 (2003) (concurring); *Walker v. Georgia*, 555 U.S. 979, 987 (2008) (concurring); *Graham v. Florida*, 560 U.S. 48, 99 (2010) (dissenting); *Miller v. Alabama*, 567 U.S. 460, 503–4 (2012) (dissenting); *Glossip v. Gross*, 135 S. Ct. 2726, 2751 (2015) (concurring). The only instance where Thomas defends the proportionality principle is in the context of fines. *United States v. Bajakajian*, 524 U.S. 321, 336–37 (1998); *Timbs v. Indiana*, 203 L.E. 2d 11, 23 (2019) (concurring).

23. *Alleyne v. United States*, 570 U.S. 99, 109 (2013).

24. Jan Crawford Greenburg, *Supreme Conflict: The Inside Story of the Struggle for Control of the United States Supreme Court* (New York: Penguin, 2007, 2008), 120.

25. In addition to the prisoners' rights cases discussed below, see *Foucha v. Louisiana*, 504 U.S. 71, 102, 118n13 (1992) (dissenting); *Riggins v. Nevada*, 504 U.S. 127, 146 (1992) (dissenting); *Dogget v. United States*, 505 U.S. 647, 659 (1992) (dissenting); *Graham v. Collins*, 506 U.S. 461, 478–500 (1993) (concurring); *McFarland v. Scott*, 512 U.S. 849, 870–73 (1994) (dissenting); *Thomas v. Keohane, Warden*, 516 U.S. 99, 116–21 (1996) (dissenting); *O'Dell v. Netherland*, 521 U.S. 151, 153 (1997); *Mitchell v. United States*, 526 U.S. 314, 341–43 (1999) (dissenting); *Florida v. White*, 526 U.S. 559 (1999); *Knight v. Florida*, 528 U.S. 990 (1999) (concurring in denial of

certiorari); *Tyler v. Cain*, 533 U.S. 656 (2001); *Foster v. Florida*, 537 U.S. 990 (2002) (concurring in denial of certiorari); *Chavez v. Martinez*, 538 U.S. 760 (2003); *Groh v. Ramirez*, 540 U.S. 551, 571 (2004) (dissenting); *United States v. Patane*, 542 U.S. 630 (2004); *Halbert v. Michigan*, 545 U.S. 605, 624 (2005) (dissenting); *Deck v. Missouri*, 544 U.S. 622, 635 (2005) (dissenting); *Georgia v. Randolph*, 547 U.S. 103, 145 (2006) (dissenting); *Samson v. California*, 547 U.S. 843 (2006); *Kansas v. Marsh*, 548 U.S. 163, 181 (2006); *Rothgery v. Gillespie County*, 554 U.S. 191, 218 (2008) (dissenting); *Giles v. California*, 554 U.S. 353, 377–78 (2008) (concurring); *Thompson v. McNeil*, 556 U.S. 1114, 1116, 1118 (2009) (concurring in denial of certiorari); *Cone v. Bell*, 556 U.S. 449, 486 (2009) (dissenting); *Connick v. Thompson*, 563 U.S. 51 (2011); *Cullen v. Pinholster*, 563 U.S. 170 (2011); *Williams v. Illinois*, 567 U.S. 50, 103 (2012) (concurring); *Missouri v. McNeely*, 569 U.S. 141, 176 (2013) (dissenting); *Peugh v. United States*, 569 U.S. 530, 551 (2013) (dissenting); *Salinas v. Texas*, 570 U.S. 178, 191 (2013) (concurring); *Fernandez v. California*, 571 U.S. 292, 309 (2014) (concurring); *Navarette v. California*, 572 U.S. 393 (2014); *United States v. Bryant*, 136 S. Ct. 1954, 1967 (2016) (concurring); *Utah v. Strieff*, 136 S. Ct. 2056, 2059 (2016); *Birchfield v. North Dakota*, 136 S. Ct. 2160, 2196 (2016) (concurring in part and dissenting in part); *Lee v. United States*, 137 S. Ct. 1958, 1969 (2017) (dissenting); *Carpenter v. United States*, 138 S. Ct. 2206, 2235 (2018) (dissenting); *Rosales-Mireles v. United States*, 138 S. Ct. 1897, 1911 (2018) (dissenting); *District of Columbia v. Wesby*, 138 S. Ct. 537 (2018); Christopher E. Smith, "Rights Behind Bars: The Distinctive Viewpoint of Justice Clarence Thomas," *University of Detroit Mercy Law Review* 88 (2011), 829–72; Eric L. Muller, "Where, But for the Grace of God, Goes He? The Search for Empathy in the Criminal Jurisprudence of Clarence Thomas," *Constitutional Comment* 15 (1998), 225–50; Rossum, *Understanding Clarence Thomas*, 142–79; Mark A. Graber, "Clarence Thomas and the Perils of Amateur History," in *Rehnquist Justice: Understanding the Court Dynamic*, ed. Earl M. Maltz (Lawrence: University Press of Kansas, 2003), 81–83, 86.

26. *Hudson v. McMillian*, 503 U.S. 1, 28 (1992) (dissenting); *Overton v. Bazzetta*, 539 U.S. 126, 142, 144 (2003) (concurring); *Beard v. Banks*, 548 U.S. 521, 537 (2006) (concurring).

27. *Hudson v. McMillian*, 503 U.S. 1, 4, 19, 28 (1992) (dissenting).

28. *Farmer v. Brennan*, 511 U.S. 825, 858–859 (1994), (concurring); *Baze and Bowling v. Rees*, 553 U.S. 35, 100–101 (2008) (concurring).

29. *Farmer v. Brennan*, 511 U.S. 825, 859 (1994) (concurring). In a footnote to a later case, Thomas slightly qualified this position: "Sentencing a criminal to a term of imprisonment may, under state law, carry with it the implied delegation to prison officials to discipline and otherwise supervise the criminal while he is incarcerated. Thus, restrictions imposed by prison officials may also be a part of the sentence, provided that those officials are not acting *ultra vires* with respect to the discretion given them, by implication, in a sentence."

He went on to write: "Restrictions that are rationally connected to the running of a prison, that are designed to avoid adverse impacts on guards, inmates, or prison resources, that cannot be replaced by 'ready alternatives,' and that leave inmates with alternative means of accomplishing what the restrictions prohibit, are presumptively included within a sentence of imprisonment." *Overton v. Bazzetta*, 539 U.S. 126, 140–42 (2003) (concurring). Also see *Beard v. Banks*, 548 U.S. 521, 537 (2006) (concurring).

30. *Hudson v. McMillian*, 503 U.S. 1, 18 (1992) (dissenting); Greenburg, *Supreme Conflict*, 119–20.

31. *Helling v. McKinney*, 509 U.S. 25, 40, 42 (1993) (dissenting). Also see *Hope v. Pelzer*, 536 U.S. 730, 758n12 (2002) (dissenting); *Overton v. Bazzetta*, 539 U.S. 126, 145 (2003) (concurring); *Beard v. Banks*, 548 U.S. 521, 537 (2006) (concurring); *Erickson v. Pardus*, 551 U.S. 89, 95 (2007) (dissenting); *Wilkins v. Gaddy*, 559 U.S. 34, 40 (2010) (concurring).

32. *Hudson v. McMillian*, 503 U.S. 1, 28 (1992) (dissenting).

33. *Farmer v. Brennan*, 511 U.S. 825, 858–59 (1994) (concurring).

34. Thomas, "'Rights Revolution,'" 13.

35. *Miller-El v. Cockrell*, 537 U.S. 322, 361–63, 368, 370 (2003) (dissenting); *Miller-El v. Dretke*, 543 U.S. 231, 275, 279, 285–91 (2005) (dissenting); *Snyder v. Louisiana*, 552 U.S. 472, 486 (2008) (dissenting); *Walker v. Georgia*, 555 U.S. 979, 988 (2008) (concurring in denial of certiorari); *Foster v. Chatman*, 136 S. Ct. 1737, 1765–69 (2016) (dissenting).

36. See, for example, *Graham v. Collins*, 506 U.S. 461, 481 (1993) (concurring); *Davis v. Minnesota*, 511 U.S. 1115, 1117–18 (1994) (dissenting from denial of writ of certiorari); *Davis v. Ayala*, 135 S. Ct. 2187, 2210 (2015) (concurring); *Buck v. Davis*, 137 S. Ct. 759, 784–85 (2017) (dissenting).

37. *Utah v. Strieff*, 136 S. Ct. 2056, 2063 (2016).

38. *Utah v. Strieff*, 136 S. Ct. 2056, 2068 (Sotomayor, dissenting).

39. *Utah v. Strieff*, 136 S. Ct. 2056, 2069 (2016) (Sotomayor, dissenting).

40. *Utah v. Strieff*, 136 S. Ct. 2056, 2070–2071 (2016) (Sotomayor, dissenting).

41. Thomas, "The New Intolerance," Law Day Address, Walter F. George School of Law, Mercer University (May 1993), http://www.americanrhetoric.com/speeches/clarencethomasthenewintolerance.htm.

42. Thomas, "The New Intolerance."

43. Thomas, "Why Black Americans Should Look to Conservative Policies," 11.

44. James Forman Jr., *Locking Up Our Own: Crime and Punishment in Black America* (New York: Farrar, Straus & Giroux, 2017), 113–14.

45. Randall Kennedy, *Race, Crime, and the Law* (New York: Vintage, 1998); Forman, *Locking Up Our Own*, 126–29.

46. Jeffrey Rosen, "Moving On," *New Yorker* (April 29/May 6, 1996), 67. Beyond the question of African American victims of crime, Thomas believes that there is a class dimension to the Court's liberal jurisprudence. The Court is indifferent to the victims of crime (and ordinary citizens' need for armed self-defense), says Thomas, because it enjoys a gilded protection from crime. The

justices "work in marbled halls, guarded constantly by a vigilant and dedicated police force." *Peruta v. California*, 137 S. Ct. 1995, 1999 (2017) (dissenting from denial of certiorari).

47. Thomas, *My Grandfather's Son: A Memoir* (New York: HarperPerennial, 2007), 94–95.

48. *Chicago v. Morales*, 527 U.S. 41, 98–99 (1999) (dissenting); Tracy L. Meares and Dan M. Kahan, "The Wages of Antiquated Procedural Thinking: A Critique of *Chicago v. Morales*," *University of Chicago Legal Forum* (1998), 199.

49. *Chicago v. Morales*, 527 U.S. 41, 109–11, 115 (1999) (dissenting).

50. Forman, *Locking Up Our Own*, 107–10; Charles E. Menifield, Geiguen Shin, and Logan Strother, "Do White Law Enforcement Officers Target Minority Suspects?," *Public Administration Review* (2018), 1–12. On the racial underpinnings of police discretion, see David Cole, *No Equal Justice: Race and Class in the American Criminal Justice System* (New York: New Press, 1999), 41–52; Kennedy, *Race, Crime, and the Law*, 136–67.

51. *Chicago v. Morales*, 527 U.S. 41, 109–10 (1999) (dissenting).

52. Thomas, "'Rights Revolution,'" 12.

53. *Chicago v. Morales*, 527 U.S. 41, 111 (1999) (dissenting). One should not assume that Thomas is always indifferent to charges of abuse of discretionary power. In *Graham v. Collins* (1993), he rehearsed at length how "behind the Court's condemnation of unguided discretion" in the administration of the death penalty "lay the specter of racial prejudice—the paradigmatic capricious and irrational sentencing factor." When it comes to punishment, as opposed to policing, Thomas can summon pages of complex, compelling exegesis to explain the dangers of racially motivated discretionary state power. And while the overall point of his opinion in *Graham* was to endorse a mandatory sentencing scheme for the death penalty, thereby eliminating the power to suspend a death sentence in individual cases, it is telling that he focused his argument on the need to remove "the unfettered discretion of the jury to save the defendant from death." For "to withhold the death penalty out of sympathy for a defendant who is a member of a favored group is no different from a decision to impose the penalty on the basis of negative bias." *Graham v. Collins*, 506 U.S. 461, 484, 495 (1993) (concurring). Also see *Miller v. Alabama*, 567 U.S. 460, 506 (2012) (dissenting); *Glossip v. Gross*, 135 S. Ct. 2726, 2755 (2015) (concurring).

54. Thomas, "No Room at the Inn: The Loneliness of the Black Conservative," in *Black and Right: The Bold New Voice of Black Conservatives in America*, ed. Stan Faryna, Brad Stetson, and Joseph G. Conti (Westport, CT: Praeger, 1997), 4; Jane Mayer and Jill Abramson, *Strange Justice: The Selling of Clarence Thomas* (Boston: Houghton Mifflin, 1994), 32; Thomas, Savannah State Address, 31; Thomas, "Victims and Heroes," 671.

55. Thomas, "Victims and Heroes," 672.

56. *Chicago v. Morales*, 527 U.S. 41, 103, 107 (1999) (dissenting).

57. Thomas, "Freedom: A Responsibility, Not a Right," 11–12.

58. For an excellent discussion of this feature of the literature, see Quinn Slobo-dian, *Globalists: The End of Empire and the Birth of Neoliberalism* (Cambridge, MA: Harvard University Press, 2018), 5–7.

59. Melinda Cooper, *Family Values: Between Neoliberalism and the New Social Conservatism* (Brooklyn, NY: Zone Books, 2017).

60. Thomas, "Black America Under the Reagan Administration," 36–37.

61. *Chicago v. Morales*, 527 U.S. 41, 115 (1999) (dissenting).

62. Thomas, "'Rights Revolution,'" 12.

63. *Chicago v. Morales*, 527 U.S. 41, 115 (1999) (dissenting).

64. *Jones v. Flowers*, 547 U.S. 220, 248 (2006) (dissenting).

65. Thomas, "New Intolerance."

66. Thomas, "'Rights Revolution,'" 12–13.

67. Ibid., 12, 13.

68. *Chicago v. Morales*, 527 U.S. 41, 104 (1999) (dissenting). In the 2019 *Timbs v. Indiana* case, there is a glancing reference to the role of vagrancy statutes in the backlash against emancipation, but Thomas seems not to have noticed the discrepancy between that reference and his earlier discussion in *Chicago v. Morales*. *Timbs v. Indiana*, 203 L.E. 2d 11, 27–28 (2019) (concurring).

69. Thomas, "'Rights Revolution,'" 13.

70. Ibid., 13.

71. Thomas, "Victims and Heroes," 679.

72. Thomas, "'Rights Revolution,'" 12.

73. Thomas, "Why Federalism Matters," *Drake Law Review* 48 (2000), 234; Graber, "Clarence Thomas and the Perils of Amateur History," 84; Mark A. Graber, "Clarence Thomas," *Biographical Encyclopedia of the Supreme Court: The Lives and Legal Philosophies of the Justices*, ed. Melvin I. Urof-sky (Washington, DC: CQ Press, 2006), 542–53.

74. Joseph E. Lowndes, *From the New Deal to the New Right: Race and the Southern Origins of Modern Conservatism* (New Haven, CT: Yale University Press, 2008), 30–34, 49–54; Barry Goldwater, *The Conscience of a Conservative* (Princeton, NJ: Princeton University Press, 1960), 17–23.

75. *U.S. Term Limits v. Thornton*, 514 U.S. 779, 846 (1995) (dissenting).

76. *U.S. Term Limits v. Thornton*, 514 U.S. 779, 846, 848, 858, 859 (1995) (dissenting).

77. *U.S. Term Limits v. Thornton*, 514 U.S. 779, 849, 859, 860 (1995) (dissenting).

78. Thomas, "Why Federalism Matters," 234–37; Graber, "Clarence Thomas and the Perils of Amateur History," 77–79.

79. *McDonald v. City of Chicago*, 561 U.S. 742, 841 (2010) (concurring).

80. Thomas also wishes to empower the states in order to restrict the power of the federal government to regulate the economy. Enhancing the power of the states to regulate their internal economies has the potential effect of constraining the ability of the federal government, under the Commerce Clause and other statutory provisions, to preempt the ability of the states to do so. The effect of these opinions, if unencumbered by the sorts of First Amendment challenges

discussed in chapter 6, would be to return the United States to an antebellum state-centered jurisprudence of political economy. *Wyeth v. Levine*, 555 U.S. 555, 583–88 (2009) (concurring); *Gobeille v. Liberty Mutual Insurance Company*, 136 S. Ct. 936, 949 (2016) (concurring); *Upstate Citizens for Equality v. United States*, 199 L. Ed. 2d 372, 373 (2017) (dissenting from denial of certiorari); *Murphy v. NCAA*, 138 S. Ct. 1461, 1485 (2018) (concurring).

81. Thomas, "'Rights Revolution,'" 13; *McFarland v. Scott*, 512 U.S. 849, 872 (1994) (dissenting).

82. Thomas, "Why Federalism Matters," 236. Thomas sets out the connections between his concerns about federalism and crime and punishment, between preserving the balance of power between the states and national government and enhancing the punitive power of the states, in many cases: *O'Neal v. McAninch*, 513 U.S. 432, 447–48 (1995) (dissenting); *Lewis v. Casey*, 518 U.S. 343, 385–88 (1996) (concurring); *Pennsylvania Board of Probation and Parole v. Scott*, 524 U.S. 357, 369 (1998); *Smith v. Robbins*, 528 U.S. 259, 274 (2000); *Shafer v. South Carolina*, 532 U.S. 36, 58 (2001) (dissenting); *Kelly v. South Carolina*, 534 U.S. 246, 265 (2002) (dissenting); *United States v. Comstock*, 560 U.S. 126, 164 (2010) (dissenting); *United States v. Kebodeaux*, 570 U.S. 387, 407, 413 (2013) (dissenting); *County of Maricopa v. Lopez-Valenzuela*, 135 S. Ct. 2046 (2015) (dissenting from denial of certiorari); *Lynch v. Arizona*, 136 S. Ct. 1818, 1822 (2016) (dissenting); *David Anthony Taylor v. United States*, 136 S. Ct. 2074, 2088 (2016) (dissenting); *Davila v. Davis*, 137 S. Ct. 2058, 2069–70 (2017); *Collins v. Virginia*, 138 S. Ct. 1663, 1680 (2018) (concurring).

83. Thomas, "'Rights Revolution,'" 12.

84. In several opinions, Thomas expresses different versions of this discomfort with any attempt to swap out the punitive power of the state for a more general liberal or therapeutic approach to governance. In an early opinion involving questions of sovereign immunity, Thomas took great exception to the notion that social workers are equivalent or analogous to prosecutors. In two later opinions, he affirmed his concern that the federal government may be usurping the police powers of the state through its use of the Commerce Clause. *Hoffman v. Harris*, 114 S. Ct. 1631, 1632–33 (1994) (dissenting from denial of certiorari); *Alderman v. United States*, 526 U.S. 1163 (2011) (dissenting from denial of certiorari); *David Anthony Taylor v. United States*, 136 S. Ct. 2074, 2089 (2016) (dissenting).

85. Thomas, "Judging," *University of Kansas Law Review* 45 (1996), 5.

86. Thomas, *My Grandfather's Son*, 27–28.

87. Ibid., 27.

EPILOGUE

1. Josiah Nott, "Instincts of Races," in *Defending Slavery: Proslavery Thought in the Old South: A Brief History with Documents*, ed. Paul Finkelman (Boston: Bedford/St. Martin's, 2003), 206.

2. Jessica Blatt, *Race and the Making of American Political Science* (Philadelphia: University of Pennsylvania Press, 2018); Karen E. Fields and Barbara J. Fields, *Racecraft: The Soul of Inequality in American Life* (New York: Verso, 2012), 95–103, 120–21.

3. Thomas, "The New Intolerance," Law Day Address, Walter F. George School of Law, Mercer University (May 1993), http://www.americanrhetoric.com /speeches/clarencethomasthenewintolerance.htm.

ACKNOWLEDGMENTS

Six years ago, Melvin Rogers and Jack Turner asked me to write an article on Clarence Thomas for an anthology of essays they were preparing on African American political thought. Having recently completed a controversial book on conservatism, which consumed nearly as much of my attention after its publication as it had before, I wasn't keen to take up another project on the right. But as I was getting ready to say no, Rogers Smith stepped in and convinced me to say yes. Once I finished that article and shared its contents with Steve Fraser, Steve saw its possibilities as a book, which he urged me to pursue. Had it not been for this serendipity of strong arm and suggestion I'd never have written this book.

Along the way, I have been fortunate in getting good advice and close reading from a number of colleagues and friends. I was introduced to Cedric Johnson's *Revolutionaries to Race Leaders* by a suggestion on Facebook and immediately saw how it might help me make sense of Thomas. Cedric then heard me present the argument in its earliest phases and discussed it with me throughout its middle phases. In the book's final (or what I thought was final) phase, Cedric took it upon himself to read the entire manuscript and send me nine single-spaced pages of detailed critique. While I'm certain this work does not meet the stringency of his standards, had it not been for these interventions *The Enigma of Clarence Thomas* would have turned out a poorer book.

I am also indebted to Keith Whittington. Not only did Keith read the entire manuscript and offer helpful comments throughout, but he also fielded literally dozens of inquiries from me—as many as four or five in a single day—about various matters, large and small, of constitutional law and the Court. Each time, he responded with generosity and care, averting some embarrassing errors and hasty conclusions on my part.

Tom Sugrue and Martha Biondi, two of the civil rights movement's finest historians, pushed me on specific historical claims about Thomas's role in the black freedom struggle, recommended reading after reading, patiently answered my questions, no matter how naïve, and performed that role we so often crave in academia but so seldom get: the sympathetic yet scrupulous reader. Mike Dorf read an early version of Part II, offered trenchant and detailed feedback, and then, when I returned for more, proved to be an invaluable guide through thickets as dense as the Dormant Commerce Clause and as impassable as the Takings Clause. Jessica Blatt, Daria Rothmayr, and Amy Kapczynski read the entire manuscript in its penultimate incarnation, providing me with the requisite combination of caution and correction that I needed to refine and finalize the arguments of the book.

Multiple other readers lent their time, talent, and expertise to this project, reading chunks of the manuscript with an eye toward saving me from myself or helping me through some of its thornier passages. Many thanks go to Tommie Shelby, Andy Koppelman, John Palattella, Jed Purdy, Aziz Rana, Bonnie Honig, Sam Moyn, Tim Barker, Rob Mickey, Scott Saul, Greg Grandin, Jeremy Kessler, Charles Petersen, Melvin Rogers, Jack Turner, Steve Fraser, Rogers Smith, Jodi Dean, Adina Hoffman, Alex Gourevitch, and Ellen Tremper.

Throughout the research and writing of this book, I have presented portions of it at department workshops, law school seminars, and university conferences. Had it not been for invitations from Melvin Rogers and Jack Turner to the University of Washington; Bonnie Honig,

Alex Gourevitch, Brian Meeks, and Amanda Anderson to Brown (three times); Jamila Michener and Aziz Rana to Cornell and Cornell Law School; Margo Schlanger to the University of Michigan Law School; Davide Panagia to UCLA; Jacob Selwood to Georgia State University; Jodi Dean to Hobart and William Smith Colleges; Adom Getachew to the University of Chicago; David Forrest to Oberlin; Jackson Lears to Rutgers; Paul Frymer to Princeton; and Gary Gerstle to Cambridge, I would not have had the prodding I needed to write this book. Nor would I have received the excellent feedback I got from my discussants—Michelle Smith, Sam Bagenstos, Lucas Pinheiro, Amna Akbarton, and Gary Gerstle—and my hosts, as well as from Andrew Dilts, Sina Jo, Joshua Dienstag, Jason Frank, Larry Glickman, Bob Hockett, William O'Neill, Paul Passavant, Sankar Muthu, Patchen Markell, Jennifer Pitts, Melissa Lane, Stan Katz, Paul Starr, Andre Willis (whose well-timed question about black nationalism sat with me for years, leading to big changes in chapters 1 and 4), David Sehat, Alex Sayf Cummings, Don Herzog, and many others.

As a professor at a cash-starved public university, I could not have written this book without the material support of several individuals who gave me access to resources I never would have had access to otherwise. Charles Petersen and Paisley Currah helped me out with multiple requests; the generosity of Jeremy Kessler has been unmatched.

Speaking of cash-starved public universities, I am indebted to so many close friends and colleagues throughout CUNY, but special mention goes to Paisley Currah, Carolina Bank-Muñoz, Moustafa Bayoumi, Michelle Anderson, and above all, for countless reasons, Ellen Tremper.

And speaking of friends, Alex Gourevitch and Seth Ackerman deserve special mention for indulging me in endless hours of conversation about Thomas, which have helped orient me in so many ways. Their influence is evident throughout this book; if even a quarter of their intelligence is too, I'll be pleased.

I received invaluable research assistance from Jeenie Kahng and Andrew Shanahan, both of whom sought to make sure that there wasn't something in the vast archive of Thomas's opinions that I had overlooked; as it turned out, there was, and the final manuscript has been much improved by their efforts. Andrew went above and beyond the call of duty, working with me in the final stages of this manuscript's preparation on all manner of fact- and footnote-checking, patiently answering my many queries about proper methods of legal citation and other issues, and preparing brief memos for me on some challenging material. At the age of ten, Carol Brahm-Robin undertook her first research project, amassing a database for me of Thomas's law clerks and their roles under Trump.

In the last year of this project, I had the extraordinary luck to receive a fellowship from the Cullman Center for Scholars and Writers at the New York Public Library. Not only was I given access to the Library's untold resources, particularly at the Schomburg Center, not only was I was given time and a room of my own to write, but I also was given the gift of a group of writers and scholars—David Bell, Jennifer Croft, Mary Dearborn, Ada Ferrer, Vona Goarke, francine j. harris, Faith Hillis, Martha Hodes, Brooke Holmes, Karan Mahajan, Marisa Silver, Kirmen Uribe, Amanda Vaill, and Frances Wilson—whom I've come to think of as family. And at the center of that family are the three people who make it all possible: Salvatore Scibona, Lauren Goldenberg, and Paul Delaverdac. The fellowship—the humor, intelligence, conversation, warmth, and support—of these men and women has been as wonderful as it was unexpected.

I've been working with editors at newspapers and magazines—some of them the most gifted of their generation—for nearly two decades. But I never have had the experience that I've had working with Sara Bershtel at Metropolitan Books. Sara's sense of writing is impeccable: in her attention to pacing, ensuring that every element of the book is in its proper place; in her devotion to the arc of an argument, that it gather the necessary force; in her fidelity to the facts and logic of the story. Focusing on the smallest details, she never loses sight of the larger structure, and vice versa. Sara never stopped insisting, until we were nearly done, that I hadn't yet figured out what this book was about. I thought she was wrong, but she turned out to be right. It has been a wonder—and an education—for me to see this book get made and remade under her watch.

In the last year of our working together, Sara was joined by Grigory Tovbis. When Grigory took his pen to the page, it was as if the narrative of a case, previously obscure, suddenly loomed into view, like the vision of outer space you get from one of those ships in *Star Wars* when it's been cast into hyperdrive. Grigory would cut, and suddenly I'd see. Grigory is also responsible for one of the most important editorial interventions I've ever received: "This paragraph used the word 'things' nine times in its first seven sentences."

And for Laura and Carol? "There are, indeed, things that cannot be put into words. They make themselves manifest."

INDEX

ABOUT THE AUTHOR

COREY ROBIN is the author of *The Reactionary Mind: Conservatism from Edmund Burke to Donald Trump* and *Fear: The History of a Political Idea*. He teaches political science at Brooklyn College and the CUNY Graduate Center. Robin's writing has appeared in the *New York Times*, the *New Yorker*, *Harper's*, and the *London Review of Books*, among other publications, and has been translated into thirteen languages. He lives in Brooklyn, New York.